THE
SIMPLE
FLUTE

From A to Z

Michel Debost
Illustrated by Jeanne Debost-Roth

OXFORD
UNIVERSITY PRESS

2002

OXFORD
UNIVERSITY PRESS

Oxford   New York

Athens   Auckland   Bangkok   Bogotá   Buenos Aires   Cape Town
Chennai   Dar es Salaam   Delhi   Florence   Hong Kong   Istanbul   Karachi
Kolkata   Kuala Lumpur   Madrid   Melbourne   Mexico City   Mumbai   Nairobi
Paris   São Paulo   Shanghai   Singapore   Taipei   Tokyo   Toronto   Warsaw

and associated companies in
Berlin   Ibadan

Copyright © 2002 by Oxford University Press

Published by Oxford University Press, Inc.
198 Madison Avenue, New York, New York 10016

Oxford is a registered trademark of Oxford University Press.

Library of Congress Cataloging-in-Publication Data
Debost, Michel.
[Simple flûte. English]
The simple flute : from A to Z / Michel Debost.
    p.   cm.
Translated from French.
Includes bibliographical references.
ISBN 978-0-19-514521-2

1. Flute—Instruction and study.   I. Title.
MT340 .D4313   2002
788.3'2193—dc21   2001033831

19 18 17 16 15 14 13 12 11 10

Printed in the United States of America
on acid-free paper

CONTENTS

THE SIMPLE FLUTE

Suzano

_____

Lent 2008

Mt-Vernon, GA

A TO Z IN FORM OF INTRODUCTION

Alphabetical order for entries in this book has been chosen for various reasons. The main one is that such a book is not meant to be read like a novel, drink in hand under the lamp. It is a book for lovers of the divine pipe, for those fascinated by actual contact with the flute, with instrumental playing as well as musical function in mind, for its poetic mysteries as well as for its technical secrets.

I have been playing the flute for close to sixty years. Yet nothing is indifferent to me that involves the flute. Hopefully it will be so as long as I have a breath, or a tooth, left. I take nothing for granted either, and each day brings new questions and renewed pleasures.

Separating into "logical" compartments different aspects of musical art (technique, tone, articulation, interpretation, etc.) seems to me arbitrary. I cannot see the border between questions. The art of the flute is not a chest of isolated little drawers with one aspect of playing locked in each one. Musicality does not start where technique stops, if it ever stops.

There is no possible practice of articulation without a cultivated tone, any more than there can be a valid reflection on tone without a living consciousness of the breath. There is no significant instrumental work without a musical project, and there can be no meaningful interpretation without valid instrumental playing.

"Art is but feeling. Yet, without the science of volumes, of proportions, of colors, without the ability of the hand, the liveliest feeling is paralyzed. What would become of the greatest poet in a foreign land, whose tongue he knew nothing about?"[1]

Alphabetical organization, therefore, seemed to me more practical for a "flute in hand" reading.

Another reason relates to the attention span of your average flutist. Mine does not go much beyond a thousand words, or about two typewritten pages. Such is the size of most of my subjects, to which are added a few illustrations, musical examples, and sketches by Jeanne Debost-Roth. She has the necessary know-how and patience, being the daughter and wife of flute players.

If interest is aroused by an entry, the implied subjects are indexed, again in alphabetical order, at the end of each entry, so that a curious reader may easily find them in cross-reference. Some ideas will be repeated for the same reason, sometimes word for word: cross-reference. The repetitions are not unintended. Teaching is, like conducting, glorified redundancy. After the teacher has repeated the same axiom a hundred times, the student will need to hear it for the hundred and first time.

Music is whole, and to serve it one must explore the secret paths that link aes-

1. Auguste Rodin (1840–1917) in *L'Art* (Paris: Bernard Grasset: 1911).

thetics and technique, content and form, matter and spirit. Instrumental playing, in my own terminology, is precisely all that. To work on "technique" without thinking about tone, vibrato without bothering with intonation, phrasing without articulation? A false consideration for logic presides over the serialization of practice. Logic is not always common sense.

Certain words or phrases will seem idiosyncratic and unclear. They do relate to concepts that I hope will become clear.

Air brush: The stream of air between the lips' aperture and the striking edge of the embouchure plate, as compared to the artist's brush.

Air column: One continuous unit from the inner part of the body to the tip of the foot joint.

Air management: The economy and control of blown air according to length of phrases and need of dynamics.

Air speed: The rate of airflow, in direct ratio to pressure and in inverse ratio to volume.

Apnea: Holding the breath after inhalation.

Appoggio: A technique used by singers to create balance between support and air control.

Bridge: The connection between the low and middle ranges (B–D, C–D) where fingerings go from one or two fingers (B, C) to all fingers (D–D♯).

Cough point (or sneeze point): The point in the abdomen, lower than the navel, felt during coughing (or sneezing).

Finger phrasing: Making music with the fingers as much as with the sound. The opposite of slam-and-squeeze.

Finger tonguing: A procedure whereby the airflow is set in motion without the tongue. The key closest to the desired note is snapped lightly (without any tonguing).

Fulcrums: Three points vital to the stability of the flute:

1. The first joint of the left index finger.
2. The tip of the right thumb.
3. The point of contact of the chin to the lip plate. None of the three fulcrums contribute to fingering notes.

Gas-leak sound: Thin, wheezy sound. Produced with pinched lips and air pressure.

Jawboning: Constant use of the jaw during flute playing.

"Hhaah" sound: Sound produced when the throat is open upon inhaling. It also implies that abdominal support, not the chest, powers the breathing,

Little devils: Three critical fingers whose action is often contrary to that of the other fingers:

1. The left index finger (octave key).
2. The right pinky.
3. The left pinky.

Middle breath: Something less than a full inhalation. A partial inhalation involving the abdomen but not the upper respiratory agents (chest and shoulders). A breath proportionate to the amount of air needed for the phrase being started. "If you don't need a big breath, don't take one."

Shifting: A slight movement in the center of gravity that causes the air to change speed naturally.

Silent key: A non–tone producing key used for balance or fingering anticipation.

Slam-and-squeeze: The action of bringing down the fingers forcefully on the flute (generating unwanted noise) and pressing them tightly (slowing down the fingers' lift).

Stepping-stones: Hinge notes or fragments helping to deal with technical difficulties, usually a note where downward fingers and rhythm coincide. In the construction of interpretation, harmonic or structural landmarks that help pacing in variations in dynamic level (crescendo, diminuendo) or in tempo (rallentando, accelerando) or harmonic progression.

Tenuto, Sostenuto, Ritenuto: A process related to appoggio:

- *Tenuto*: Stability on the chin through the left hand.
- *Sostenuto*: Support by the abdominal muscles.
- *Ritenuto*: Resistance to the collapse of the rib cage.

Timbre: The coloring of the sound. Like the voice, it is totally personal. It varies according to the number of partials (harmonics) in the sound.

Turbo-sound: The result of blowing a large volume of air without focus.

A flutomaniac bibliography will be included at the end, incomplete by nature, since every year sees a new crop. I will not fail to mention the sources, old and recent, from which I have drunk, even if some have served as repellent. Thus, it will be possible to know all and the contrary of all.

Finally, I do not aim at universality, even if it existed in any area. This research concerns my own findings, but it is not the Bible.

ACCOMPANIMENT

The phrase "collaborative playing" has a politically correct ring that gives accompaniment the stigma of menial labor. Likewise, the plumbing at your school is no longer in the care of the traditional janitor; it is kept in condition by a maintenance technician.

But let us call a cat a cat. Accompaniment is not a dirty word. If I accompany you to the movies or to a concert, it is not to carry your books or your popcorn, it is to share a moment and an experience. Our best reward, as musicians, is sharing great works with others—in the orchestra, in the band, in a small group or with a keyboard. When we look forward to a performance, we have to be ready with our part, obviously, but that is not enough. We have to know what our partners are doing and try to resurrect what the composer had in mind.

The secret is in the score. Before you even try to perform with others, look at the score; write in your own part who will lead this passage; who starts first; who cuts off this chord; who is likely to need time to breathe; who has a tendency to rush (it's the flute!); how the harmony evolves and how it affects the tuning of chords; and so on. A score is like a beautiful landscape: you can see it under different kinds of light, and there is always something to discover.

Then try to listen to a recording—not to copy tempos or breaths, but to get a general view, as if you were not a player, but a listener. Play the recording with the flute part as you have annotated it. Then listen to it again with the score. If it is a piano score, keep your eyes on the keyboard staves since you know the flute line, don't you? If it is a group score, listen for everything but the flute, although it is, I agree with you, the center of the world. . . .

When you play duets, which is a fun way to practice reading and ensemble playing, train yourself to read your part while listening to the other line. You might make a few more mistakes in your part at first, but you will be amazed, in the long run, at how you can restabilize near-disasters and balance the music. Am I leader? Am I accompanist? Listen, look, feel. . . . After all, the best teacher (and cheapest) you will ever have is you.

In ensemble playing, there is no winner or loser, no master or slave: "I played my part well, so my conscience is clear." Fine, but all must share the score for the music to be served. A chain is only as strong as its weakest link.

When we are accompanied by keyboard (mostly piano or harpsichord), as well as by harp and guitar, awareness of that score is also crucial. One of my favorite traps, as my students well know, is to play a line and ask them to identify it. They soon suspect that it is something in the piano score of the piece they are currently studying.

Or, "What is the piano playing during this passage?" Is it purely rhythmic, is it contrapuntal, or is it . . . silence? Each accompanying texture shows you what the composer wants or allows you.

Looking at the piano (orchestra) score, we see different patterns:

Here the flute is accompanied by repeated eighth notes: the tempo is steady. Elsewhere, the piano is playing quarters: the passage is more cantabile and flexible. There the flute is alone: a certain freedom is in order.

Consider a piece we all love, the Mozart Concerto in G Major, K. 313. Whether in the orchestra score or in the piano part, we find a mine of information. It will have great impact on our interpretation and on our efficiency (see Accompaniment ex. 1, page 7).

First the flute is alone; you have a bit of leeway for the scale pattern in thirds. Then the repeated eighth notes show that you cannot waver. You have become the accompanist, because there is no way that fourteen violinists (or even one pianist) will follow you if the rhythm is not firm.

Even more so (see Accompaniment ex. 2, page 8).

The scale pattern in thirds with grace notes is written in a way suggesting hes-

Accompaniment Example 1. Mozart, Concerto in G Major, K. 313,
first movement, measures 60–66

itancy, but the second measure, once again, has a dominant rhythmic beat that
must be followed by the solo instrument.

In measure 72, the flute is totally alone, allowing you to make a dynamic progression on the five Ds. In measure 73, the accompaniment is in flexible slurred
eighth notes, as in measure 75. The reappearance of steady eighths in the next
measure indicates a return to strict rhythmic tempo (see Accompaniment exx. 3
and 4, page 9).

Mozart intended the flute to be alone on its first phrase, indicating that it has

Accompaniment Example 2. Mozart, Concerto in G Major, K. 313,
first movement, measures 70–76

a tentative character. Each time it appears it is up to us to play it in as many different moods as our inspiration desires: soft or loud, lyrical or subdued. . . . But
as soon as the strings enter in sixteenth notes, they indicate a pace that will sound
natural if the flute does not try to play slower than the orchestra or the piano.
Wise are flutists who accept compromise with a dozen orchestra players (or a pianist) instead of trying to inflict themselves upon them.

It is interesting to see also how for the last appearance of this phrase, the flute
is no longer alone. This indicates that the solo instrument should follow the violins (or the conductor, or both). Ensemble will be more efficient.

For the flute, it's the same music. However, it is shadowed by the accompaniment that underlines the flute line and that somewhat restricts the freedom of
the two previous identical patterns.

Accompaniment Example 3. Mozart, Concerto in G Major,
K. 313, second movement, measures 10–12

Accompaniment Example 4. Mozart, Concerto in G major,
KV 313, second movement, last entrance

"The player should play with the bass, not the bass with the player."[1]

Now consider the development of this movement (see Accompaniment ex. 5, page 10).

Three Es start it. The second one is left alone by Mozart to allow a certain dynamic and rhythmic suspension. But one measure later the same three-E pattern is accompanied by a steady stream of sixteenth notes. Even if our tempo is slow and our humor cantabile, we must be with the bass line.

1. Trevor Wye, *Marcel Moyse—An Extraordinary Man: A Musical Biography* (Cedar Falls, Iowa: Winzer Press, 1993).

Accompaniment Example 5. Mozart, Concerto in G Major,
K. 313, second movement, measures 16–18

Dynamics are also affected by the context. Obviously, if you are alone, you will have no problem cutting through, and you may risk playing softer. The composer again is telling you that you are somewhat free. However, if the traffic is heavy in the accompaniment, then you have to work at the balance to make yourself heard, regardless of your intended dynamic.

The most efficient way to make music is to consider the letter and the spirit of music and the people who recreate it with you, as a soloist or as an accompanist. Egos often get in the way, but conflicts for preeminence are only political. If you deserve the limelight, people will know sooner or later.

In a nutshell:

Do not think that the flute line exists by itself. Live with the score. Analyze it, and serve it. Knowing is reinventing. Read the score and listen to it, not for your line but for everything else.

Please refer also to:

Dynamics   Silence
Freedom   Score
Interpretation

ACOUSTICS

One of the most obstinate complaints I heard from musicians during my orchestral life (besides moaning about the conductors) was that the acoustics of the hall were too much this, too little that, and in general not flattering enough.

Flutists, like other players, are so preoccupied by their sound that often they are unable or unwilling to have an objective ear. They "look" at themselves play without listening.

My opinion is that we must play, regardless. Few people play the rehearsal like the concert. The hall itself resonates differently with and without an audience. The only option is to adapt on the spot to the concert venue. In other words, musicians should have their ears twenty feet away, as it were, and they should "play the hall." The return is what they must assess.

A dead-sounding studio will do justice to the cascades of notes in an allegro that would be totally drowned out at the same tempo in a church. The same studio flattens the delicious inflections of an adagio played in a church, whose reverberation will increase further the sensual pleasure of the flutist and perhaps of the audience. We must therefore adapt tempi to venues.

The effects of performance stress tend to make us ill at ease and to exaggerate what we perceive as unsatisfactory. Then experience and conditioned reflexes set in and we adapt. This is one more reason that few things can be set in stone in terms of interpretation.

The acoustics of a resonant hall are deceptive. It is very possible that the listener is not as happy as the player and vice versa. Usually the presence of wood among building materials has a favorable effect on acoustics and resonance. The hall's volume, shape, and dimensions have their importance. Still, acoustics is far from being an exact science. It's an art. Unfortunately, the best analysis and celebrated acousticians have produced a lot of horrors. In Europe, in America, and in Australia, some beautiful concert halls have been built to great expense and have turned out to be musical disasters. On the other hand, Leipzig's Neue Gewandhaus has the appearance of a monument to Stalinism or of a blockhouse of gray concrete. But the acoustics are excellent.

Things might be better if all these experts thought about music and musicians before their own posterity in the slick pages of architectural reviews.

> ### *In a nutshell:*
>
> Listen to the return from the hall. Don't judge only from the way you think you play. Be your own listener. Adapt.
>
> #### *Please refer also to:*
>
> Dynamics
> Interpretation
> Tempo

AGOGIC

Slight changes occur during a human instrumental[2] execution. Agogic[3] is the combination of the natural tendency of dynamics to affect tempo and rhythm, and vice versa.

It concerns, for a great part, these natural phenomena:

- An accelerando invites a crescendo, whereas a diminuendo tends to drag.
- A stretched tempo increases the effect of a harmonic progression toward an accent.
- Upbeats are characterized by a more animated and lighter dynamic (weak beat) than downbeats (strong beats), which are by nature heavier and more stretched.
- Short values (sixteenths) in a fast tempo invite an even quicker pace, but the same values, in a slow movement, tend to drag.
- Long notes decay naturally if they are not sustained.
- Rubato allows phrasing to "speak" the music by imperceptibly stealing here the time that will be returned there.
- Silence attracts sound just as gravity affects mass.

It is important to know about agogic, either to go along with it to enhance performance or to control it when it threatens to disfigure the musical discourse. Instruments have their own agogic. Cellos and bassoons thrive in their lower range, whereas flutes and violins find their best singing voice in their middle and upper-middle registers. These natural characteristics help to color and pace music effectively.

However, the composer sometimes uses deliberate awkwardness in extreme

---

2. As opposed to mechanic or electronic.

3. Used and defined for the first time by Hugo Riemann (1849–1919), the music theoretician and philosopher, in *Musikalische Dynamik und Agogik* (Hamburg: Rahter, 1884).

ranges to imply strain, or to enhance a nostalgic mood. A famous example is the opening of *The Rite of Spring*.[4] This haunting wail puts the listener (and the bassoonist) in an eerie and mysterious mood. The same notes scored for the flute or the clarinet instead would have a soothing color. Difficulty is here part of music.

Lento, tempo rubato

Agogic Example 1. Stravinsky, *Le sacre du printemps*

The perils of altitude also create an excitement that explains the way opera audiences respond to great tenors as they soar into heroic high notes. The trumpet has the same effect.

It is tempting for young players to search for the loudest flute, so they can emulate CDs. Cooper[5] says that of ten head joints he offers, the loudest are the most popular. Sometimes power is achieved at the expense of flexibility and beauty.

From the point of view of interpretation, a flutist must recognize the inherent characteristics of his instrument. He may use them by going along with the agogic of the flute: using staccato as an echo for legato, allowing the sound to diminish or increase naturally, changing colors on identical patterns, enhancing the innately poetic character of the flute—in short, implementing everything that serves music.

On the other hand, knowing the agogic of the instrument will help the flutist find solutions that do not come naturally: delicate attacks, playing loud in the low range and soft in the ledger lines, preventing the premature increase of a progression, keeping long notes alive, controlling a tendency to rush—in short, mastering instrumental playing while keeping in mind the aesthetic goal of music.

> ### In a nutshell
>
> Agogic: Quasi-innate circumstances of music, instruments, and performers. You must recognize it to control it and use it to enhance interpretation.

---

4. Igor Stravinsky (1882–1971), composer.
5. Albert Cooper (1926–), flute maker.

Please refer also to:

Accents   Rubato
Metronome   Tempo

AIR COLUMN

In my terminology, the air column is not only the air inside the instrument, nor is it the flow of air from the lungs to the lips. The air column is a continuous unit from the inner part of the body to the tip of the foot joint. Thereafter it unfortunately escapes our control, even if the medium (air) keeps resonating.

The physical definition of musical sound is a vibration[6] carried by a medium (air). I define the air column as every part of the body or of the instrument in contact, directly or indirectly, with air. This includes the air not only in the lungs and in the mouth, but also in the cavities of the nose, forehead, and inner ear that singers, with good reason, call resonators. Everyone's voice or flute tone is unique, due in great part to the characteristic sound components of these resonators. Resonance of the sound implies that none of the various elements of the air column counteracts the others: diaphragm, throat, mouth, nose, and nose cavities.[7] Moyse used to compare the air column to a fountain. If it is well set, the flow is smooth and regular. If it is too weak, it breaks. If it is too strong, it splashes.

Throat

The throat is the narrowest passage and the most unconscious obstacle to the free flow of the air column. When we are worried or upset, our spoken voice changes: it becomes coarse or forced. This is the result of the throat's contraction, preventing the free play of the vocal cords. In the performing arts, nervous tension is often responsible.

Likewise, when we raise our shoulders, the voice sounds more pinched. On the path of the air column, the throat acts as a gorge or rapids.[8] The smoothly flowing river must suddenly narrow its course, and the same volume of water must flow through a narrow bottleneck. With a great amount of turbulence and white water, the stream fights its way through the obstacle. Further downstream the valley widens once more, and the body of water is again serene.

6. This vibration is not the same as vibrato.

7. Richard Miller, *The Structure of Singing: System and Art in Vocal Technique* (New York: Schirmer Books, 1986).

8. The word *gorge* in French, with the same spelling and meaning, means also the throat, in its primary sense.

At the slightest nervous tension, the throat tightens and squeezes the air column, producing a choked sound. The same phenomenon occurs when we lift
our shoulders in an instinctive defensive gesture or because of poor posture.
How can we alleviate this problem? By emulating the process of yawning upon
breathing as well as upon blowing.

Everything is connected back there. Our ears pop when we change altitudes
in a plane because pressure differs on either side of the eardrums. Blowing our
nose, swallowing, or yawning corrects this imbalance from the inside.

Yawning

When we yawn, our body tells us to relax, to forget our problems, to sleep, to feel
good: the shoulders fall, the throat opens, the ears pop, and the abdomen's movements no longer restrict the lungs' inflation. Yawning reproduces naturally a correct breathing procedure and a sensation of comfort.

Nose

When we suffer from a respiratory problem such as a cold, we have the impression that our tone is as stuffy as our nose. Our perception is altered because the
inner ear, the sinuses, and the pharynx[9] cannot resonate.

To avoid cracking a difficult note—one played *piano* in the high register or *forte*
in the low register—the "explosion" of air hitting the edge of the embouchure
can be blunted by releasing a small amount of air through the nose just before
the attack. This precaution sets the air column in motion. It does not prevent a
precise attack—quite the contrary. Compare this to the violin bow: it moves
slightly before the note speaks, unless a very strong attack is required. In this
case, the bow hits and bites the string.

To open the sound, try to open your nose. You can even try to stretch your ears
from the inside. Spread out your nostrils: you feel your throat also opening up,
and all the hollow cavities of the head start to resonate. It is the same process as
yawning: it feels good and contributes to the opening of the sound.

Another use of nasal air release: while playing, just before a breath, you may
want to empty your lungs to get fresh oxygen.

Control of your blowing, and inhaling through the nose is the first step toward
continuous blowing, commonly known as circular breathing.

Mouth

Some are of the opinion that the shape we give to the mouth cavity affects the
sound. Inflating or vibrating the cheeks would provide more resonance. I do not

---

9. The cavity situated at the back of the mouth that connects the nose, the throat, and the inner
ear.

share this theory for more than one reason: flapping cheeks affect focus and take some of the direction out of the air column. Fast register changes (arpeggios) do not permit this without danger, especially under stress. Still, if it really works for you, why not?

Diaphragm

The diaphragm is often considered a conscious element of the air column that we could, at will, command to do what we tell it. That is a well-meaning misconception. The diaphragm goes down when we inhale and up when we exhale, in a completely automatic fashion that ends with our life. When we hold our breath, we stop its movement, for little more than a minute, by the action not of the diaphragm itself, but of the muscles around it, mainly the abdominal and chest muscles. These respiratory muscles can hinder the automatic play of the diaphragm. To inhale, all tension in the abdomen must be let go by "dropping" it. Upon exhaling (blowing) the chest muscles must keep the rib cage expanded to counteract their own elasticity and weight, as well as the pressure generated by the abdominal muscles. For this reason, after a big breath, the first concern should be not to blow until the initial third of the breath has been spent through natural resilience and gravity working on the rib cage.

This is an important point in teaching beginners, and even some advanced players: they always complain they don't have enough breath, when, in fact, their blowing needs to be better managed. My concept of air management is symbolized by *Tenuto* (stability of the flute on the chin), *Sostenuto* (support from the abdomen), *Ritenuto* (counteracting the collapse of the thorax with the chest muscles). Think more of the way you blow than about how you breathe. Breathing is the most natural activity. Open your mouth and let the air in. Blowing is where art is. Air management is what produces music and expression, whereas breathing is often a dirty noise.

> ### In a nutshell:
>
> Think of air as the vehicle of your sound. Put every molecule of air in resonance with your sound by opening all parts of the respiratory system, especially throat and nose. Don't think that tone starts at the embouchure and dies at the foot joint.
>
> Use muscle control not to force volume, but to open all the resonators. Releasing air through the nose helps difficult attacks. Open your nose to open your sound. Release air pressure for special effects and circular blowing, also for emptying the lungs while playing.

Please refer also to:

Air, Hot and Cold   Circular Blowing
Air Management   Focus
Air Speed   Lips
Appoggio   Resonance
Attacks   *Tenuto, Sostenuto, Ritenuto*
Blowing   Turbo-Sound
Breathing

AIR SPEED

When we play a wide interval, say, wider than a fourth, our first reflex is to move the chin or the lips to shift the angle of attack of the air brush. If it works for you, even when you are out of shape or nervous, of course, do it. My problem with that process is its relative unreliability at the wrong moment, under stress. No doubt the lips provide guidance, but the energy comes from the strong air-column muscles. We need to give more or less speed to the air, and to involve the whole body in the playing process.

When we rise in the range of the flute, instead of messing with the embouchure only, we should, as it were, sink into the ground. We feel very heavy, the shoulders are low, and the abdominal belt is firm thanks to the strong leg muscles. The higher you play, the lower your center of gravity should be.

When you want to descend with an equivalent interval, you relax the abdominal belt before lipping and jawboning.

Hot Air, Cold Air

A strange thing happens when we change the air speed. Nobody has been able to explain to me why our air brush is cold when we blow fast, as if to cool a cup of coffee, whereas, when frost bites our hands, we slowly exhale some hot air into them to warm them up.

Try these experiments:

- When you are cold, blow into your cupped hands. Your throat and mouth are wide open, and the air is hot, almost at body temperature. If you aim at a cold surface (a window or someone's glasses), it fogs up.
- A game we used to play as children: blow the same way through someone's woolen sweater. The air really seems even hotter.

When your cocoa or coffee is too hot, you blow to cool it off. You pinch your lips to make an air brush similar to the one we use for our flute playing.

My question is: why is slow, open-throat air hot, and fast, closed-lip air cold? Is it the difference in speed? But why? It's the same air; it must start from the lungs at the same temperature. Has it something to do with panting, like a dog?

Whatever the answer, it helps us:

- Fast air — cold air — descending center of gravity — intervals ascending — high notes.
- Slow air — hot air — relaxed belt — open throat — intervals descending — low notes.

This simple demonstration will help you to feel the relationship between air speed, support, and resistance at the level of the embouchure. It is also very useful for young flutists.

On wide slurs, up or down, one must change the air speed to compensate for the possible break in the air column and in the sound wave.

In a nutshell:

Play from the ground up. Use your feet more than your lips for tone production. The energy of your tone starts low in the abdomen. Leg muscles contribute to that effort. The air column contributes at each level to air speed. Its last step is at the air brush, where the lips act as an intermediary, not as a force.

Please refer also to:

Air Column	Lips
Air Management	Muscles, Strong and Weak
Appoggio	*Tenuto, Sostenuto, Ritenuto*
Center of Gravity	Turbo-Sound
Intervals	

ALIGNMENT

The outer edge of the embouchure hole, the leading edge on which we blow, should be roughly on a straight line running through the middle of the tone holes. It is advisable for people who are unsure of their position to mark this with a drop of nail polish on the head joint and on the brand-mark ring.

Alignment Figure 1

However, certain experienced players have found it more comfortable to open, that is, turn out, or to cover, that is, turn in the embouchure. This is a matter of taste and convenience. If it works for you, do it!

If the amount of deviation one way or another makes you produce a sound that is too thin and reedy, chances are you are covering too much. If it is too breathy and out of focus, then your opening might be exaggerated.

One of the advantages of the French system is that you have to have an average alignment of the headjoint for the fingers to cover the holes on the ring keys. It is hard to understand why students are supposed to learn on closed-hole instruments that encourage bad habits and then graduate to French-system flutes after they have developed such bad hand positions that it is terribly painful to change them. More makers should offer cheap French-model flutes, so that more people can start with reasonable finger placement. (However, I think the offset G, as Boehm devised it, is a better solution for young hands.) Once you know what you are doing, then you can make an informed decision. Open holes do not really make that much of a difference.

I purposefully do not have marks any more. I do align roughly as mentioned above, but often correct slightly one way or the other. I have noticed that I fidget with it more when I am nervous for a performance than when I feel normal.

The important thing is not to make it a fetish. Just correct as needed. Thank God, the flute is not a precise machine.

Foot Joint Alignment

The rod of the foot joint should also be aligned on that straight line running through the middle of the tone holes.

Alignment Figure 2. D tear drop (nineteenth century and l. lot.)

Alignment Figure 3. D spatula (modern)

The C♯ key should be separated from the D♯, contrary to what is currently the fashion among flute makers. The old teardrop was more efficient: you did not risk leaking the D♯ key when your pinky went over to work both C♯ key and rollers. If you even barely touch the D♯ key, the extreme notes of the flute, either low C♯, C, and B, or super-high D, will not speak, regardless of your chinning and face contortions. What you get is at best nothing, or worse, a loud crack in the sound.

For certain low-note sequences, turning in the foot can help flutists with a short pinky to feel more comfortable with a slightly altered alignment. As soon as possible, they return to the basic foot alignment.

Even the gizmo can get in the way of the pinky outreach to the C. Whereas closing the B is a definite help for some high notes, such as A, C, and D, this can be achieved by touching the B roller. If the gizmo is to be completely comfortable, it should be built turning away from where the pinky will sit.

Head Joint Alignment

The tone is not the only area that is affected by the head joint alignment. The position of the fingers can be a problem. When the head is turned too far outward, the hands must play on keys at an inward angle. On the other hand, if the head is turned inward, the sound is covered and the chin must be jutted out so that the fingers work in a normal, practically horizontal plane.

My suggestion is to stay in the basic alignment, adjusting a few degrees one way or the other. Do not be dogmatic about a precise place, but don't jeopardize your playing and comfort by indulging in bad habits.

The ideal body alignment is a very personal thing, once you know how to play. Until then, do what your teacher says; there must be a reason for it. Productive and enjoyable flute playing is based on common sense, comfort, and pleasure.

In a nutshell:

Hand position is the justification of proper alignment. Adapt the hands to the flute, not vice versa. Breaking too far from the basic alignment can lead to tense instrumental playing, and sometimes to pain.

Please refer also to:

Boehm System   Hands
Fetishes   Slam-and-Squeeze
Flutes

APPOGGIATURA

Of two slurred notes, the second is almost always less intense than the first, because in general the first one is an appoggiatura (from the Italian *appoggiare*). The word means "to lean upon," either because the note is outside the harmony (1) or part of a dissonant chord (2), creating tension, or because it is leading to (3) or longing for resolution and release (4).

Appoggiatura Example 1. Mozart, Oboe Concerto in
C Major, K. 314, second movement

From the point of view of instrumental playing, it must be kept in mind that a lifting finger (A2 to B♭2, or E2 to F2) will resolve naturally. But falling fingers (B♭2 to A2, or F2 to E2) have an organic tendency to reinforce the resolution. This is one more reason to avoid slam-and-squeeze. The fingers must also take part in phrasing. Sonority is vital, but try to play without the hands.

An appoggiatura may be indicated as a grace note (1) or written out (2). Identify it in your discovery of the piece.

Appoggiatura Example 2. Mozart, Concerto in
G Major, K. 313, third movement

The release of an appoggiatura can be very long and diluted, sometimes comically, in rococo or flute romantic repertoire such as Boehm or Doppler. Still, the harmonic tension (1) must live through it, until the release point is found (2). None of the ornamental notes (3) should have more energy than the appoggiatura and no less than the release note (4).

I think of the appoggiatura as a coiled spring. One leans upon it to accumulate

Appoggiatura Example 3. Mozart, Oboe Concerto in C, K. 314, second movement

energy. When one lets go, the stored power is released, and the spring hums. For this reason the build-up of an accent (2), the tension between the notes (1), should be used instead of vibrato. Upon release (3), the vibrato should make up for the spent energy to keep the release alive. On either side of the rest, the identical notes (=) have the same intensity, but not the same vibrato.

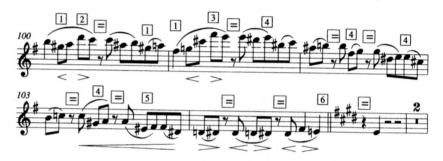

Appoggiatura Example 4. Brahms, Symphony No. 4, Finale

Another idea to construct this passage is to take time with the increase of tension (1). Let the energy build up almost by itself (2), and culminate (3). Then do not linger anymore (4), (5) until the end (6) or the start of a new progression (5). The sign (=) means we should match the sound on either side of the breath.

The appoggiatura acts as the tonic accent of a spoken word. The resolution of an appoggiatura is like a silent syllable:

French: "J'aim(e) ma bell(e) flut(e)."
English: "I lov(e) a nic(e) flut(e) ton(e)."
Italian: "Mi piac(e) un(') bell(') suono."
German: "Ich lieb(e)," "Flöt(e)," etc.

> ### In a nutshell:
>
> Appoggiaturas express tension and release. In linear fashion, they make harmony melodic. Learn how to resolve them with fingers, not only with sound.

> *Please refer also to:*
>
> Accents   Metronome
> Fingers   Rubato

APPOGGIO

Appoggio is an air-management technique used by singers of the Italian school. The English "breath support" is not an adequate translation. Appoggio is a system of combining and isometrically balancing the abdominal and chest muscles' action in the inhaling procedure as well as in the exhaling and tone-producing phenomenon.

"To sustain a given note, the air should be expelled slowly; to attain this end, the respiratory (inspiratory) muscles, by continuing their action, strive to retain the air in the lungs, and oppose their action to that of the expiratory muscles, which is called *lotta vocale* or vocal struggle."[10] Upon blowing, the technique of appoggio,[11] meaning the act of leaning in Italian, is the process that would come closest to what is mistakenly meant by diaphragmatic support.

If the intercostal[12] muscles did not isometrically balance it, the support of the abdominal muscles, without opposition, would lead to a rapid deflation of the lungs. Appoggio prevents the collapse of the chest. Schematically, the singer or flutist's effort is to not blow but to realize this inner balance. "After breathing in as far as possible, we must use considerable inspiratory force to keep the air from going out with a sigh. . . . You have to brake your exhaling, using inspiratory muscles to hold back, to keep the chest volume from decreasing too rapidly because of its own elasticity."[13]

The techniques of *Tenuto, Sostenuto, Ritenuto*" and *appoggio* are sophisticated. There are rewards to this quest. Once the techniques have become natural, they become an element of ease in playing in all ranges, of pleasure, of dominating the torments of fright, and of serving phrasing and music.

Tenuto, Sostenuto, Ritenuto

What I call *Tenuto* (*tenu*, or held) is the need for embouchure stability on the chin. The weak muscles (facial, labial, and intercostal) are the most obvious playing muscles, but use of the strong ones (abdominals, leg, and left arm) is indispensable to the production of musical sound. Tonal focalization and density are aided

10. Francesco Lambert, *The Art of Singing,* quoted by Miller.
11. Miller.
12. Between the ribs.
13. Miller.

by the lips, to be sure, but the main agent is the left arm. Flapping cheeks do not help focus and control of the tone in the extreme low or high ranges.

The first joint of the left forefinger is the first fulcrum of the flute. It provides the stability vital for technique and articulation, but also for tone production. All the old illustrations of transverse flute players through the ages show this position: left forefinger halfway down, balancing the flute's body. Jaw movements and lips contribute to tone production, but stability at this point is essential.

Support does not imply the diaphragm. Support is the abdominal muscles' involvement in the blowing process. This is *Sostenuto* (*soutenu*, or supported). When we lift a suitcase or lean against a car with the upper body, our powerful leg muscles contribute to the effort of the abdominals. The cough point, or sneeze point, situated just below the navel, is the seat of the most intense energy, strengthened by the action of the thighs.

Therefore I advise the use of the legs (when standing) to provide support. For the seated flutist, I do not agree with the military posture: chin up, shoulders up, elbows high, and buns on the edge of the chair. Instead, try sitting with the kidneys reclining gently against the lower part of the chair back, pushing the tummy out, and feeling the ground under the feet to complement the support.

Ritenuto (*retenu*, or withheld) is the mechanism of the upper chest muscles, which counterbalance the abdominal muscles of support so that air is not flushed out all at once. Our main effort in playing is actually to not blow and to maintain the expansion of the rib cage, to resist its collapse.

In a nutshell:

Abdominal support is the motor of playing. However, it would cause all the air to be spent rapidly if it were not counterbalanced by chest muscles preventing the collapse of the thorax. Stability on the chin helps air management by contributing to create a focused tone while saving air and coloring the sound.

Please refer also to:

Air column	Isometrics
Blowing	Muscles
Breathing	Stability
Diaphragm	

ARPEGGIO

The fundamental note of an arpeggio needs to resonate: it is not in bad style, therefore, to hold it a little, and even to give it a little vibrato. Especially when it is slurred, an arpeggio should not be seen as a staircase whose steps would be pushed away one by one by jutting the chin (figure 1), but as a chain (figure 2) whose links would be the notes wrapping onto one another in a seamless stream of sound.

Arpeggio Example 1

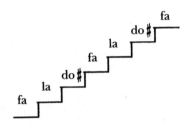

Arpeggio Figure 1

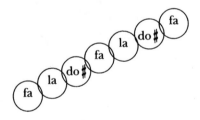

Arpeggio Figure 2

The highest point always seems the hardest. This is purely psychological, for if this note were part of an arpeggio reaching higher, it would not be a problem. Three things must be kept in mind:

- The higher the note, the lower the center of gravity should be. As the arpeggio rises, you should feel that you are sinking into the floor. The power that you feel in your abdominal wall comes also from your legs, just as when you lift a heavy object. If you are sitting, your lower back contributes to the legs' involvement.

- A slight lip movement may accompany this support. However, jutting the chin becomes useless, even detrimental to the sound's focus, because it is exaggerated in time of stress.
- Fingers, especially little devil no. 1, which works our octave key, are vital for a smooth arpeggio. You must phrase with your fingers and anticipate their motion so that there is no delay in their action. No amount of slamming of the fingers will replace this. Furthermore, slamming shakes the embouchure, another problem in arpeggios.

Practice daily exercise no. 10 in the Taffanel-Gaubert *Dix-sept exercices journaliers*.[14] These triads are best played slurred, slowly and freely. Speed is not the issue here.

In a difficult arpeggio, the lowest notes must be nourished. They should act as a diving board, helping you to spring up from the fundamental instead of producing an effort just to reach for the upper note. The highest note is like a release after the effort produced on the next to last degree, comparable to the climber's last step at the mountain's summit: a reward after the long climb.

In a nutshell:

Involve your whole body in your playing, from the ground up. Your sound is the result of it all. Focus and nourish the fundamental. Do not confuse a timely tuning correction by the lips with constant chinning.

Please refer also to:

Center of Gravity	Little Devils
Finger Phrasing	Slam-and-Squeeze
Intervals	Stability

ARTICULATION

Articulation implies the word *article*, a locution allowing the language to be clearer, more legible, more . . . articulate. Newspaper headlines use no articles: "Mother Robs Bank for Son's Bail." A whole story in six words, but hardly an example for musical interpretation.

Each musical phrase can be taken as a spoken sentence, each element of this

---

14. Paul Taffanel and Philippe Gaubert, *Dix-sept grands exercices journaliers de mécanisme pour flûte* (Paris: Alphonse Leduc, 1923).

phrase as a word, and each note as a syllable. This, in turn, consists of consonants and vowels.

The sound equivalent of any syllable is unique to each language. Consider the imaginary words *tude* and *ture* (for example, in lati*tude* and minia*ture*): it is difficult to compare the dryness of the French *u*, the guttural German *ü*, or *y*, the velvet of the Italian and Spanish *ou*, the wet English *you*. The wonder of sounds!

The consonant *t* is more or less dental; in the *r*, we hear all the different flavors: the rasp of the German and French and the roll of bel canto in Italian, Spanish, and the ancient French that can still be heard in some French-speaking provinces and lands (such as Canada and Lebanon). The brogues of Ireland and Scotland and the local tongues of England roll around like a mouthful of pearls. The *r* seems to be the stumbling block of Japan, where *r* and *l* are pronounced almost identically. Modern English speakers find it hard to deal with either the rolled or the guttural *r*. Learning a foreign tongue or two opens one's mental scope; for a musician, and particularly for a flutist, it is a charming and helpful tool for articulation and for a natural phrasing.

In sung prosody (words and music) the consonant has the articulating function, colored by the sustained sound of the vowel. Solfège (do, ré, mi) is none other than a syllabic codification to help singing.

To achieve ensemble in the attack, a group of varied instruments (strings, woodwinds, brass) must get rid, as it were, of the consonant to let the common sound blossom on the vowel.

What syllables can be used to conceptualize flute articulation?

The consonant can be *t* in all forms of single tonguing; *k* for short double tonguing; *d* for *louré* (sometimes called legato in North America); *g* for mellow double tonguing; and *d* for composite single tonguing. The possible consonants are numerous. Even *p* is useful for a soft articulation without the tongue. The only issues are comfort, efficacy, and clarity, not dogma.

Choices for the vowel are more limited: *a*, as in *bar*, sings well in the long notes but can be sluggish for fast runs; *e*, short as in *pet* or long as in *where*, is more nimble for staccato passages in single, double, and triple tonguing.

The *i* of *bid* or *kiss* is probably the most commonly used sound in any language. Certain theories contend that Latin tongues lend themselves better to a clear articulation. However, there is no special trick or magic wand: I know some English-speaking flutists who have no problem with tonguing. Ransom Wilson, for example, is one of the fastest tongues in the west.

Whatever one's native tongue, nothing replaces or resists intelligent study and regular practice. One must have an idea of the musical goal. Then articulation must be practiced to become natural; for instance, in groups of four or six notes, or repeated notes, two or three at a time, on the Taffanel-Gaubert scales.[15]

Subdivision of staccato passages into these groups helps to synchronize tongue

15. Taffanel-Gaubert, daily exercise no. 4.

and fingers. Rhythm must be the common denominator for both: they relate to it instead of to each other:

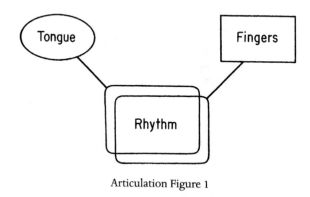

Articulation Figure 1

Quantz[16] dedicates a whole chapter, with many illustrations, to the use of *tiri* (*ti* short, *ri* longer) at a time when the *r* was normally rolled throughout Europe. Today, *di* would be most commonly used in composite tonguing instead of *ri*. Then as now, it is an extremely convenient and musical means of articulation.

Finally, unwritten inequality *(inégal)* was a common baroque practice. It consists, roughly, of emphasizing the first note in a group of two, three, or four equal notes. The typical pattern is with two sixteenth notes in binary measure. It was unwritten because it was understood by cultivated musicians before 1800. Quantz advises the player to articulate it with the syllables *did'll*, as in *diddle*. Unwritten inequality is still in use today in jazz and traditional music, but it has fallen out of use in classical playing. However, it remains a useful tool for "speaking" fast runs grouped by two smoothly and flexibly.

The degree of articulation should vary in reverse order of the range: repeated notes in the low register tend to sound continuous. It is a good idea to separate them slightly more than one would the same figure in the middle and high registers.

In the case of an isolated articulation, an upbeat, for instance, a dotted note does not always mean a pointed attack with the tip of the tongue, but that the note is framed by a bit of air on either side, and, most important, that it is lighter than the downbeat it introduces. This effect of lightness is constant in baroque and classical music, as in the siciliano from J. S. Bach's Sonata in E Major, BWV 1035, and can still be found in Schubert's upbeats.

---

16. Johann Joachim Quantz, *Essay of a Method for Playing the Transverse Flute, Accompanied by Several Remarks of Service for the Improvement of Good Taste in Practical Music,* a trans. with introduction and notes by Edward R. Reilly (London: Faber and Faber, 1966).

Articulation Example 1

Articulation Example 2. Schubert, Theme and
variations, on "Ihr Blümlein Alle, op. 160

Many elements of interpretation are not explicit. Too many annotations on a
score would weigh down the musical text, as can be seen in so many abusive editions of baroque repertoire. To a cultured musician, the "good taste" dear to our
musical ancestors was precisely all that was implicit, all that went without saying.
"Culture is what's left when everything has been forgotten."[17]

Articulation is a technical tool. As such, it is a means to an end. Imagination
and meaning are the guiding force.

In a nutshell:

Articulation should become second nature. Through
practice on scales, we should be able to use various syllables and different tongue movements without having to
think how we do them. Starting the tone on an attack is
different from the actual tonguing of articulation. Meaning is the goal of articulation. There are no secrets, just
common sense and practice.

Please refer also to:

Attacks	Phrasing
Baroque	Rhythm
Composite Tonguing	Scale Game
Double Tonguing	Single Tonguing
Unwritten Inequality	

---

17. Edouard Herriot (1872–1957), French politician, in *Discours à la Chambre des Députés*
(Speeches at the Chamber).

ATTACKS

This word has an aggressive connotation, but is well understood by most wind players. Singing coaches prefer to use the word "onset."[18]

The French language's idiomatic *tu* attack cannot be reproduced in English. At best, a *tu* replica would be *too*, a muddy attack, or worse yet, *tew*. Both, however, are better than the *ta* or *da* jaw-dropping sound that some people advise, to disastrous effect: there is no direction in the tone, no follow-through with the airstream. Yet, the *ta* or *da* can be useful on some dark long notes.

Therefore we are left with the *ti* (pronounced "tea" in English.) At least it slightly pulls back the corners of the lips, to me more necessary than relaxing the cheeks. It contributes to focusing the tone and to reliable articulation.

The movement of the tongue is not a percussive one, as the "French" tonguing is sometimes misconstrued. It is the venting of an orifice behind which pressure has built up, as in the venting of an eight-foot organ pipe:

- If you open the valve and then blow the bellows, you get a wheezy, comical whimper.
- If you send air without stopping the pipe first, you cannot control the articulation.

Doesn't that remind you of the flute? "Throughout all this, the tongue plays an essential part, but it must be remembered that it is simply a kind of spring valve that contains and releases the appropriate impulse of pressure of air behind it."[19]

In other words, tone production does not involve the tongue. Moreover, you must keep in mind that whatever syllable is used for attacks, the actual sound is carried by the vowel, not by the consonant, which provides the attack or articulation.

So get rid of the consonant and sing the vowel. If you try to make the consonant coincide with the piano's attack, your tone and balance will be killed and the apparent ensemble will be problematic. The vowel is the vehicle of the sound:

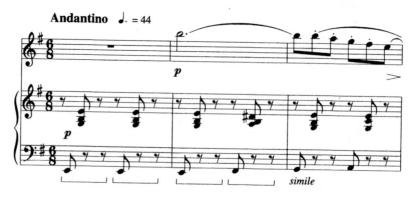

Attacks Example 1. Fauré, *Fantaisie*, Andantino,
with piano accompaniment, first three bars

18. Miller.
19. John Krell, *Kincaidiana: A Flute Player's Notebook* (Culver City, Calif.: Trio Associates, 1973).

A simultaneous ensemble attack by varied instruments (strings, woodwinds, and brass) is difficult. The group must, as it were, get rid of the consonant to let the common sound blossom on the vowel. The impression of togetherness (ensemble) will not be coming only from the simultaneity of the attack (consonant) but more through the feeling that all the individual sounds come alive at the same moment, with the vowel.

I had to develop my own attack procedure during my thirty-year orchestral career. At the Orchestre de Paris, some of the greatest conductors were our guests. The greatest were not always the clearest. Some were alchemists of orchestral sound, so I thought it was better to live with it than complain. A challenge improves the performance and the performer.

I noticed that violinists' bow is almost always in motion before the onset of the sound. So is the vibrato. Listening, looking, and trying were my good teachers.

Practicing Attacks

Attacks Example 2

This exercise is inspired by Moyse's *De la sonorité*.[20] Play slow attacks from the low tonic of the major keys of E, E♭, D, C♯, and C, all the way to the highest notes and back again. This incites you not to breathe too much between notes. For the low notes, use finger tonguing.[21]

I do not like the term attack very much because of the aggressiveness it implies. In fact, many broken notes are due to the stiffness of the attack. When one thinks of a *f* or *ff* attack, automatically the movement of the tongue is powerful, precise, and brutal. Hence, the result is often a break on delicate notes (E^2 and $E3$, and $F\sharp^3$) or, on the lowest notes, nothing. On the other hand, when a *p* or *pp* note is started, the attack tends to be sluggish and shy, and the result, with all the insecurity and stress it entails, disappointing. As is often the case, we must invert our reflexes: a *pp* attack in the high register requires a lot of support and energy. For *mf* and louder, we must release the airflow and let go to develop the sound.

In *mf, f,* and *ff* dynamics, the sound has its own life. The attack is helped by this natural energy. Even without tonguing, the sound comes alive, perhaps even better than with a big tongue movement. Conversely, in *mp, p,* and *pp* dynamics, the tongue action will have to be quick and precise to compensate for the lack of natural energy in the sound.

---

20. Marcel Moyse, *De la sonorité: Art et technique* (Paris: Alphonse Leduc, 1934).
21. With due respect, I advise against doing the same pattern slurred because of the risk of too much jawboning.

How can we achieve this?

When the tongue moves to a tricky attack, the air must be already flowing, albeit imperceptibly, through the nose. When released lightly in this manner, the air column is in smooth motion. The tongue is visible between the lips. It blocks the aperture.

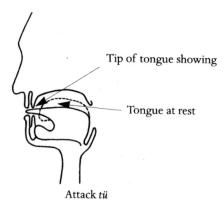

Tip of tongue showing

Tongue at rest

Attack *tü*

Attacks Figure 1

Upon attack, the tongue is pulled back swiftly. Even if for some reason the French attack is taboo, the tongue should be as close as possible to the air brush. Its travel should be as short as possible. If the tongue is too far back in the mouth, chances are that the attack will be cloudy, rough, or too loud.

The attack, therefore, is not percussion by the tongue, but a quick and precise withdrawal. No roughness is necessary, except for special and deliberate effects, as in some music of the second half of the twentieth century.

Low Register Attacks, *forte* and *fortissimo*

In the low register, the bottom notes often do not come out because the tongue precedes the fingers.

If you do not hear your own low notes, it means they have not been played. You have the best seat in the house. Give yourself time so that you, at least, hear them. Blowing more will not help. On the contrary, hold back and give the sound a very small amount of time so that you hear it. Think of singing more than of forcing or hitting.

A slight slap of the key closest to the note to be played can replace the actual tonguing.[22] Powerful attacks are controlled better on a middle breath[23] than on a big inhalation.

The shoulders should be low. There should be a good contact of the lip plate

22. This is called finger tonguing.

23. Middle breath: a partial inhalation involving the abdomen but not the upper respiratory agents (chest and shoulders).

with the chin fulcrum. Tone production comes more from abdominal support than from the lips. Precision of attack owes more to air speed than to the tongue. In the standing position, one's weight should be firmly on the feet. In the sitting position, it would rest on the lower back.

When we start a low passage after a rest, the lowest notes tend to "resist" on a loud attack. This can be helped with finger tonguing: the first note is set in resonance not at all by the tongue, but by a faint percussion of the finger closest to the desired note.

Attacks Example 3. Mendelssohn, *A Midsummernight's Dream*, Scherzo

This has nothing to do with the systematic slamming of the left ring finger that is often so loud and offensive. It does not contradict my disapproval of slam-and-squeeze. It also helps to think of the attack note.

High Register Attacks, *piano* and *pianissimo*

Delicate attacks are performed best on middle breath. Support must be even more powerful in *piano* and *pianissimo*: one must have the feeling of sinking into the ground (standing) or into the chair (sitting.) In both cases, the abdomen is pushed outward. In order to control the air stream, the abdominal pressure is counterbalanced by appoggio and by *Tenuto, Sostenuto, Ritenuto*. After air starts to be released through the nose, the backward motion of the tongue is swift and gentle.

When a big breath is needed, at the start of a long phrase, a flutist should set the air column in motion by releasing a bit of air through the nose to avoid the explosion that will break notes. If the length of the phrase is comfortable, do not breathe too much. Play using middle breath. As a general rule, don't take a huge breath if you don't need it. This applies to attacks also.

When an attack follows a short rest (such as a sixteenth-note rest in a tempo of quarter note = 120), it is advisable to breathe early on the longer rest and to blow on the short rest. This extremely common pattern comes naturally after we practice it in our daily scales. Otherwise our attack might be late and explosive if it is not broken outright.

Scale Game:

Attacks Example 4a

Attacks Example 4b

Finally, a difficult attack, like a difficult interval, works better if it is timed or measured. Some flutists sort of stutter on an untimed attack, as if they had trouble making up their minds. If, on the contrary, the attack is timed ("three, four, go"), all the reflexes involved, breath, tongue, and finger relate to the ----- ---- denominator of rhythm.

> ### *In a nutshell:*
>
> An attack is not percussion, but the venting of an aperture. Prepare the blowing before the attack. Don't take a huge breath if you don't need to; it causes bad attacks. Use discreet finger movement to set the air column in motion. Time your delicate attacks.
>
> ### *Please refer also to:*
>
> Air Speed
> Articulation
> Finger Tonguing
> Fulcrums
> Middle Breath
> Stability
> *Tenuto, Sostenuto, Ritenuto*

BEGINNERS

Common sense at an early stage will bear flute fruit in the long term. Semi-advanced flutists and their teachers lose many hours correcting bad habits that early care could have avoided. Past the first six months of playing, my principles are not dogmatic: efficiency, comfort, pleasure, and beauty. If it works, do it and teach it. Do what you preach, and preach what you do.

Those first six months, however, are crucial. Teacher and beginner should not be afraid of proceeding very slowly at first. Impatience, as well as family pressure, wants to jump ahead and hear results. But the future can be jeopardized by haste. Look how slowly and carefully young violinists start out. The method chosen should reflect this concern. My preference goes to the most progressive, not to the fastest.[1]

The typical beginner has had no musical training. It is important that she or he be taught notation and rudiments of theory right along with the first instrumental discoveries. A method book is not enough. Often it prints what to do, but rarely does it show how to do it. The teacher is the essential example. Since young people learn mostly from imitation, the teacher should be constantly demonstrating and playing along.

Producing a Tone

At first play with the mouthpiece only. Soon play with both hands on the flute:

1. Right hand around trademark, left hand as usual.

Beginners Figure 1

2. Right hand over low B (or low C), left hand as usual.

Beginners Figure 2

3. Both hands as usual, only left hand plays, only right pinky is down.

Beginners Figure 3

Play simple tunes this way:

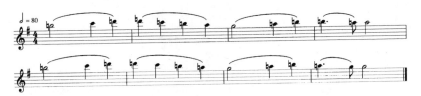

Beginners Example 1. Beethoven, "Ode to Joy" (in G Major)

1. Henry Altès, *Célèbre méthode de Flûte,* facsimile ed. by Jean-Pierre Rampal and Alain Marion (Paris: Allo Music, 1979).

Beginners Example 2. Saint-Saëns, *Danse macabre*

Beginners Example 3. Chabrier, *España*

Don't try to play long tones yet. Instead, play sounds one second long (quarter note = 60) neither loud nor soft, but with a clear attack right away. The tip of the tongue shows before the air is blown, then is pulled back as if to spit out a seed. This vents the small aperture that directs the air brush, and it helps to form the half-smile necessary for a proper direction. I still don't understand why this tonguing is anathema in certain circles. It should not be always used for a series of repeated notes, but to form the first tone, it works.

The frown is sometimes advised, but it does not come naturally. The half-smile is a better way. The flute airflow is comparable to cooling a hot spoonful or blowing out the last candle of a birthday cake. Who does not like to do that?

Breathing

Blowing is, at first, more important than breathing. Don't take in more breath than you need to play tones of one second. To feel the short breaths that you need at first, lie down on your back; in this position you cannot breathe using your shoulders. Your tummy goes up and down—that's good.

Posture

The most logical way, again, is your natural posture when you read a bulletin board or wait for the bus: no raised shoulders or elbows.

Instruments

It is hard to understand why students are supposed to learn on instruments that encourage bad habits, such as covered-key flutes. By the time they graduate to the French system they have developed bad hand positions that are terribly frustrating to change. More makers should offer cheap French-model flutes (with open keys) so that more people can start with reasonable finger placement. One excellent feature of the cheaper flutes, however, is the offset G sharp. It is much easier on small hands.

Hand Position

The teacher should adopt the most natural position. I do not like to see cocked wrists: they lead to tendinitis. As much as possible, the tendons of both arms should stay aligned with the fingers.

Left Hand

Pinch your right ear with your left hand. Your wrist is aligned: play the flute the same way.

Right Hand

Try picking up a book lying flat on a high shelf. Your wrist is aligned with your right arm and with your fingers. These are almost flat, and the thumb is positioned somewhere opposite the forefinger and the middle finger. They are more or less flat, and that is good. If they were too rounded out, as is sometimes taught, you would be squeezing the instrument with the right hand. Lifting squeezing fingers requires more effort than flat ones. This in turn could, in the long run, create stress on the tendons all the way up the right arm.

Stability

It will be a blessing if, early on, the beginner feels the stability of the lip plate on the chin. The lips should be relaxed, not loose. The chin should not jut forward or extend toward the lip plate. Instead, the flute should be brought to the chin by the stability generated by the main points of balance: first joint of left forefinger, right thumb.

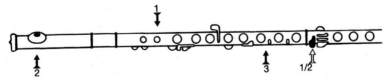

Beginners Figure 4

The First Pieces

It is most important for a beginner to hear the teacher play the same things, or accompany them. The teacher should not hesitate to stay a long time on simple tunes such as "Three Blind Mice" or "Frère Jacques" or the ones given earlier.

Repetitiousness is not usually a problem for the first six months. Full pieces will come much later. At first, love starts with playing the flute, not so much with playing the music. At a young age, the aesthetic reward of great music comes after the exquisite pleasure of playing the beloved flute. Some fifty years later, my own delight survives and flourishes.

> ### *In a nutshell:*
>
> Proceed slowly with beautiful tunes that have movement. Long tones are difficult and tedious. Breathe just enough to play a few notes. Big breaths are hard to control. Always give a tonguing on the first note.
> Once the fingers are placed logically, comfort and stability are the issue. A good stability with the fulcrums does not mean tightness. Do not "slam-and-squeeze."
>
> #### *Please refer also to:*
>
> | | |
> |---|---|
> | Blowing | Position |
> | Comfort | Posture |
> | Fulcrums | Slam-and-Squeeze |
> | Hands | Stability |
> | Lips | |

BLOWING LONG PHRASES

There is no answer to the sophistic question, "Which came first, the chicken or the egg?" For us it translates to: "Which is first: blowing or breathing?" Breathing, of course, and yet it is the blowing that creates a sound. If you don't know how to blow, your breathing will be just an organic act, a vital but musically void necessity. Still, it seems that most of us are worried more by the intake of air than with the management of its release.

Examples of breath management problems abound in our solo repertoire: the first three movements of Bach's Partita in A Minor, BWV 1013; the opening solo in Mozart's Concerto in D Major, K. 314; and in Poulenc's Sonata, the opening phrase of the Cantilena.

We find it in the orchestral repertoire also: among other places, in Ravel's *Bolero* and the beginning of Beethoven's Fourth Symphony. The latter is never mentioned, but it was my personal nightmare: one single B♭ held for what seems like hours by one flute (no second to help out), two clarinets, and two bassoons over three octaves. The more famous the conductor, the slower the tempo. . . . Pitch problems, breath management problems, attack problems. I preferred some of the technically "difficult" excerpts.

Most often required for auditions are the Scherzo from Mendelssohn's *Midsummer Night's Dream* and Debussy's *Prélude à l'Après-midi d'un Faune*. I would like to illustrate my ideas with the *Faune*, but most of what I have to say would apply to other examples as well

Blowing long phrases Example 1

When you are playing *L'Après-midi d'un faune* in a concert situation, it is not so important if you breathe before the end of the first phrase. In an audition for an orchestral position, however, it is more or less expected that the opening, when the flute is totally alone, should be uninterrupted. Circular breathing (actually circular blowing) does not work here very well. So don't linger on the long notes, and manage your air.

Even if you are in shape to go the whole nine yards in one breath, the music you are making is still the most important issue. By the time you have reached the end of the second bar, no one knows, except you perhaps, whether you will make it to the end of the phrase without breathing. Still, after these fifteen or twenty seconds, your listeners will have a pretty good idea of how they like your music, breath or no. The length of your breath must not be at the expense of tone quality. You must find timbre and color with very little expenditure of air.

This is what we will try to achieve first. The actual inhaling process will be addressed later.

Good air management goes with my alliterative concept of *Tenuto, Sostenuto,*

Ritenuto (in French, *tenu, soutenu, retenu*; to keep the rhyme, in English it would be "held, upheld, withheld," although "upheld" is better described by our well-known "support," which everyone talks about).

"Support," for me, does not imply the diaphragm. It is an involvement of the abdominal muscles in the blowing process. When we lift a suitcase or push against a stalled car with the upper body, our powerful leg muscles contribute to the effort of the abdominals. The cough or sneeze point, situated just below the navel, is the seat of the most intense energy, strengthened by the action of the thighs. Therefore I advise the use of the legs (when standing) to provide support. For the seated flutist, I do not agree with military posture: chin up, shoulders straight and elbows high, buns on the edge of the chair. Instead, try sitting with the kidneys reclining gently against the lower part of the chair back, pushing the tummy out for support and feeling the ground under the feet to complement the support.

Instead of the weak muscles (facial and labial), use your strong ones (abdominal, leg, and left arm) to produce musical sound. I call this *Tenuto*. I believe that focus and tonal density are helped by the lips, to be sure, but that the main agent is the left arm.

The first joint of the left forefinger is the fulcrum of the flute. It provides the stability vital not only for technique and articulation, but also for the production of sonority. All the old illustrations of transverse flute players through the ages show this position—left forefinger halfway down, balancing the body of the flute. The jaw movements and the lips contribute to tone production, but stability at this point is essential.

To physically feel the *Tenuto* effect, try to cross your right hand over the left, which stays in place for this experiment.

Blowing long phrases Figure 1

Wrapping your right hand without tightness around the trademark between the lip plate and the first keys, play a few notes (low or high), for instance: "Three Blind Mice" in G, with the left hand alone. After a first feeling of awkwardness, you will feel the added control on the focus without spending too much air. You can also play the first bar of the *Faune*, repeating it three or four times in a loop until you run out of breath.[2]

Now let us consider the actual start of the piece. The deliberately bland C# has no natural center because there are no fingers holding the flute. It has a beautiful reedy quality, blue-gray, hollow, slightly fragile and out of tune.

2. For this, the A# must be fingered by the left thumb, on and off, which is excellent training for the use of thumb B♭.

Let's assume that the inhaling process, which we will discuss elsewhere, is complete. As soon as possible after you have filled up with air, you should start playing. To hold a huge quantity of air, you must block your breath, which tends to make your attack explosive upon release. When you are in an audition, no problem: you are the boss. In concert, if the conductor knows his stuff (it happens!) he should give a small sign for you to fire at will instead of the usual downbeat, which interferes with your inhaling sequence. You can always talk it over with the conductor (but not in the rehearsal: it might look as if you were teaching him his job, or worse yet, that you are having a problem). This piece is often placed right after intermission; it cannot start the concert, nor can it end the first half, nor can it be the last work at the finish (not noisy enough). So it is difficult to concentrate because of movements and conversations in the audience as well as in the orchestra.

So you have started to play. Now comes the withholding (*Ritenuto*). Your main effort now is to not blow and to maintain the expansion of your rib cage to resist its collapse. By sheer elasticity of the cartilage in your chest and the natural weight of the bone in your shoulders, some air will be let out. The withholding is actually an effort to maintain the air cavity open, to counteract the support muscles in the lower body. With support and no withholding, the chest empties quickly and the phrase cannot be held to its end.

Do not blow at first: this is the secret. Until the end of the second measure, release the chest air sparingly. Do not spend it, save it. When you realize you are short of air, it is usually too late. It is how you manage your airflow at the very start of the phrase that makes the difference.[3]

Then for the second and third measures, "normal" blowing is in order, supporting with the abdomen. For the final notes, you can think of making a *crescendo* because air is running out, and this ultimate support helps keep the sound in tune.[4] Finally, if you are on good terms, ask the first oboe to connect his A♯ with yours preferably sooner than later, and to play it not too sharp, to match yours, because you might have a tendency to go flat at the end of your apnea.

Now we must retrace our steps to the inhaling procedure. I say inhaling because it is a deliberate process as opposed to the natural breathing function.

First, as stress control and as a way to reoxygenate your blood, ventilate by taking a few deep inhalations,[5] producing the "hhaah" sound and cooling your deep throat. When we are making a physical effort, we are out of breath for the same reason: our blood needs more oxygen for our red blood cells to bring repair to the muscle cells.

Second, expel every ounce of air possible, with an audible (to you) "sschss . . .

---

3. Air management reminds me of personal finance management: it is wiser to save your salary when you get it than be reduced to poverty before the next paycheck.

4. If you realize at the end of the third measure that you might come out short, the most musical breath to take is in the fourth measure between the two Bs.

5. Dogs, who do not sweat, must pant to eliminate excess body heat. Panting is also taught in so-called painless childbirth.

tchhh," ending with collapsed chest, low shoulders, and abdomen totally pushed in.

Third, start inhaling slowly through the nose, filling the chest cavity and every little nook and cranny in the upper torso. I advise doing this upper process first because the chest muscles work more slowly than the abdominals and because intake through the nose corresponds to upper breathing.

Fourth, open the mouth and throat, expanding the belt area, inhale to produce the "hhaah" sound, then play right away.

Preparation: 1. ventilate ca. 5"—2. expel all air—3. upper breathing ca. 5"—4. abdominal breathing ca. 3"—5. start immediately

Très modéré

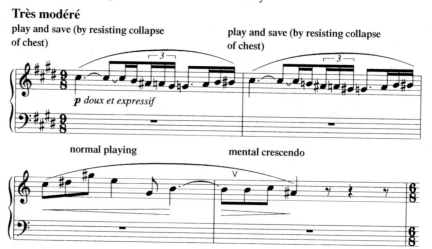

Blowing long phrases Example 2. Debussy, *Prélude à l'après-midi d'un faune*

As I have said, you should not use this lengthy process every time you breathe, but only when you need to conduct a long phrase, such as in *L'Après-midi d'un Faune*.[6] It does not take more than a few seconds when you master this technique.

Blowing on an Attack

For a low attack *forte* or a high one *piano*, a late onset of the air might jeopardize the quality of the first note and the ensemble of the whole passage. If you have time, it is always a good idea to breathe early and to be already blowing when the first note is articulated.

Blowing long phrases Example 3. Beethoven, *Leonore* Overture no. 3

6. Historical note: *Prélude à l'Après-midi d'un Faune* was premiered on 23 December 1894. The flutist was Georges Barrère, then eighteen years old! The record does not show whether he breathed in the first phrase, but the piece's success was immediate and enormous: it had to be encored.

Another helpful procedure is to time your blowing, even when you are practicing. In the above excerpt, this would mean that your breath would occupy the half-note rest (v), and that you will blowing on the quarter-note rest (ʌ). Since the opening passage is short, you need not breathe very much. That way, your blowing on middle breath will be smoother and more reliable for the low D.

Practice these stop-and-go attacks during the Scale Game.

Blowing long phrases Example 4. Scale Game #28 and #30

> ## *In a nutshell:*
>
> The key to good air management is knowing how not to blow. Support, of course, is the first thing that comes to mind, but it must be balanced by air economy, especially at the start of playing. A forceful exhalation does not produce the best sound.
>
> ### *Please refer also to:*
>
> | | |
> |---|---|
> | Breathing | Isometrics |
> | Center of Gravity | Stability |
> | Cough Point | *Tenuto, Sostenuto, Ritenuto* |

BREATHING I

Generalities

Breathing is such an obsession with wind players that it is seen as a mechanism distinct from instrumental playing and as an entity that you could practice outside of a musical context. We have a psychological hang-up about breathing. We are afraid of silence. Upon taking a breath, we leave the last note almost with regret, as if the sound of the flute should always be heard without interruption. It is true that we have a handicap compared to reed players, who often have too much air.

I have trouble believing that one can buy machines to improve breathing. It is as if exercise machines advertised with beautiful models were the secret of eternal health.

Breathe as you would without a flute on your lips. Go back to simplicity. When you read a bulletin board, do you lift your shoulders? Do you stand at attention? Breathe as you would when you wait for the bus.

Middle Breath

Do not systematically take a full breath if the length of the phrase you have to play does not require it. Use what I call "middle breath." Your air will be more manageable, your rib cage will not extend fully, and your shoulders will not rise. Listen to your tone: even if the focus is good from the start, it improves after a second or two in middle breath, because the airflow is smoother, the mouth cavity and the throat more relaxed. Place little breaths (gasps), unmarked, unheard, wherever you can, like a fish opening its mouth as it moves along.

Sometimes, the mechanics of breathing seem more important than blowing. For instance, "circular breathing" is actually uninterrupted blowing. You may feel comfortable with your breathing, but what is the use of good breathing if you don't know how to blow? My approach is that if you produce a good tone, you are on the right track for breathing. The contrary, however, is not always true: you may be breathing well and still produce an ugly noise.

The basic act of breathing is simple enough: drop your shoulders, open the throat with the "hhaah" sound, relax the abdominal wall, and emulate the mechanics of yawning. When we are reading a bulletin board instead of music, our breath is "normal," noiseless and comfortable. As soon as we begin to play, our air intake becomes noisy, contrived, and stressful. We don't take our time, we don't make the "hhaah" sound to feel cold air in our deep throat, we leave the tongue in the way, and we try to go beyond our capacity. My purpose here is not only "how" to breathe, but "where" and "how much." What happens to the music before, during, and after the breath?

It seems that most flutists think the air intake must always be huge, and that the musical thing to do is to hold the breath forever. While it might sometimes be vital to do so, one should not systematically fill up. Let us compare music to the spoken language. When asked if he has a breathing secret, Rampal replied: "No, I just open my mouth. Do you have a breathing secret when you speak? No, you open your mouth, you breathe. When you're talking, you naturally breathe between phrases, as you need it. In music, it's the same."[7] Are you going to take the same breath to recite: "Now is the time for all good men to come to the aid of their country" as to say "Ciao!" or to whisper "Good night" to a sleepy infant?

A middle breath is easier to manage than a huge one in the extreme ranges (*p*, *pp* in the high register, *f*, *ff* in the low notes). For staccato low attacks, don't

---

7. "J. P. Rampal on Making Music," *Flute Talk*, vol. 10, no. 9, 7 (May/June 1991): 8–13.

breathe too much. Take a middle breath, play middle breath, and take short gasps between articulations. Your attacks and staccato will break less. These gasping breaths are very helpful in rhythmic passages. They are barely audible, they add to the articulation, and they allow us to fill up before a long uninterrupted segment:

Breathing Example 1. Bach, Sonata in E Minor,
BWV 1034, second movement, beginning

Take little gasps after the first and fifth note of each measure. "Gasp" twice per measure at first, then at measure 16 you will be able to play the whole passage without breathing.

There are almost as many ways to breathe as there are musical examples, but let us consider certain logical axioms: where to breathe, and where not to breathe. Once you have understood the breathing process, the way is paved to the musical goal. Breathing is only one of the means, albeit an essential one, to that end. "Having a clear musical image rather than thinking of the physical means is the best way to produce music. This entails breathing naturally."[8]

In a nutshell

Breathe to play as you breathe to speak. Good blowing leads to good breathing, but not always vice versa. Musical breathing is like punctuation. Breathe more often like a fish than like a whale. A middle breath is more manageable than a huge one. Balance your tone on either side of the breath and keep a smooth musical line. Use small breaths to enhance shaping.

Please refer also to:

Air Management	Scale Game
Attacks	Staccato
Gasps	Stress
"Hhaah" Sound	Synchronization
Intervals	

---

8. Kathleen Goll Wilson, "Concepts of Phrase Breathings," *Flute Talk*, vol. 10, no. 6 (February 1991): 10–12.

BREATHING 2

Mechanics of Breathing

Pulling in the tummy during inhalation is the result of education and of attitude control that a screaming infant cares nothing about. This look is fine for fashion models, but for breathing it is hopeless. Standing at attention, tummy tucked in, chin up, and eyes to the horizon is superb for a Marine on the parade ground but is not a good idea while playing the flute.

Here is a simple exercise to feel a true abdominal inhalation: sit with knees and feet joined; bring your elbows to your knees while exhaling. When you inhale, your torso cannot move and your breathing is really abdominal. Of course, it is not advisable to play in this position!

Now lie on your back. In this position, you cannot raise your shoulders upon inhalation. However, you can raise your tummy freely. This is the most natural and the best breathing procedure. Duplicate it while standing.

Try to avoid the impression of inflating your lung cavity. Atmospheric pressure does that by a bellows effect when you create a void inside your lungs. Nothing should stand in the way of fresh air. The bellows effect explains why our breath is shorter at high altitudes. Because of the lower atmospheric pressure, the same chest movement gives us less air.

Short panting breaths are very helpful in rhythmic passages: they are barely audible, they add to the articulation, and they allow us to fill up before a long uninterrupted segment. This implies that you use the abdominal belt to huff-huff little gasps. Start panting between eighth notes early in the piece, before you start running out, because the longer you postpone your inevitable breathing, the noisier it will be.

The "Hhaah" Sound

If you breathed with clenched teeth, you would do a very poor inhalation. You would be breathing with high shoulders. You would produce a strong hissing noise, perceptible from a distance and your teeth would feel cold. If you opened your jaws but left your tongue in the path of incoming air, you would get a slightly better inhalation (although it would still be placed in the upper part of your chest). You would feel the cool air inside your mouth, but you would still make this unpleasant sucking noise that flutists often produce. A sucking noise at air intake shows that your mouth and your throat are closed and that your tongue is in the way.

Now if you feel cold air on your Adam's apple, and if you hear the sound "hhaah," you are breathing fully. The abdominal belt is released and you take in a maximum of air with a minimum of noise.

Good breathing is what you do when you yawn (open throat, low shoulders). Proper blowing is what you do when you cough or sneeze (support with the abdominal muscles). Don't worry about your diaphragm. It goes up, it goes down; it goes down, it goes up. Like Timothy Tim's ten pink toes, it goes wherever the air goes. Only a contrary action of the abdominal muscles or stiff raised shoulders can hinder it.

Yet we must sometimes be able to play a long phrase such as the first phrase of *Prélude à l'Après-midi d'un Faune*[9] in one breath. Many conductors see it as an important test. After thirty years in an orchestra, I consider the *Faune* (nicknamed *L'après-midi* in English-speaking orchestras) the most difficult of orchestral solos. Flutists capable of sustaining the longest phrase are not always those with the biggest chest cavity, but those who manage their air most efficiently. The answer is not in circular blowing,[10] which I confess to not mastering perfectly. If the sound is out of focus and mismanaged, "circular breathing" will not hide the fact that air economy is not mastered.

A good idea for oxygenating quickly, before a demanding passage and during the course of a piece, is panting. It is repeated gasping, comparable to what dogs have to do on a hot day. They cannot sweat, so they use this method to eliminate water to lower their body temperature, even if they are not running.

1. Before inhaling, empty your chest cavity completely.[11]
2. Then, through the nose, slowly fill the upper part of your chest cavity, keeping the abdomen flat.
3. When you are about to play, drop (release) your abdominal belt, and inhale with the "hhaah" sound. You feel the cold air deep in your throat, indicating that your throat is open.
4. Start playing right away to avoid blocking the sound.

This process seems long, but does not take more than a couple of seconds.

Imagine you were not using your mouth. It would seem as though air would pass through the skin of the neck at the lowest point where the cold is felt.

Some wind instrumentalists perform the abdominal breathing first and the upper (or thoracic) breathing last. This conforms to the yoga doctrine.[12] I advise the opposite because upper breathing is a relatively slow process, whereas abdominal (or low) breathing is fast. It can be placed at the last fraction of a second, avoiding blocking the air and risking a broken attack.

Nerves do not affect only fingers and saliva secretion. As far as I am concerned, short breath is the main syndrome. Don't be too optimistic. Even during practice, breathe more often than you hope you will need. Your listeners might not notice an extra breath. They might notice if you faint.

---

9. Claude Debussy (1862–1918).
10. Improperly called "circular breathing."
11. A small part called residual or remnant air cannot be evacuated.
12. A Hindu school of thought involved with control of the body to achieve communion with the spirit of the universe. Inhalation is one of its central concepts.

> ### *In a nutshell:*
>
> Inhale as you yawn waiting for the bus: low shoulders, open throat. Make up for an insufficient air volume by placing your intake as low as possible, where you feel the cold air. If your breathing is noisy, you are not breathing as well as with the "hhaah" sound.
>
> ### *Please refer also to:*
>
> | Abdominal muscles | Gasps |
> |---|---|
> | Attacks | Support |
> | Blowing | Throat |
> | Breathing | |

BREATHING 3

Where Not to Breathe

My basic philosophy about breathing is simple: if you don't need a big breath, don't take one. When you say: "Cool!" you only need a sip of air. But when you tell someone, "I just did not have time to open my flute case since my last lesson," you need a lot of air, and a lot of nerve.

Don't breathe in the following places:

- Before a resolution or during harmonic tension (appoggiaturas, seventh chords, and dissonances).

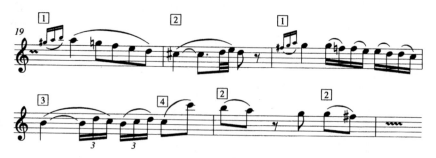

Breathing (Where not to breathe) Example 1. Mozart, Oboe Concerto in C Major, K. 314, second movement

Do not breathe after the C♯ before the triplets.

- Before a perfect cadence, except in certain baroque endings, when a slight wait before the last note emphasizes the conclusion.
- Breathing on bar lines is usually not good: it creates a rupture in the line, a sort of hiccup. But there are exceptions, as when the harmony progresses in whole or half measures or in arpeggios.
- On a short rest: if you can, do not breathe just before a fast run or scale. There are a million examples of this.
- If you have relatively long rests (quarter or eighth) followed by sixteenth rests, you should not breathe on the short rest. If you do, you are going to be late on ensemble and clumsy on synchronization of tongue and fingers.

A good way to train for this is to integrate it into your daily practice on scales.

Breathe on the previous quarter rest and blow on the sixteenth rest.

Breathing (Where not to breathe) Example 2

(The v sign indicates breathing; the one above the short rest indicates blowing.)

Breathe more than you need in practice. In actual performance, it will be easy to stretch your air if you feel good. But if you stretch it too thin, you might be forced to make catastrophic breaks. I learned long ago from my own experience that stage fright affects the breath first. Something technical is often easier.

In a nutshell:

Interrupt the phrase as little as possible. It is not a matter of holding a line forever as much as matching color and sound. Good blowing leads to good breathing, but not always vice versa. The issue is music, not Olympic records. Use the haahh sound if you have time. Elsewhere, little sniffs and gasps will help you and and the music's clarity.

> ## Please refer also to:
>
> | | |
> |---|---|
> | Attacks | Scale Game |
> | Color | Staccato |
> | "Hhaah" Sound | Stress |
> | Middle Breath | Synchronization |
> | Phrasing | |

BREATHING 4

Where to Breathe

There is of course the obvious musical punctuation:

- After a tonal resolution.
- After a perfect cadence.
- Between two staccato notes.
- Between two notes of the same name. It will also help to articulate them.
- On a syncopation:

Breathing (Where to breathe) Example 1. Bach, Sonata in B Minor,
BWV 1030, second movement, measure 13 to end

The gasps reinforce the tension build-up or release of the syncopations. You can almost breathe on each syncopation. It helps you and the music too. In other words, the rhythmic character of a piece lends itself to many little breaths. Rampal gave magnificent examples of this in many of his recordings (the Bolling suite and post-baroque concertos by Stamitz and Benda, among others). It is said that Gaubert was also a master at stealing gasps here and there without being heard.

The problem is compounded when the passage is slurred or fast. If it must be interrupted for a biological reason, here are a few ideas:

- Chose a place where the music is not offended too much and match the tone on either side of the breath, for instance in the Sarabande of Bach's Partita in A Minor, BWV 1013, or in the opening bars of the second movement of the Martinu Sonata.
- Breathe with your ears. If you must interrupt the line, your ears should tell you how to deal with the sound and the phrase just before and just after the breath, especially if is not a musically obvious place. Do not systematically taper off on the release before the breath. Think of matching the dynamics in the very recent past and in the very near future.
- Do not to hit the following note just because you filled up and are no longer threatened by immediate asphyxiation.

In other words, always breathe in the direction of the phrase, whether it is ascending or descending. I am not trying to say that you can breathe anywhere. The line must continue through the silence of the breath, just like a cloud or a tree can hide the trajectory of a bird in flight from your view for a moment.

In the Allemande from the Bach *Partita*, do not sit on the notes following the breaths. In this very difficult work, one hears too often a diminuendo followed by a sucking noise and then an accent. Here, again, match the notes on either side of the breath.

To practice this, play a few notes beyond your intended breath, then repeat the last notes you have just heard yourself play, this time with a breath. Try to musically balance the tone on either side of the break as if there had been no interruption. If the line is increasing, the previous note should not taper off before you breathe, and the note following should be in direct progression with the context. Conversely, when the line decreases, don't let the perspective of your breath affect the remaining energy of your tone. The note following should not be suddenly louder than the previous phrase.

Integrate small gasps into your daily practice on scales. Breathe after the first note in a group of four or eight notes and, again, match the tone on either side of the breath.

Breathe comfortably when you are alone and the accompaniment is suspended. This implies that you can slightly shorten the note before the break without tapering it. When your breath is, by necessity, not in the best musical place, using the accompaniment as a shield can hide it. On an accompaniment chord, your gasp is lost in the resonance of the piano. For this reason as well as many others, you must have studied the whole score, not only the flute part.

When you have no choice but to breathe or die, it is better to speed up just before the breath than to come to a full stop and slow down after. A slight rush on the three notes preceding the break will give you just that little bit more time to stay on course.

In an avalanche of notes, it is preferable to contract a few notes than to take some out. A good example of this is Variation 5 of Schubert's Introduction and Variations on "Ihr Blümlein Alle," op. 160.

These little cheats give you a split second to breathe. They are barely notice-able, and 911 need not be called.

In a nutshell:

Breathe to play as you breathe to speak. Good blowing leads to good breathing, but not always vice versa. Musical breathing is like punctuation. Breathe more often like a fish than like a whale. A middle breath is more manage-able than a huge one. Balance your tone on either side of the breath, and keep a smooth musical line. Use small breaths (gasps) to enhance shaping.

Please refer also to:

Attacks	Scale Game
Circular Blowing	Staccato
"Hhaah" Sound	Stress
Language	Synchronization
Middle Breath	

BRIDGE

In the course of twenty-four hours in the life of a flutist, the break between low and medium ranges is breached hundreds of times. Yet it is still one of the criti-cal points of instrumental playing, especially when it must be slurred slowly. It shows once more how deceptive is the assumption that "only fast is difficult." After more than half a century of playing the flute, I still have to think ahead and work at making the bridge smooth and musical, but it brings rewards.

The problem lies in the fact that we have to go from two handfuls of fingers (D2) to only one or two (C2) and back. To make matters worse, these happen to be our dear little devils no. 1 and no. 2. "The second octave C–D, for instance, re-quires an extremely complex coordination of seven fingers and a thumb (an ex-change that can be simplified by anticipating the D with the second and third fin-gers of the right hand while playing the C and vice versa)."[13] And, I may add, not using the right pinky.

The bridge question does not arise only for the C2–D2 break. It is also implicit in the following:

13. Krell.

Andante

Bridge Example 1

For all these combinations, a better smoothness in the passage of the bridge will be achieved at no expense of tone quality—quite to the contrary—by using the balance provided by the right ring finger:

Bridge Figure 1. Right hand for these notes

In the case of most intervals involving D2—namely the Bridge—the right pinky (little devil no. 2) can be left unused, because it is usually more of a nuisance than a necessity. Of course, if D♯ or E♭ are played, the right pinky comes down, but it is still the right ring finger that provides the comfortable balance. Actually, a stiff right pinky pressed hard on the D♯ key is no longer the element of stability that it is intended to be, but a painful liability. Remember, an open D♯ key is absolutely vital on only six notes:

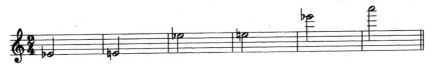

Bridge Example 2

Many purists will object that preparing finger combinations is a cop out, and that leaving a finger on a "silent key"[14] (such as the right ring finger) is an offense to purity. Strangely enough, it is often the same people, invoking the same correctness, who insist on forbidding the use of the Briccialdi thumb B♭ key or the side lever for a smoother B♭ and on always using the "real" B♭ fingering. Yet, in this instance, the right forefinger is closing two "silent keys" for no other purpose than to activate the B♭ tone hole. By preparing the bridge, you are not putting more " silent keys" down than in the "real" B♭ fingering.

This is not just a technical detail: smooth phrasing is a musical necessity. There is no good instrumental playing without a musical perspective, and vice versa. Furthermore, one can readily see that the stability of the embouchure is often shaken upon the passing of the bridge and that the improved steadiness of the lip plate at this point is a definite musical asset.

14. "Silent" or "dead" key: a non–tone producing key.

In a nutshell:

Be inventive with your fingerings. The smoothness of the break from low to middle ranges and the stability of the embouchure depend on you.

Please refer also to:

Finger Antagonisms	Finger Phrasing
Little Devils	Silent Keys

CENTER OF GRAVITY

A flute player's center of gravity is neither the diaphragm nor the plexus, but a point below the navel that you feel when you sneeze or cough. When we sneeze or cough, a considerable amount of energy is concentrated at this point in a short time, since we are trying to expel something. This energy is similar to what we call support, except for the fact that it must be sustained to conduct tone. When you shift slightly this center of gravity, even by imperceptibly moving your balance from one foot to another or feeling your weight on the floor, the air speed becomes faster or slower and provides the basic means of tone production in all ranges. Only then should the lips intervene to guide the air brush.

Air support can be compared to the sensation we have in our abdominal muscles while moving a heavy object: the tummy juts forward (and not backward, as is sometimes prescribed.) We have the impression that very strong muscles are producing the essential force, as in tone production. The center of gravity is ever lower. There is no energy in the upper body, and the shoulders must be low. Air support has its origin at this center of gravity, which is also the cough or sneeze point. Consciousness of its localization is vital. The famous diaphragm that everyone talks about, rightly or wrongly, is much higher, and no one has control over it. "The center of gravity must be found as close as possible to the ground, i.e. in the lower abdomen."[1]

The Chastain Maneuver

While sitting comfortably with both feet flat on the ground, play a lower note *mf* with an average vibrato until you are happy with your tone. Then start the exercise. At the count of three, stand up. After a few tries, you feel that the shift in

---

1. Michel Ricquier, *Traité méthodique de pédagogie instrumentale,* pref. Maurice André (Paris: Gérard Billaudot, 1982).

your center of gravity has made the octave smooth, even, and in tune without your having had to mess with the embouchure. If the two notes of the interval are fingered differently, the shift must synchronize the thrust of the legs, the fingers, and the beat.

While the Chastain maneuver obviously cannot be used in public, it is designed to make one feel the work of the strong lower muscles instead of relying on the lips and the jaw. It also helps to realize that low shoulders come naturally and are vital for comfort and control.

The same effect can be obtained, while standing, by imperceptibly flexing the knees during the first note of the interval, then, in time, "pushing the ground away." The higher the range of the interval, the more one must "sink into the ground." Likewise to play softly—p/pp—and in tune in the ledger lines.

While sitting, the belt or abdominal muscles are pushed out, and one can use the leg muscles to accompany this thrust. While playing in the sitting position, the center of gravity's placement is similar, if less obvious. In my opinion, it is not bad to have the lower back resting against the lower part of the chair's back, feet flat on the floor, feeling that the cough or sneeze point is close to the chair's seat and feeling that the tummy is pushed out. Low shoulders, of course, and stability of the embouchure on the chin are necessary under all circumstances.

A low center of gravity helps to control intonation in playing f/ff; lowering one's center of gravity, "sinking into the ground (or chair)," playing with low shoulders, opening one's throat, and, as a last resort, directing the air brush into the flute all contribute to controlling sharpness.

On the other hand, in playing p/pp, relative lack of energy in the air column tends to result in a flattening of the pitch, in every range, particularly in decreasing or tapering long terminal notes. A low center of gravity will improve this. We should have the impression that we are "pushing the ground away" and keeping up the air speed. Controlled vibrato helps to animate the airflow.

I have noticed that a shift to a lower center of gravity occurs when a certain amount of weight is added, as in the last three months of a pregnancy.[2] The sound tends to become wider, fatter. This is due in my opinion to a modification in the stance and posture to compensate for the added weight. It is possible to emulate this, whatever your gender. Take a large shopping bag in which you put between five and ten pounds of phone books or dictionaries. Run a large belt through the handles and hang it around your neck. I agree it is awkward at first, but try to play anyway: your tone focuses differently, and, in my opinion, broadens, because you are playing with a lower center of gravity.

My students are familiar with my leaning against their sternum[3] to encourage them to involve their whole body behind their playing. Their immediate reflex is to resist with their legs, thereby lowering their center of gravity.

2. I do not advise this for a purely experimental purpose.
3. Breastbone.

Hara

This Japanese word means belly, as in *hara-kiri*.[4] Japanese martial arts have long fascinated Western culture. *Judo*,[5] *jiu-jitsu*,[6] and *Karate*,[7] as well as *aikido*, archery, and fencing, have been exported from Japan into Europe and America. They were adapted for spiritual evolution and for commercial use. Some Japanese are quietly amused about Westerners' infatuation with Asian disciplines. To hear their advocates, they are a cure for your aches and pains, and for the wounds of the soul. Like snake oil, they are good for what you got. After all, why not, if it does not hurt. Such claims also come from flute professors (no one excluded), Alexander technicians, Feldenkrais practitioners, yoga instructors, and exercise machine salesmen, to name a few.

The practice of *hara*, like yoga, has the merit of relating directly to the everyday practice of a wind instrument. We will leave aside the spiritual and philosophical aspects of *hara* to focus on its postural and blowing implications.

"It is impossible to find internal equilibrium—the psychic center of gravity—without having found the center of gravity of the body." It is placed at the cough or sneeze point, a couple of inches below the navel and about halfway into the abdomen. "Many people position themselves at the chest level. The 'chest forward/shoulders back/tummy in' is not a natural posture. It is the typical attitude of someone who wants to assume a personality, a demeanor that is not his own. . . . This attitude will entail further chest breathing that has a negative influence on the psyche."[8]

Hara can be practiced quite easily. While standing on the full soles of both feet, you must let all your weight hang down vertically, shoulders low and heavy without constraint, abdomen relaxed. As you breathe comfortably, there are no chest or shoulder movements. You really feel the pull of gravity throughout your body. Now place one of your hands below the navel and cough. The point where you feel the energy is your *hara*. When we are "in our *hara*," we breathe better, blow better, and tire less, because the *hara* and our center of gravity are an inexhaustible source of power and pleasure.

---

4. *Hara* (bowels)-*kiri* (cutting); *The Concise Oxford Dictionary* (New York: Oxford University Press, 1990).

5. *Ju* (gentle)-*do* (way).

6. *Ju* (gentle)-*jitsu* (skill).

7. *Kara* (empty)-*te* (hand).

8. Ricquier.

> ### *In a nutshell:*
>
> Feel the power concentrated below the navel as you cough. Think of the way you produce the sound from this point instead of somewhere in the upper body. The wider an interval, the more you must use the center of gravity and the shifting of the air speed before doing facial movements. A phrase conducted with this awareness and smooth fingers involves you fully.
>
> ### *Please refer also to:*
>
> | | |
> |---|---|
> | Cough Point | Shoulders |
> | Diaphragm | Stability |
> | Dynamics | Stress Control |
> | Intonation | *Tenuto, Sostenuto, Ritenuto* |
> | Posture | |

CIRCULAR BLOWING

This is also called, somewhat improperly, circular breathing. Labeled a "contemporary" technique, it is probably as ancient as wind instrument playing itself. Its use can be witnessed at all latitudes—Africa and Asia, for instance. In its principle, it is comparable to the bagpipes of the British Isles, to the *biniou* of Celtic French Brittany, and to the various similar instruments of the European continent. Here, air is periodically stocked by mouth into a sheepskin or goatskin bag compressed by the player's arm.

One of the circular blowing techniques reproduces this principle. The air bag is the blown-out cheeks. A reed independent of the mouth replaces the embouchure. The Muslim world's *rajta*[9] players use this technique, recommended also by some present flutists.[10] I have never been able to use this blown-out cheek process without considerably altering the sound. I recommend another way. It calls for the mouth cavity's air projection through a quick forward movement of the tongue without cheek inflation.

To get used to this technique, it is necessary, first, to educate the respiratory reflexes without the flute through the steps described in the following diagram. It

9. A sort of oboe with a leather reed.

10. Robert Dick, *The Other Flute: A Performance Manual of Contemporary Techniques* (New York: Oxford University Press, 1975), and *Circular Breathing for the Flutist* (New York: Multiple Breath Music Co., 1987).

must be kept in mind that circular blowing will be constituted by short periods of normal blowing (approximately five seconds) between very short (one-half second) nasal intakes. During the latter, the tongue's forward thrust, pronounced *ffffoot*, makes up for the normal blowing's interruption.

It must be added that circular blowing is not a panacea. Even when well performed, it is scarcely efficient during long held notes or piano passages. As far as I am concerned, it only works during multiple note patterns above the staff.

Finally, musical punctuation brought about by well-lived breathing is a necessity. It might seem interesting to play the Allemande in the Bach Partita, BWV1013, without breathing audibly, but it is the listener who might risk asphyxiation.

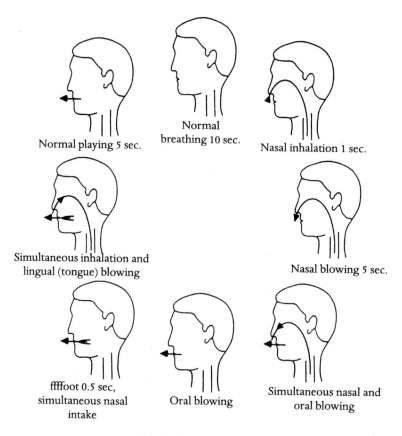

Normal playing 5 sec.

Normal breathing 10 sec.

Nasal inhalation 1 sec.

Simultaneous inhalation and lingual (tongue) blowing

Nasal blowing 5 sec.

ffffoot 0.5 sec, simultaneous nasal intake

Oral blowing

Simultaneous nasal and oral blowing

Circular blowing Figure 1

In a nutshell:

Circular blowing is more appropriate than circular breathing. It represents an assist and a good education of respiratory reflexes.

Please refer also to:

Air Brush	Breathing
Blowing	Cheeks

CONCENTRATION, RELAXATION

Flute players have so many times been told that they must relax that they forgo all stability of the instrument-holding posture and end up doing lip acrobatics, straining the weak facial muscles. These muscles are not meant for that. Playing with a loose flute and slapping fingers and not calling into action the strong leg muscles, the abdominals, and the arm muscles (biceps) is not logical and efficient instrumental playing. These have been called the energy muscles; they enable standing, walking, running, pushing, and lifting. They are well within their power when we play the flute and for this reason do not generate tension and the problems of overuse.

One of the goals of practice is to achieve the greatest relaxation with total concentration.

Ask an unsuspecting person to relax: the shoulders fall, the hands hang by the side, the body goes into a slouch, the eyes lose their spark, sleep is close at hand. The personality is all but snuffed out. Now tell another one to concentrate: every muscle tightens, the forehead wrinkles, the neck stiffens, the eyes glow, the body stands at attention. The person is awake and ready for action, but nervous tension threatens to hinder performance. The ideal would be a combination of both: a sharp mind in a calm body. We cannot relax everything at once. If we did, instrumental playing would fall apart; the flute would float out of control.

Relaxation, to be productive, must come with concentration. You can relax only after you know what muscles, what actions, and what thoughts actually hinder your playing. You can only fix what you know does not work. It is a sort of journey toward the inside, a survey of one's physical and nervous capabilities, a selective use of our muscles. To understand relaxation, first work at something that does not require force or induce stress—for instance, intervals. At the point of passage, hold down the fingers that do not have to move, but relieve the pressure on the one(s) that will give you the interval, usually the key closest to the embouchure. Never slam the fingers on the way down: this will make you tenser and will make the lifting of the fingers harder. Lifting is harder than slamming, so concentrate on not applying more pressure on the way down. Use more finger speed on the way up, while the immobile fingers hold the flute.

When a difficulty arises, nervous tension builds up, causing contraction of the throat, an attempt to produce the tone with the lips, using the tongue as percussion and grasping the keys with the fingers. Concentration helps to know which areas need stability so that other obstacles can loosen up.

Practicing Concentration

Start with a passage a few seconds long. Put your thoughts together for the same amount of time. Release the tension built up by your focusing by playing in a short burst. Scales in stop-and-go mode are good training.

Technical difficulties are of two sorts. One is pure reading. The other is finger antagonism, when two fingers or sets of fingers work in opposite directions. Concentration is identifying at a glance the problem and knowing how to fix it. Sight-reading is also excellent concentration training. Decide that you are not going to stop. Force yourself to look ahead instead of reminiscing about the mistakes you just made. Keep your mind on the road ahead, not on the rear view mirror.

Difficulty in a flute lick is usually confined to two or three awkward notes. Practice this passage slowly, but even when you are up to tempo, feel those notes come and go under your fingers, sing them, and live with them for a fleeting moment.

In a nutshell:

The thought process of relaxation starts with consciousness of every aspect of playing. Then a conscious loosening of the obstacles to a free flow of air: tight throat, unsteady chin, pinched lips, grasping fingers.

Please refer also to:

Appoggio	Posture
Fulcrums	Sight-Reading
Muscles, Strong and Weak	Stability

DIAPHRAGM

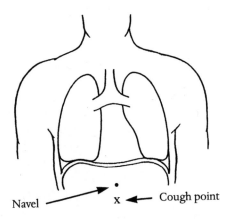

Navel ———→ x ←——— Cough point

Diaphragm Figure 1

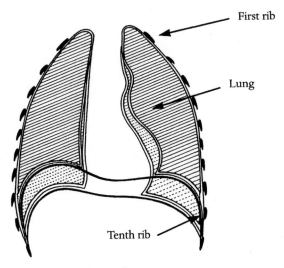

First rib

Lung

Tenth rib

Diaphragm Figure 2. The diaphragm is placed quite high relative to the cough point (x). A sketch of the thorax shows diaphragmatic contraction (inhalation—unshaded down) and relaxation (exhalation—shaded up).[1]

The term "diaphragm" is often used as a catchall for the mechanisms of breathing and playing. Who has not heard, or even said: "Support with your diaphragm" or "Breathe with your diaphragm" or "Position yourself on your diaphragm" or even "Vibrate with your diaphragm?"

1. From Cunningham's *Manual of Practical Anatomy*, qtd. in Richard Miller, *The Structure of Singing: System and Art in Vocal Techniques* (New York: Schirmer Books, 1986).

The diaphragm is a reflex muscle. It does not respond to willpower, try as we may. Its cycles, like those of most of the vital organs that operate when we sleep, dream, or play the flute, are beyond our control. Basically, it goes down upon breathing (inhaling) and up while blowing (exhaling). Should it do otherwise, flute playing and all other activities would just stop: death would ensue in short order.

Since there is no sensory perception of the movements or position of the diaphragm, at any time, there is no way that we can control them. I remember very well feeling dumb and insensitive, as a student almost as much as now, when I could neither feel nor respond to professors' commands regarding my friend the diaphragm. Only when studying medicine, a project quickly aborted by my acceptance to the Paris Conservatory, did I understand that the playing concept of diaphragmatic technique was scientifically incorrect. It was a well-meaning approach to the phenomena of breathing and blowing.

Involuntary, the movements of the diaphragm are conditioned, freed, or hindered by all the muscles, lower or upper, surrounding it. Inhalation on a tucked-in tummy has the abdominal muscles compressing the viscera. They will prevent the diaphragm from its full normal downward movement. Efficient breathing should actually imply the release of all tension in the abdomen. A purely thoracic inhalation will result in high shoulders and constricted throat and airway. An overly extended rib cage will tend to collapse under its own gravity and elasticity. The act of yawning gives a good feeling for correct breathing procedure: wide-open throat, abdominal relaxation, fullness of air, and a perception of pleasure.

Upon blowing, the technique of appoggio,[2] meaning "the act of leaning" in Italian, is the process that would come closest to the common meaning of diaphragm. Appoggio is a technique for breath management used by singers of the Italian school. It is not accurately translated in English by the words "breath support." It is a system of combining and balancing the action of the abdominal and chest muscles in the inhaling procedure as well as the dual phenomena of exhaling and sound production. The support of the abdominal muscles, without opposition, would lead to a rapid deflation of the lungs. The intercostal muscles (between the ribs) must counterbalance it. They actually prevent the collapse of the chest. Schematically, the singer or flutist's effort is to not exhale, in order to achieve this inner balance. Once mastered, this equilibrium opens new horizons to the sound and a feeling of bliss.

Appoggio implies conscious muscular actions, as opposed to the unconscious play of the diaphragm.

2. Miller, *The Structure of Singing.*

> ### *In a nutshell:*
>
> Do not mistake the diaphragm for the muscles that help
> or hinder it. You can act on the latter, not on the former.
> Yawning is not polite, but it feels so good!
>
> ### *Please refer also to:*
>
> | | |
> |---|---|
> | Appoggio | *Tenuto, Sostenuto, Ritenuto* |
> | Blowing | Yawning |
> | Breathing | |

DYNAMICS

Do not judge your dynamics by your efforts but by what you are hearing. You might think you are playing *pianissimo* because you've stopped supporting, but you hear an approximate sound with a doubtful intonation. Or you are blowing like mad but your sound is narrow and forced.

Teachers rarely explain their request to play louder or softer. Hence flutists have a tendency to do what is evident: push to play loud and disintegrate to play soft. For once, our natural reflexes are totally deceptive.

The problem with dynamics is that they never exist by themselves. They are like the painter's palette. They are useless if they don't relate to the musical content as much as to objective conditions of instrumental playing. What to make of an orchestral instrumentalist who plays so softly that we can't hear him or her? Or of another who blasts so loud (acoustically or electronically) that he or she drowns out all the rest?

When a crooner whispers a tender ballad to a crowd, ten thousand listeners perceive him as sweet and intimate. His amplifiers are anything but that. In contrast, in the middle of a hundred-strong orchestra, a lonely nonamplified flute plays the first phrase of Ravel's *Bolero*. As the first step of a seemingly endless crescendo, it must start very, very softly and still be heard at the back of the hall.

The listener's impression should be: "How can the flutist play *pp* so mysteriously and magically and still project?" The listener's reaction should *not* be: "I can't hear the flute. The flutist must be playing *pp*!"

Soft dynamics cannot project and stay in tune if a half-inflated carnival balloon, without support or energy, plays them. On the contrary, a forced tone and an air volume big enough to bend a tree will not always produce a "big sound." What I call "turbo-sound" is precisely that: an enormous quantity of air without timbre or focus.

Our concern here is not to determine where to place the dynamics. This is the domain of interpretation. What we are seeking is the way to control dynamics and perform them spontaneously.

Forte and fortissimo

Playing loud requires little effort because the sound is carried by its own energy. However, we must remove all the obstacles to the air column. A tight throat is like rapids in a mountain stream—we will "yawn" the sound and open wide the throat. Shoulders held high strangle even our spoken voice—we will play with low shoulders. Lack of support restricts the airflow—we will blow from the lowest possible point, the cough or sneeze point.

Projection requires a low center of gravity—we will place ourselves low on our chair or "heavy" on our feet and play from the ground up.

Uncontrolled vibrato wastes air, timbre, and focus—in playing *f*, we will moderate the vibrato by trying to keep it inside the tone.

Pinched lips choke the sound—we will leave them relaxed while stabilizing the embouchure with fulcrum no. 1, the first joint of the left index finger.

For intonation in playing *f/ff*, lowering one's center of gravity, playing with low shoulders, opening one's throat, and as a last resort, rolling in the flute, all contribute to controlling sharpness.

Piano and pianissimo

To play *p* and especially *pp* requires a lot of concentration and, yes, effort. We must compensate for the lack of natural energy in the sound.

When a flutist plays *f/ff*, the sound is animated by its own natural energy. However, as soon as the intensity of the tone diminishes, this almost spontaneous energy tends to vanish. It is in the nature of things and the agogic of the flute: soft sound becomes difficult to control, most of all in the ledger-line notes, in the attacks and in the held notes where intonation falters. This lack of natural energy in *p*, *pp* playing must be remedied in an almost artificial way by providing the sound with an internal and hidden energy. It is one of the greatest difficulties of flute playing.

The throat must not close—we will try to open all the cavities of the ears and sinuses to enhance resonance but not loudness. The last thing we want to lessen is support but we must counteract it to avoid the collapse of the chest and the "free exhaust" of air.

Phrasing with the lips does not make a small airflow easy to manage—we will keep a stable embouchure and phrase with the fingers close to the keys.

The agogic of soft flute sound tends to kill vibrato—we will animate the soft dynamics with relatively more vibrato in *p/pp* than in *f/ff* playing.

Ask flutists to play *p* or *pp*. Often you will notice that their very demeanor shows that support is no longer present. This reflex must be inverted; it takes more effort to play *p* than *f*.

Crescendo, Diminuendo

Management of crescendos and diminuendos should take into consideration the following:

As intensity increases, we will gradually leave the soft-playing mode. We might feel that by pushing and forcing we are playing louder. There is a certain measure of truth here, but the most obvious consequence is the raising of the pitch.

We also have a tendency to culminate our dynamic progressions too soon. The word *"crescendo"*[3] implies that we are at a lesser level of intensity and that we must preserve enough space to reach a climax. We should let the flute do the first part of the crescendo naturally. Then gradually we can relax and open the tone as we reach the goal.

"Diminuendo" is actually an indication that intensity is still relatively strong; we can keep it at this level for part of the diminuendo. Once more the agogic tendency is to diminish too soon after a climax or a loud dynamic. We must play with mental binoculars in order to guess where our playing will reach its minimum, as a bird lands after a graceful flight. As we diminish, the elements of soft playing come back into action gradually: more support, more *Tenuto, Ritenuto, Sostenuto*, less volume, but more air speed and more vibrato to animate the tone.

Tenuto, Sostenuto, Ritenuto

Support is even more important in *p* than in *f*. We have to play *Sostenuto*. However, support is not enough: if some withholding mechanism does not counterbalance support, the lungs empty too quickly, producing an airy, unfocused tone. We also need *Ritenuto*.

Control of *p* or *pp* requires also a steady embouchure. Obviously a floating lip plate will make insecurity even worse—the left arm will provide *Tenuto*.

The blowing procedure will be the same as in appoggio: a balance of forces between abdominal muscles providing support and pectoral muscles preventing the collapse of the chest. By using appoggio the air speed can be sustained; thus pitch can be better controlled without having to change the embouchure all the time.

As far as fingers are concerned, if the dynamic is *p* or *pp*, the natural reflex is to have weaker and less precise movements. On the contrary, I think that the softer one plays, the more swiftly and precisely the fingers must move. This is not intended to mean that the fingers must slam and squeeze.

In a wide interval played *p*, smoothness often does not depend upon the obvious "down" fingers, but on one "up" finger, usually the one venting the hole closest to the embouchure. This is the finger that must work lightly and fast.

The same idea holds for attacks: the tongue's movement must be all the more precise and faster as the dynamic is softer. This is particularly true for woodwind

---

3. The suffix –*ndo*, called the gerundive, means "in the process of" in Italian.

chords in classical and romantic symphonies. The conductor's beat is less vigorous when he wants a round, soft ensemble sound. If his gesture is strong, for precision, he will naturally get a sort of percussive attack unless the woodwinds are able to release the sound precisely but softly.

On a delicate ensemble attack, I start to blow gently through the nose to start the airflow. My tongue is slightly apparent between my lips, closing the aperture where the air brush passes. At the moment the chord starts to form, a quick movement of the tongue toward the back releases the already flowing air. The tongue works as a valve releasing a fluid more than as percussion. This way, I avoid the explosion consequent to blocked air being released suddenly by tonguing.

I find it useful, for the coordination of my reflexes for a p attack, to tap lightly, without tonguing, the key closest to the note I want to play. This slight tap sets the air column in vibration inside the tube. It serves as a common denominator for my attack process and as a trigger for the movement of my tongue backward.

In staccato passages, the shorter span of each note results in naturally lower dynamics. It is therefore a good idea to play the desired soft passages[4] more staccato than the loud ones.

Vibrato helps to animate the sound in soft phrases, preventing breaks in the slurs. It seems to give an imaginary speed and life to the air.

Warm Air, Cold Air

Warm air corresponds to a large volume of air associated with lack of direction and low air speed. Fast air speed and sense of direction, on the contrary, carry cold air. These concepts are extremely useful for the success of dynamics. With practice, they will soon become second nature.

Release

Many long notes don't have a printed diminuendo, but we are tempted to do one anyway. Don't press your luck. If it's not written, don't do it. If I were to die for lack of breath at the end of a long note, that would be the perfect taper, the ideal organic diminuendo.

For one thing, the tone should not be throttled on a diminuendo. On the contrary, the speed of air must be maintained, and one should support even more, keep the vibrato going, hold the flute steady, and in fact think crescendo to keep the intonation from falling. At the end of a long note, especially a high one p, pp, the release is especially delicate.

Even if a diminuendo is not indicated, the note will eventually decrease anyway. Running out of breath will be the perfect release provided the air is sup-

---

4. For instance, in a baroque reiteration, imitation, or echo.

ported until silence. If we just try to diminish the air speed, two things are bound
to happen:

- The tone falls uncontrollably to the nearest harmonic, a sad noise to complete a poetic ending.
- Even if it does not, the intonation can suffer dire consequences that lip and jaw movements will control with difficulty.

My advice:

- If the composer did not write a diminuendo, don't do one.
- If there is one, don't start that final note in the softest dynamic you want to reach on release.
- Be sure that stability from the abdominal muscles and the left arm is still present after the note has reached silence.
- If at all possible, stabilize with "silent keys" (for instance, the B♭ lever or side key on G3 and D3), so that the fingers of both hands are on the flute.
- Don't move. "It ain't over 'till it's over."[5] The slightest physical movement may destroy the fragile suspension. Furthermore, the fraction of silence following the release of a final note creates some of the most moving moments of music.

Even if you have time, don't breathe just before the last few notes. Sometimes
this does not feel comfortable or natural, but it will force you to support to get
the last ounces of air out, thereby preventing the fall or intonation problems described earlier. If you are definitely out of air, stop playing. Breathe silently without moving to give the visual impression that you haven't stopped. Then call 911.
   The relationship between music and dynamics is not only the fruit of inspiration. It can be practiced. I must admit it is very tempting to use repertoire for this
purpose in spite of the many stylistic implications and sheer length of the pieces.
Short phrases such as those in Moyse's *Vingt-quatre petites études mélodiques*[6] are
extremely valuable for the study of dynamics alongside phrasing and intonation.
   Dynamics are not mere entities. They must be coherent with interpretation
and meaning. For each work, we should try to match dynamics and demands
such as distance, range, and context with the inner character of the music.
   Images of relative dynamics:

fff	Calling someone across a crowded street
ff	Calling someone over two stair landings
f	Addressing a classroom without amplification
mf	A group conversation around a table
mp	A one-on-one conversation
p	A telephone conversation

5. Yogi Berra (active late twentieth century). Well-known American philosopher.
6. Paris: Alphonse Leduc, 1932.

pp A love conversation, a confidence

ppp A stage whisper with enough energy to fill the hall

Your imagination is as good as mine.

In a nutshell:

Playing soft requires more effort than playing loud. Soft tone and phrases need stability. Vibrato helps the soft intervals. There need not be change at the level of the lips and embouchure. Control of blowing is essential. Take into consideration that staccato results in softer dynamics.

Please refer also to:

Agogic	*Tenuto, Sostenuto, Ritenuto*
Air Speed	Vibrato
Dynamics	Warm Air, Cold Air
Slam-and-squeeze	

EMBOUCHURE

A good, stable, and flexible embouchure position should be the same for all registers.

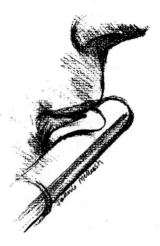

Embouchure Figure 1. Drawing Jeanie Mellersh

Chin and lip gymnastics are counterproductive, especially under stress.

Flute sound is created by the air brush hitting the outside wall of the embouchure hole. Turbulence is created as part of the air brush's energy is transformed into vibration,[1] which resonates according to the length of the tube. The rest of the air stream escapes out of the embouchure hole.

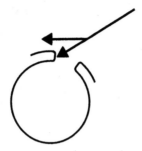

Embouchure Figure 2

Below the outside rim of that hole is the wall, whose height is critical. Its measurements and the shape of the head-joint tube constitute the art of head-joint making. The material[2] of the chimney, also referred to as the riser, and the undercutting of the lip plate are flute makers' trade secrets and the object of endless speculation among flutists.

A thorough discussion of all embouchure-making matters is beyond the scope of this work. There are some acoustically objective elements, and, to be sure, as many preferences as there are flute players.

Embouchure Position

Who says that your embouchure has to be dead center, at right angles with the flute? Pythagoras? Archimedes? If your position works (be it as crooked as mine), keep it there. Don't confuse logic and symmetry with ease and comfort; they are not necessarily roommates.

During that first lesson, Kincaid noticed that my embouchure was not exactly centered. In fact, it was quite crooked. He told me to look in a mirror while I practiced and to center the embouchure. When I returned the following week, I had the embouchure in the proper place, but had very little control over it. He thought for a while, and then had me play many things (loud, soft, high, low) with my embouchure in its original position. Finally, he told me to do it my way. Many years later . . . he called me over to where he was talking with

---

1. Not to be mistaken with vibrato.
2. Gold or gold alloys, for instance, on silver head joints.

some concertgoers. They had been asking him about correct embouchure, and Kincaid asked me to face the people and play for them. My guess is that his answer to them was "whatever works."[3]

Angle of Attack

As soon as the air brush clears the lips, it tends to disperse, to lose its direction and focus. This is the reason why, for each flutist, there is one ideal angle of attack, according to preference, lip configuration, and dental implantation. If the distance between the lip aperture and the embouchure's outer edge is too great, one produces what I call "turbo sound": large air flow, a need to breathe often, lack of timbre in the low register, ill-defined articulation, difficulty in controlling intonation,[4] and a hollow sound in general. Conversely, if the angle of attack is too closed and the lips too close to the tone edge, one gets the "gas leak" effect: shrill sound, saturated with foreign noises, brittle attacks, lack of flexibility in intonation and color, and narrow dynamic range. Therefore, each player must find by trial and error an average angle of attack on comfortable notes, such as D2 or G2.

However, once this average position has been found, it is not necessary, in my view, to change it constantly. It is possible to go step by step though the whole range of the flute without jawboning or facial gymnastics. The sound's modulation, in intervals as well as in arpeggios, can be achieved by shifting the air speed and the center of gravity, jawboning and lipping coming into play only to refine intonation.

In a nutshell:

Embouchure position is only one of the parameters of flute playing. Do not be obsessed with it and your head joint. If an offset position works for you, keep it. Your ears are more important than your lips. An average angle of attack allows you to modulate your sound in range and in color without jeopardizing reliability.

Please refer also to:

Air Brush	Flutes
Air Speed	Intervals
Arpeggios	Intonation, Intonations
Center of Gravity	Jawboning
Dynamics	

---

3. Robert Cole, in his recollections about William Kincaid, "William Kincaid," *Flutist Quarterly* (Fall 1995): 44–48.

4. Sharp in loud dynamics and flat in soft.

ÉTUDES

At every stage of our development, whether amateur or professional, we want, or we are requested, to play studies (or études). The range is wide: from Berbiguier to Jeanjean, by way of the Boehm caprices, all the Andersen *études* (ten books!), de Lorenzo, the Bach *studies*, the Donjon *études de Salon*, the Fürstenau *Bouquet des tons*, the Paganini violin caprices transcribed for flute, and the Karg-Elert caprices. All different, they all have something in common: they are supposed to make us play better, but they are not designed to be performed in public.

Études are different from basic exercises such as scales or tone work. Daily instrumental work hones our playing skills, day in and day out, regardless of our level. Études are temporary fodder, changing every week or at every lesson.

Kincaid always requested Berbiguier's *Dix-huit exercices*; Moyse used Andersen's op. 15. Tom Nyfenger insisted adamantly on "perfection." This is something that I confess having never accomplished: perfection in an étude (or in anything, for that matter).

What is perfection anyway? Playing all the notes? Running through them with a metronome?

At the risk of once more swimming against the current, I have to say that the benefits of studies are elsewhere: perfection is not the issue for me, unless we had études by Chopin and Debussy like the ones pianists play on their recitals.

I think that flute études are super for sight-reading, for training in concentration, in will power and in the art of approximation. For real sight-reading, a methodical approach is in order, albeit in a very short time:

- What is the key (and its changes)?
- What are the meter and tempo?
- What are the fastest runs and slowest notes?
- What is the basic rhythmic unit (quarter, eighth, etc.)?

This strategy applies when tackling an étude. It is amazing to see how many people start practicing even before looking. For an étude, this preliminary survey must be refined, pencil in hand. Indicate the chromatic passages: you won't even have to read them. When a line is in two voices, see which one is melodic and which is accompaniment: usually you have to read only one of the two. Indicate facilitating fingerings, on and off, such as thumb B♭. Breaths should be thought out, even if you change them later. Be wise in this respect; there is no reward for breaking breath records in an étude. Write in a few accidentals, the most annoying ones. Finally, double-check the key of each passage; you will avoid many wrong notes.

Do a run-through when you start that day's practice. Decide: "I won't stop, repeat, I won't stop." Read ahead. The old sailing ships had a saying: "One hand for the ship, one for the sailor." For musicians, it would be: "One eye for the reading, one for the playing."

At the end of the read-through, circle the "bad" passages in pencil.

When you do work on this étude, start your practice from the end, line by line. It is common to know the first six lines of a study quite well, but come the recapitulation and its changes, we run out of concentration and start thinking of anything but the matter at hand. I speak from experience.

Concentration is the most difficult thing to acquire and to teach. Three or four minutes of intense mental focus are more important than the repetition needed to bring a study to "perfection."

Developing this skill is one of the rewards of sight-reading (*prima vista*) and of a weekly étude, where the purpose is an improvement of the brain, not the immediate result of a study.

In a nutshell:

More important than momentary perfection in an étude are the skill to read and prepare a piece in a short time and the willpower to keep going.

Please refer also to:

Breathing	Notes
Concentration	Sight-Reading

FINGERINGS

Facilitating Fingerings for High Passing Notes

Only finger-activated keys for the second note of each triplet are shown. The first note of each group is not indicated and is always "normal" fingering. The facilitating principle is that fingers move in the same direction, not antagonistically.

Facilitating fingerings for high passing notes Figure 1

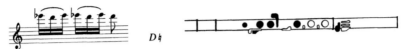

Facilitating fingerings for high passing notes Figure 2

Facilitating fingerings for high passing notes Figure 3

Facilitating fingerings for high passing notes Figure 4

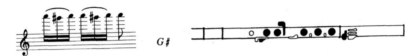

Facilitating fingerings for high passing notes Figure 5

Facilitating fingerings for high passing notes Figure 6

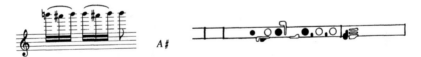

Facilitating fingerings for highpassing notes Figure 7

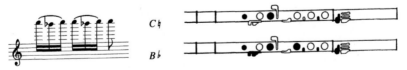

Facilitating fingerings for high passing notes Figure 8a and 8b

This fingering shows both notes because both fingerings are alternate.

"Harmonic" Fingerings

These scales, where only the left hand is active, can be played in the normal position or with hands crossed to demonstrate stability, as illustrated in the chapters on beginners and stability.

Harmonic fingerings Example 1

Some Alternate Fingerings for Stability, Tuning, Facility, Color, and Timbre

Only fingered keys are shown. Black means finger down, white means finger up, and gray means the key is optional. Half black, half white key: finger is either on the rim of the key or pulled back to show the open ring, the key being depressed (French-system flutes).

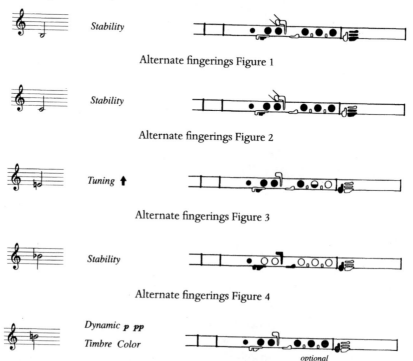

Alternate fingerings Figure 1

Alternate fingerings Figure 2

Alternate fingerings Figure 3

Alternate fingerings Figure 4

Alternate fingerings Figure 5a

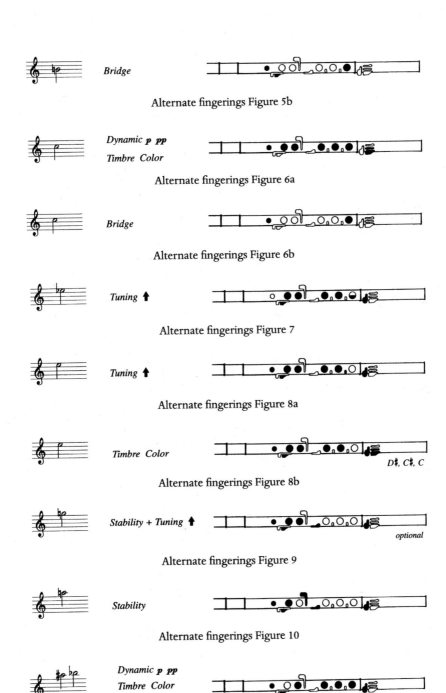

Bridge

Alternate fingerings Figure 5b

Dynamic **p** **pp**
Timbre Color

Alternate fingerings Figure 6a

Bridge

Alternate fingerings Figure 6b

Tuning ⬆

Alternate fingerings Figure 7

Tuning ⬆

Alternate fingerings Figure 8a

Timbre Color

D♯, C♯, C

Alternate fingerings Figure 8b

Stability + Tuning ⬆

optional

Alternate fingerings Figure 9

Stability

Alternate fingerings Figure 10

Dynamic **p** **pp**
Timbre Color
Tuning ⬆

Alternate fingerings Figure 11

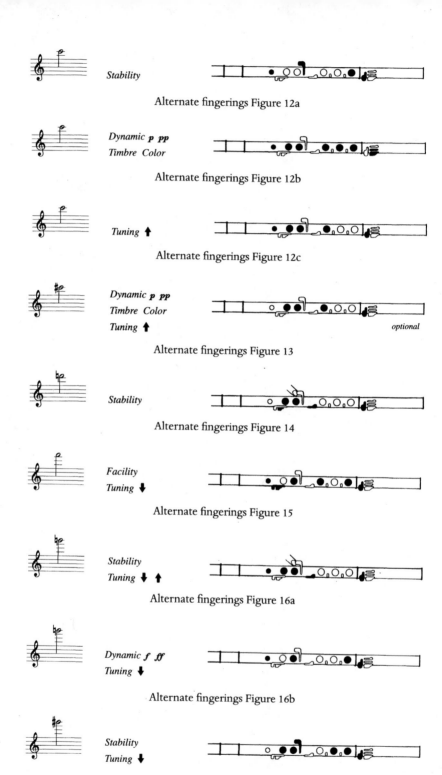

Stability

Alternate fingerings Figure 12a

Dynamic **p pp**
Timbre Color

Alternate fingerings Figure 12b

Tuning ↑

Alternate fingerings Figure 12c

Dynamic **p pp**
Timbre Color
Tuning ↑

optional

Alternate fingerings Figure 13

Stability

Alternate fingerings Figure 14

Facility
Tuning ↓

Alternate fingerings Figure 15

Stability
Tuning ↓ ↑

Alternate fingerings Figure 16a

Dynamic *f ff*
Tuning ↓

Alternate fingerings Figure 16b

Stability
Tuning ↓

Alternate fingerings Figure 17

 *Stability*

Alternate fingerings Figure 18a

 *Dynamic **p pp***

Alternate fingerings Figure 18b

 *Dynamic **p pp***
Timbre Color

Alternate fingerings Figure 19

 Facility
*Dynamic **f ff***
Tuning ↓

optional

Alternate fingerings Figure 20

 *Dynamic **f ff***
Tuning ↓

Alternate fingerings Figure 21

 *E♭*

Alternate fingerings Figure 22

 E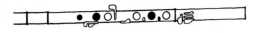

Alternate fingerings Figure 23a

 E

Alternate fingerings Figure 23b

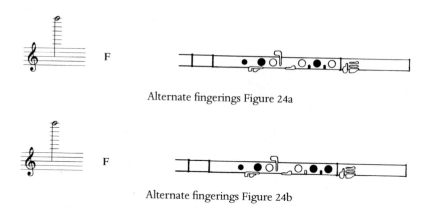

Alternate fingerings Figure 24a

Alternate fingerings Figure 24b

FINGER ANTAGONISMS

Often I feel that some of my fingers weigh a ton. This is especially obvious in trills that seem to always want to go their own way, out of context and beyond my will. Even in scale patterns and in simple arpeggios, difficulties arise when fingers work in different directions. Before being able to practice them, it is important to determine why certain patterns are more awkward than others.

"Down" fingers, through gravity and natural reflex, move faster than "up" fingers. This is one more reason to avoid slam-and-squeeze: fast movement upward, gentle landing downward. Here is a small catalog of antagonistic finger movements, in order of decreasing ease. Black keys and levers indicate finger down; white keys and levers indicate finger up; up arrows show "off" motion; and down arrows show "on" motion.

One finger of one hand in motion

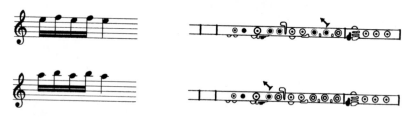

Finger antagonisms Figure 1a and 1b

Two fingers of one hand in motion in the same direction

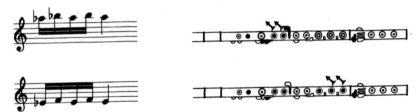

Finger antagonisms Figure 2a and 2b

Two fingers of one hand in motion in opposite directions

Finger antagonisms Figure 3

Two fingers of one hand in motion in opposite directions, with displacement of right pinky (little devil no. 2)

Finger antagonisms Figure 4

Two fingers of one hand in motion in one direction, one finger of the other in the opposite direction

Finger antagonisms Figure 5

Two fingers of one hand in motion in one direction, one finger of the other in motion

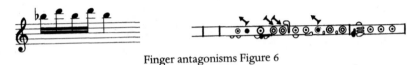

Finger antagonisms Figure 6

Two or three fingers of each hand in motion in opposite directions

Finger antagonisms Figure 7

A number of fingers of each hand in opposite directions

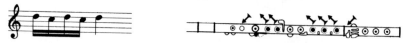

Finger antagonisms Figure 8

Repetition of these movements further increases the difficulties.

This is the reason trill fingerings aim to offer the movement of one finger, or rarely two, of one hand in one direction.

> ### In a nutshell:
>
> When many fingers are moving in contrary motion, the venting fingers (up) must work fast, whereas closing fingers (down) should not be falling hard and slam the keys. Do not hold the flute with note-producing fingers.
>
> ### Please refer also to:
>
> | | |
> |---|---|
> | Little Devils | Trills |
> | Slam-and-Squeeze | Facilitating High Passing Notes |
> | Stability | Unusual Trill Fingerings |

FINGER PHRASING

All too often we tend to identify phrasing with sound and technique with fingers, articulation being somewhere in between. Our practice is to emphasize sound as an entity to itself, relevant to the domain of musicality, whereas fingers are the attributes of virtuosity, an unavoidable and cumbersome necessity.

Yet many difficult passages are lost to poor control of the tone, because we are preoccupied only with the rapid succession of notes. On the other hand, faulty phrasing of slow lines can often be attributed to uncoordinated fingerings.

It is impossible for me to separate music from the instrumental means. Instrumental playing includes all the aspects of our dear flute: tone, fingers, articulation, slurring, pitch, vibrato, breath. . . . One may feel weaker in one area or another, but working on one without thinking about the others leads nowhere. Not even interpretation is instinctual: it responds to thought and practical solutions. There is a technique of phrasing just as there is a musical approach to instrumental problems.

I call "instrumental playing" what many people call "technique." The latter puts too much emphasis on sheer speed, the number of sixteenth notes per square foot. I think of intervals and phrases, particularly slow ones, as instrumental problems. They are a means to an end, the expression of musical feeling.

Often a slow interval is approached mainly from the point of view of sound manipulation. In a slurred phrase, the distortion of the face or of the embouchure should come as an assist only after the smoothness of the fingers has been coordinated.

How can one phrase with one's hands? I can already hear the objections.

Slapping fingers, at any speed, are an indication that instrumental playing is rough. A noisy technique is not a sophisticated one. Noise never comes from fingers lifting off the keys, but from their slapping on their way down. They make noise and rivet themselves on the keys; lifting them is then silent but difficult, sometimes painful. The first axiom for phrasing smoothly with the hands is: "Don't hold the flute with the fingers that form notes. Instead, stabilize with the three fulcrums of flute playing.[1] This way, the fingers actually playing the notes have an easier time lifting off the flute.

Of two slurred notes, the second is almost always less intense than the first, because, in general, the first one is an appoggiatura, from the Italian *appoggiare*. The word means "to lean upon," either because the note is outside of the harmony or part of a dissonant chord, or because it is leading to a release.

When, to form the second note, fingers come down, we tend to slap the downward ones. Things are smoother and more musical when the upward fingers are the most deliberate.

In the following example, the famous solo in Brahms's Fourth Symphony, it is easy to see how the plaintive second note resolves naturally when a lifting finger, indicated (1) and (3), forms it. In the passages where a finger comes down (2), however, the second note could sound stronger, if we are not careful, because of the tendency for descending fingers to slam down.

Finger phrasing Example 1

1. The first joint of the left hand, the right thumb, and of course the embouchure plate on the chin.

Even in a succession of descending intervals, as in the first movement, Adagio ma non tanto, of the Bach Sonata in E Minor, BWV 1034, we should be careful not to let the sheer weight of the falling fingers reinforce the second note.

Finally, when an interval needs to be smoothed out, before trying to lip it, we should visualize a seamless track of air going from one note to the next. A perfect slur is one where the sound wave between the two notes is not interrupted. This is achieved not by slamming fingers, but by smoothly synchronizing the connection between lifting and lowering fingers.

Venting or closing the hole closest to the embouchure, where the sound originates, interrupts the sound wave. While the octave key (C key and little devil no. 1) most often works that closest hole, the trill keyholes are even closer when involved. All fingers of the left hand, at one time or another, can be viewed as the agent of that closest hole, especially in the third octave.

One must learn how to phrase with the fingers. Phrasing achieved without any slapping of finger or key is always more beautiful. A loud finger technique results in rough phrasing. A well-practiced technique is not always the fastest, but the smoothest. Let us learn how to make music with our hands, as any modest craftsman should. The tone and the head joint are vital, no doubt, but how would you phrase without the hands?

> *In a nutshell:*
>
> Instrumental playing that sounds like an old typewriter cannot help your musicality. Think of your fingers as musical tools, not as wrestling enemies. Slow is just as hard as fast.
>
> *Please refer also to:*
>
> Fingerings   Slam-and-Squeeze
> Fulcrums   Tempo
> Rubato

FLUTES

You never hear it said that a great flutist plays a bad flute. It seems that a well-played flute improves with age. I know that when I lend one of mine, it returns with some of the defects (rarely the good qualities) of the borrower.

Physicists and acousticians will object that this is black magic. They say that only the shape and measurements of the flute, as well as the resonant medium,[2]

2. In our case, air.

matter. The effect of the tube's material would be negligible, according to them. But we flute players know there is a world of difference between metals and woods, and it is not only a matter of cost.

Antique violins improve with time. Wood is a living material and it evolves even after centuries; no doubt, the generous sound of great violinists contributes to this miracle. What about flutes?

It is true that time itself will not improve the acoustical qualities of a flute made either of German silver[3] or of sterling silver. Yet, so many old flutes possess a resonant quality of sound that seems unobtainable in newer instruments of the same make and model. One is inclined to say: "They don't make them like they used to."

To explain this, one must accept the fact that the tone quality of such a flute is the result of a hardened metal body tubing. . . . The point is that the tubing in old flutes made of non-ferrous[4] metals has hardened not with age, but with use. This is a process known as "work-hardening." As an example of the "work-hardening" phenomenon in non-ferrous metals, consider the copper tubing in our homes these days. It is very pliable when new, but whether it is used for the transport of water, oil or gas, it becomes almost brittle after a few years of use. It has become "work-hardened."[5]

Assuming they have been well made in the first place and well played, there is every reason to think that new flutes will get better as time goes on.

I am often asked: "Why are most high-quality flutes called French system?" I have to answer that no French-system flutes are made any more in France. This qualification began there 150 years ago, but sadly there are today no more French flute makers of note. Americans and Japanese are now the makers of French-system flutes. (Then again, French toast, French dressing, French fries, French letter, French vanilla, and French leave are called something else in France.)

For centuries, even millennia, flutes were a simple hollow tube pierced with holes covered by the fingers. The basic key or mode dictated the holes' position. This is the reason that non-European flutes are based on notes that seem very exotic to us.

Up to the beginning of the 1800s, European flutes were tuned to a major scale, usually D major, called a diatonic scale. The basic principle was one hole—one finger—one degree of the basic diatonic scale. This accounts for the fact that, prior to 1800, the majority of the flute repertoire was in D or G major and their relative minors. When modulations strayed too far from these, fingerings became a major problem, not unlike those of today's recorder. Deceptively simple as it may seem at first, it takes a consummate artist to play it well.

As the 1700s unfolded, flutists started adding keys to facilitate and expand the flute's technique. The first was the D♯ key used by Quantz and French players.

3. An alloy of nickel and silver.
4. Without iron content.
5. E. L. DeFord, in *DeFord Digest*.

Little by little, there were four keys, then eight, then more and more. These innovations, however, were all based on the old diatonic D scale. Flutes started looking like submachine guns, especially some of the English models, developed by Nicholson,[6] and the Gordon flute,[7] which had practically one accessory key for each accidental. The large-bore tone holes were developed as an experiment in England by Nicholson and the key mechanisms by Gordon, a dilettante flutist who served in the Gardes Suisses at the French court.

The Boehm System

Gimmicks were invented everyday. During the 1830s, a German genius appeared. Theobald Boehm, an excellent German flutist and an accomplished craftsman, designed and built the first flute, as we know it, between 1830 and 1840.

No doubt, in his time, Boehm's system was viewed as a gimmick by flutists of the old school. In fact, there was fanatic opposition to it. Imagine: a flute made not only of wood, but also of silver or German silver, capable of playing in tune, with a big tone? It was unthinkable. Yet he had a comprehensive approach, and he reinvented the mechanics of the flute.

Boehm's breakthrough was to conceive a flute based not on the diatonic but on the chromatic scale: one hole—one half-tone—one degree of the chromatic scale. Logical as he was, he theorized that his system would close or open every tone hole in sequence. The B♭ would be placed lower than the B, where our left thumb is now. The G♯ was higher than the G, hence the open G♯.

The B♭ thumb and B keys were eventually switched by Briccialdi.[8] This was the only major improvement to Boehm's system.

The French System

The French flute makers Godefroy, Louis Lot, and, later, Bonneville were the first to purchase Boehm's patents and to commercialize metal flutes. In spite of the inventor's objections, they applied their own ideas:

- Since five- and eight-keyed flutes already offered the closed G♯, they kept this feature, which made switching to the "pure" Boehm system a little easier.
- Since some of the experimental flutes already had rings, they developed open keyholes, the most visible characteristic of the French system.
- They adopted the Briccialdi key (thumb B♭) and built a few flutes with a low B.

Whereas Boehm's G and G♯ were set slightly off-center and activated by an independent rod, the French makers streamlined all of the large keys of the cen-

---

6. Charles Nicholson (1795–1837), a colorful British virtuoso.
7. William Gordon (1791–1839).
8. Giulio Briccialdi (1818–1881), Italian flute virtuoso.

ter joint into one line. My personal preference in this respect goes to the offset G/G♯, because it is mechanically better and does not require stretching the left ring finger. I have experimented with the open G♯.[9] It has great advantages but I must confess that I went back to closed G♯, finding the third-octave fingerings difficult to change at my advanced age.

The mechanics of the flute have changed very little since Boehm's system, and only the valid ones have survived: the Briccialdi key, the low B and its gizmo, the E mechanic (split E), the C♯ trill key, the closed G♯, the Brögger Mekanik.[10] But orthopedic contraptions like the Couesnon-Moyse model,[11] finger rests and crutches, the "high F♯ facilitator," the Dorus[12] G♯ key, and others have fallen by the wayside.

The Cooper Scale

The Cooper scale, devised by Albert Cooper, is the most theoretically founded improvement with respect to tuning. It is based on the Boehm schema, which describes the mathematical progression of tone-hole placement relative to basic pitch (A = 435 to A = 445). On the practical side, both the Boehm schema and the Cooper scale are at best approximations to accommodate the acoustical discrepancies between the tempered scale and the just scale.[13] The problem is that you can tamper only so much with the placement of the tone holes. Soon the whole tuning balance can be jeopardized.

Albert Cooper believes that he has gone as far as he could with respect to tuning. He has turned his attention to head joints and embouchure plates. Cooper is one of the cornerstones of modern flute making. Modest and pleasant, he is always open to new ideas and people. Ever curious and universally plagiarized, he

9. Lowering the left pinky closes the G♯ key.

10. Used as an option on Brannen-Cooper flutes. A modern development of an old idea, it applies to the center joint the double-rod mechanism of the foot joint.

11. A large-bore, covered-hole French flute (produced 1930–1960). Right-hand finger keys are compensated (thicker on the forward side than on the palm side). Left-hand finger keys are extended beyond the alignment of the body to allow the rotation of the left hand to an improved position. Aurèle Nicolet (Berlin Philharmonic), Gaston Crunelle (Paris Opéra-Comique), and a number of European flutists played this instrument. Today a similar system is used by Jeanne Baxtresser, former principal flutist of the New York Philharmonic, as a remedy for hand pain.

12. Louis Dorus (1813–1896) was the first professor to teach the Boehm System at the Paris Conservatoire (1860–1868). He devised a mechanism combining the advantages of the Boehm G♯ with the French-system closed G♯. Taffanel's portrait in the *Dix-sept grands exercices journaliers* shows such a flute. It was discontinued in part because it required a very strong spring, worked by a very weak finger, the left pinky.

13. A complicated topic. For all practical purposes, let us say that natural resonance and partials of a fundamental are not tempered. They are multiples of the fundamental's frequency. For this reason, a B♭♭ is flatter than an A, a B♭ is flatter than an A♯, etc. Likewise for G, D, and all notes. The tempered scale is a compromise to the effect that all the degrees of the chromatic scale are supposed to be equal.

actually advises his imitators. "Common sense is genius dressed in its working clothes."[14]

Embouchure plates have been built in every shape and form. Their shapes are not the only issue. Some head joints are louder, some boom in the low register; others give wings to your articulation. Most of the trade secrets lie in the hidden curvature of the head-joint tube and in the undercutting of the embouchure hole.

I have experienced many flutes: the traverso, the recorder, the metal flute as we know it, and the Boehm wooden flute that has been making sort of a comeback recently. I have a problem with this revival. I believe that you cannot make any instrument do things it was not intended for. If you are trying to make a wooden flute emulate a metal one, you risk losing the character associated with either. The only reasonable approach is to come to terms with the instrument you are playing. When the time comes to change, then love that new one. But don't try to find a flute that can do things for you by itself (huge sound, big low notes, nimble staccato). That is your problem.

To speak crudely, a flute is after all just a piece of very expensive plumbing. "In the candle, the essential is not the wax, but the light."[15]

At the risk of alienating my friends of the flute industry, I would not advise you to purchase a new flute until you know what you really need. Instead buy a second-hand one that has been played by someone, young or old, who you know plays the way you like. A well-worn flute is a good sign. Lemons usually stay in the case. I was caught once. From an antique dealer in Paris, I bought a Louis Lot, similar to the one I was playing at the time. During the late twentieth century, British "flautists" would have killed for this kind of instrument.[16] I thought I had really found a gem. It was in mint condition, as if it had not been made in 1870, but just for me a century later: no sign of wear, and sparkling. I soon discovered why: it was the proverbial lemon, probably an experimental instrument with a different scale and new embouchure design. I was lucky to unload it (at great profit) on a London dealer in such instruments.

A "previously owned" (doesn't that sound better than "used"?) flute has advantages. The price is usually more negotiable. You do not have to wait five years to try it. You may normally play it in your familiar surroundings. The binds have been played out of the mechanism. Even if it needs some pad work and is not spotlessly clean, that can easily be fixed. Besides, germ-free does not mean bug-free.

Repair

"If it ain't broke, don't fix it." Repair technicians often want every detail to look in top shape. If everything but one element works, fix that and leave the rest.

14. Ralph Waldo Emerson (1803–1882), in *Essays*.
15. Antoine de Saint-Exupéry (1900–1944), in *Citadelle* (Paris: Gallimard, 1951).
16. In the United States, around 1970, the fad was vintage Powells.

If one pad is leaking, change it. If all the pads are replaced, the result is often worse (and more costly). A newly padded flute rarely feels comfortable until after a few weeks. When an important audition or concert approaches, we become excessively sensitive to any flaw, imagined or real. Our perceptions turn catastrophic. Have the repairman adjust it, but don't overhaul it before an event. Wait until the storm is over.

My friends Étienne Vatelot and Jean-Jacques Rampal[17] look after the instruments of some of the world's great violinists. When the artists come with a worry and there is nothing wrong with the instrument, they are not contradicted. The violin is kept in the safe for a few days and returned to the virtuoso untouched, but with a technical explanation. The artist usually feels much better about himself and the violin. This is called the placebo[18] effect.

Slam-and-Squeeze

The most effective way to prevent damage to the mechanism of the flute is to avoid slam-and-squeeze. A noisy finger technique is a sure sign that an instrument is being brutalized. A flute will avenge itself. Since the music is also affected by rough treatment, working at a smooth finger technique will pay off both in quality and in musicality.

Cleaning

It has been a surprise to me that in America, one is advised to never leave a rag or a swab inside the flute. The old French flutes had a rod with an upholsterer's tassel on it. It was left inside the center joint, preferably not while playing. Jean-Pierre Rampal, among others, always did it, and so have I. Perhaps we were lucky, but we seldom have had sticky pads or needed an overhaul. After wiping most of the water out, a certain degree of humidity is maintained, and a few germs. If you feel that squeaky clean plays better, wash your headjoint in the sink.

A little moisture does not hurt. The pads and corks are still mostly natural[19] and need some humidity, as violins do. In dry environments, stringed instruments use a "dampit," a flexible green wormlike tube that releases moisture. The desirable ambient readings for good flutes, as for good cigars, are at 70 degrees temperature (20 degrees Celsius) and 70 percent humidity.

---

17. Jean-Pierre Rampal's son.
18. A medical term for a blank treatment administered to a test group.
19. Animal gut skin and cork made of oak bark.

In a nutshell:

Don't overlook second-hand flutes. Live with a flute before buying or rejecting it. Most of the playing comes from you, not the flute. Loudest does not mean best.

Please refer also to:

Embouchure   Intonation, Intonations
Finger Phrasing   Slam-and-Squeeze

FOCUS

I remember my childhood days when I started the flute. I loved to blow into it and the sound it made, but, however much I tried, I was always short of breath. It still happens sometimes. Then, teaching young players, I realized that the problem was not so much taking air in as managing its focus while blowing.

The purpose of inhaling is to produce sound. "Play well (blow well) and you will breathe well." The other way around is not always true. What is the use of breathing if the air is not focused and managed efficiently?

I have seen many articles, even books, about breathing and its mechanics, poor guys with electrodes on their chest, their throat, their abdomen. Very few words about air management or rapid breathing. Even less about music.

We are preoccupied by the mechanics of breathing and by the opinion of our flute colleagues. But the audience at large and other instrumentalists only listen to the music. Have you noticed how string players are always working on new bowings? We don't even notice whether a phrase is upbow or downbow. The same applies to our breaths. If it is well placed and executed, a breath actually contributes to the music. Don't think that an audience listens to you the way other flutists do. Don't think, while you play: "What will they say if I breathe here or there?" They are going to be critical, whatever you do.

By the time you have played the first bar, nobody knows whether you are going to breathe or not, yet everybody has a pretty good idea of what you are doing with the tone and the music. Their opinion is based on focus and musicality, not on deep-sea diving capabilities.

Our psychology deceives us: blowing a lot does not always mean producing more tone. Try playing a passage *f*, then *mf*: often *mf* sounds louder and better than *f* because we are more relaxed and more focused. Now try a short slow passage twice *mf* without breathing or change of dynamics: the sound is always better the second time.[20] Even if you feel out of air, the very fact that you have played a few seconds makes you focus better and support.

20. This is the reason why, in my Intervals 1, the same pattern is repeated twice.

The volume of your blowing is also deceptive: a huge breath is hard to manage and to focus at the onset. Therefore, if the passage you want to play loudly is short, don't breathe very much but focus the tone. Conversely, the fact that we blow little does not mean that we are playing softly. One of my charming students, when I say, "Please play *pp*," invariably retorts, "But I am barely blowing." That is the problem: *pp* requires little volume but more support than *mf* or *f*. When playing *pp*, you actually should think *ff* in terms of focus and support.

We sometimes feel that the more air comes out of our mouth, the bigger the sound. That is not quite true in spite of its apparent logic: the air inside the flute does not move, it just resonates and modulates the turbulence produced by the air stream hitting the strike edge of the lip plate. All particles of air in contact with that sound resonate, including inside our lungs and sinuses. Every flute sound is different for this reason, not because of the head joint itself. The air moves only at the strike edge. Some of it is lost in the process and moves away. It becomes that breathy part of the sound that many people resent. With a good focus, the rest of the air, hopefully the better part is transformed into vibrations. I am not the inventor of this technique: "When the airstream strikes the sharp edge of the hole, it is broken, or rather divided, so that one part goes over and beyond the hole, while the greater part, especially with a good embouchure, produces tone and acts upon the column of air enclosed by the tube, setting it into vibration."[21]

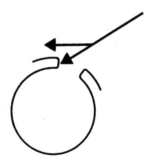

Focus Figure 1

The same principle applies to all winds, like the trumpet, where there is a lot of sound, but little air movement: a candle placed in front of the bell will not flicker.

By focus, I mean firm stability of the lip plate on the chin, and blowing inside the embouchure with a imaginary feeling that the air stream is not aimed across the embouchure hole and out, but through the diameter of the tube toward the crook of the left arm.[22]

If the distance between the air brush and the strike edge is too short, you get

21. Theobald Boehm, *The Flute and Flute-Playing in Acoustical, Technical, and Artistic Aspects*, translated and annotated by Dayton C. Miller (Cleveland: Savage Press, 1908).

22. Of course I do not mean covering or "turning in" the head joint.

a "tight" covered tone. If the gap between the lips and the strike edge is too wide, you have the "big" tone, breathy and unfocused, the "turbo sound" that seems to have some fans on these shores. If, furthermore, your cheeks are flapping about,[23] you are suffering from "loose embouchure syndrome," and you are in for trouble in the extreme registers, low and high, and on tricky attacks, $f\!f$ and pp.

Breathing is the most natural act. Breathing for the flute is like breathing for life. But focusing and air management are the art of flute playing.

In a nutshell:

Focus is essential for tone color and air management. It allows you to make the best use in terms of breath control. Don't think a strong embouchure will provide you with a strong focus. It helps, but the greatest responsibility is yours. Don't forget that the air inside your flute barely moves. There is a transport of vibration but very little transport of air.

Please refer also to:

Air Brush	Flutes
Air Speed	Intervals 1
Center of Gravity	Intonation, Intonations
Dynamics	Jawboning
Embouchure	

FREEDOM

It has been said that the worst enemy of liberty is not despotism, but anarchy. In music, an interpretation that has the appearance of freedom is sometimes chaotic because of lack of structure in the big picture and imprecision in the details of execution. I remember a few instances of Marcel Moyse's wrath, one at my expense, when a student wanted his or her personal ideas about *Syrinx* to take preeminence over the letter of Debussy's text, especially concerning the rhythm.

When you dominate your instrumental playing in every aspect of tone, vibrato, intonation, breath control, articulation, dynamics, color, finger speed, and

---

23. They cannot vibrate—the air does!

control, you become a freer musician, instead of remaining a slave to your instrumental shortcomings.

When you discipline your practice at home (or in your studio), it is not for the sake of discipline, but to improve your own music among your peers. Play scales and exercises, play slow intervals to refine your tone and your control, hone your instrumental tools, tune your own sensibility and reliability when you are alone with yourself. Alone, you have no excuse for not playing perfectly and for not mastering the notes.

The art of interpretation, however, is precisely to go beyond the signs on the paper to the emotional content. If the music we are making is not the expression of thoughts, emotions, and feelings, it is but an empty shell.

The musical vocabulary is replete with invitations to freedom: *a piacere* (at your pleasure), *ad libitum* (at will), *col canto* (with the voice), *rubato* (literally, stolen here, given back there), *seguire* (follow), *colla parte* (with the leading line), and, of course, *liberamente* (which says it all). The concerto cadenza is supposed to be improvised, in a sort of institutional freedom. This is true also of traditional jazz improvisation: it seems wonderfully free and was the spontaneous cry for liberty of an oppressed people, yet it progresses according to predictable rhythmic cells (4, 8, 16) and preset chord progressions. It is actually these codes that gave flight to the improvisers.

The more sophisticated music becomes, the more it moves away from the constraints of form and frame. The score reveals, however, how the composer shows us where to be at ease and where the rhythm must be exact, where relative solitude allows liberty, and where ensemble necessities require us to adhere to the rules of the mass.

In our orchestral repertoire, many solos give us a certain amount of freedom: Brahms's Fourth Symphony, Strauss's *Salome*, Stravinsky's *Petrouchka*, Bartók's Concerto for Orchestra (fourth movement), Ravel's *Daphnis et Chloé*, Debussy's *Prélude à l'Après-midi d'un Faune*, and more. But others are fanatically in tempo: the scherzo from Mendelssohn's *Midsummer Night's Dream*, Beethoven's *Leonore* no. 3 overture and Third Symphony ("Eroica"), Stravinsky's *L'oiseau de feu* (Firebird), Ravel's *Bolero*, Schumann's First Symphony, and many others. There are many elements of music which are too difficult, and perhaps too dangerous, to reduce to words.

But I would like to try with one of our masterpieces: Mozart's Concerto in G Major, K. 313. We are all familiar with it, mostly with piano accompaniment, which is a reduction of the orchestra.

When a steady pattern of eighth notes appears, played by the strings it is a clear indication that Mozart wants a strict rhythm. The piano would have trouble being uneven, but think of twenty strings, and one conductor, trying to keep up here with an irregular flutist.

As soon as the printed notes' visual shape changes, so does the character of the music.

The two first measures with repeated notes in the accompaniment are in strict

Freedom Example 1. Mozart, Concert in G Major,
K. 313, first movement, measures 31, 32, 33

Freedom Example 2

tempo, but already the third measure is imperceptibly more flexible, having rests and slurred patterns in the orchestra.

Consider the subsequent development (see Freedom ex. 3, page 93).

In measures 60, 62, and 64, Mozart leaves the flute alone. It is relatively free to take a bit of time, to project the sound without having to fight the accompaniment. But measures 61, 63, and 66 bring us to our basic strict eighth notes.

The following passage is interesting; we often don't know what to do with it (see Freedom ex. 4, page 94).

Again the score gives the solution: the solo grace notes in measure 70 incite us to some cute hesitation, until the eighth note pattern in measure 71 calls us back to a strict pulse. The unaccompanied measures 72 and 74 allow for some freedom to do a progression, or a regression (why not?) on the five repeated notes, whereas the slur design in measures 73 and 75 invites a certain abandon in the resolution of the half note to the quarter. But this glimpse of freedom goes back to the strict tempo in measure 76.

The slow movement's score is also evident in this respect (see Freedom exx. 5 and 6, page 95).

The introductory flute line is left alone. It can be played in more than one character: Sweet? Lyrical? *Piano*? *Forte*? Quizzical? Interrogative? It is up to us to invent

Freedom Example 3

its mood, or our own. But in the final entry, our freedom is limited by the iden-tical violin line.

However, the piano, or strings, come in on the second half of measure 11, and their regular rhythmic beat indicates that structure is back. The flutist is wise to work with the two dozen orchestra members, or even with one pianist, instead of the other way around: look at the last appearance of this motif.

It is the same music for the flute, but the presence of the accompaniment gives a frame to our freedom. In this case, it is better to follow six desks of vio-lins, and maybe the conductor, than to have to explain and rehearse a little faster here, a little wait there. It is not realistic. Take liberty when you are alone. In a typical concert rehearsal, the conductor thinks only of "his" symphony, and the

Freedom Example 4

orchestra members of the end of the rehearsal. Their last concern is the concerto, especially the flute concerto, which is always the last item on the rehearsal agenda. So, "if you can't beat 'em, join 'em." This applies also to many of our pianists.

A new development starts at measures 16–18.

It is set up by three Es. One of them, the second, is left alone by Mozart, giving us a certain leeway for dynamic and rhythmic suspension. But one measure later, the same pattern of three Es is underlined by an uninterrupted flow of sixteenth notes in the accompaniment. Even though the tempo is slow and the mood cantabile, we cannot be as free as we were the first time.

The control you have over instrumental playing allows you to play with more freedom, with a rubato that you can conduct and speak with.

Freedom Example 5. Mozart, Concerto in G Major,
K. 313, second movement, measures 10–11

Freedom Example 6. Mozart, Concerto in G Major,
K. 313, second movement, measure 60

Freedom is the dearest conquest of mankind, but it is expressed within respect for a certain number of fundamental frames that give it meaning. In music, liberty of interpretation is not only what we feel impulsively. It must be corroborated by our knowledge of the full score, and hopefully, our faithfulness to the composer's thoughts and feelings.

Freedom Example 7. Mozart, Concerto in G Major,
K. 313, second movement, measure 16–18

In a nutshell:

Freedom is not synonymous with impulse and chaos. Become freer as you know more about music and yourself. Knowing the score is the first step to a musician's inspiration.

Please refer also to:

Accompaniment Rubato
Dynamics Tempo
Interpretation

GRACE NOTES

In different cultures using a common tongue, such as English, some identical things are called by different names; the British use lorry for truck, lift for elevator, bonnet for trunk, hire for rent, and so on. They practise and labour when we practice and labor; it is their honour and our honor.

Musical notation is like all languages: the same sign does not always mean the same thing. Such is the case of grace notes, about which many treatises have been written, a real sunken treasure for doctoral divers.

Lawyers make their living by the interpretation of the Law. The interpretation of music starts with understanding the signs.

It is not my purpose to write the definitive treatise on grace notes, assuming it were possible, but to try to share what I know in a practical and musically applicable way. In the contemporary idiom, grace notes, in various numbers, "must be executed, preferably, as fast as possible."[1] This implies that they must be played at the extreme end of the allotted space, but before the next note.

The first part of the twentieth century followed the previous one's desire to make musical notation clearer and more universal so that regional and national peculiarities would not prevent publishers from selling internationally. Thus, single, double, or triple grace notes were to be played fast as an enhancement of the main note, comparable to a sigh or a surge of expression. All other passing notes are rhythmically written, implying that the composer wishes them played in time. The romantics, especially the flute romantics, had an addiction to cadenzas, embellishments, chirpings and warblings, but the grace notes were always short.

Cadenzas were written in grace notes of different values, indicating that they were to be played freely, with a vague reference to duration, but not systematically fast—for example, Doppler's *Fantaisie pastorale hongroise*, measures 27 and 28. On the other hand, for the same reason, when the notes are not grace notes, the implication is that they do refer to rhythm, however perfunctory the accompaniment—for example, *Fantaisie pastorale hongroise*, measures 11–13.

The classical era was the first to normalize the use of grace notes. The baroque practice of using grace notes to indicate an expressive accent or appoggiatura[2] was rarely used by the Mannheim school, whose innovative style inspired Mozart, Haydn, and many lesser composers. Appoggiaturas were more and more written out as the composer wanted them. Grace notes little by little came to be used to embellish or emphasize this or that note but not in the ubiquitous manner of the seventeenth and eighteenth centuries.

In keeping with the baroque tradition, a grace note was implicit just before a trill, which almost always started with the upper note, except in the case of a chromatic progression or when the upper note was already present immediately

---

1. "Le piccole note, di preferenza, devono essere eseguite il più rapidamente possibile." Performing notes for *Sequenza*, by Luciano Berio (Milan: Zerboni, 1958).
2. From the Italian *appoggiare*, meaning "to lean," hence, to emphasize.

before the trill. Another custom, carried over among others from the baroque, was that grace notes placed on repeated notes were to be performed short. This we find in our beloved Mozart concertos.

Things are not as clear for the seventeenth and eighteenth centuries, which we tend to include in the general term of baroque music. There is more than one reason for this. Over a time span of more than a hundred years, styles evolved. Furthermore, music was not performed in England or Italy as it was in France or Germany. Musical signs such as grace notes did not mean the same thing here or there. Finally, indications were sometimes vague or absent because it was assumed that good performers were familiar with the implicit ways of performance and because to the player's imagination was given a certain leeway. The trouble with editions of baroque music is that they tend to establish in hard copy one interpretation of the signs and to stress only one way of performing ornamentation, notably grace notes. Written-out ornaments are actually more awkward to read. They reflect a false sense of logic. It is much more rewarding to learn the styles and go back to the *Urtext* (original edition), hopefully the one closest to the composer's conception, and take into account the practice of the times. As far as grace notes are concerned, the generally accepted notion is that they are always long and started from the upper note and more "leaned upon" than the notes before which they are placed. This is the first step in baroque knowledge.

But just as every law has loopholes, this principle has important exceptions. Bach's Sonatas offer excellent examples.

Exception 1: A grace note is always long except when it is the appoggiatura of an appoggiatura.

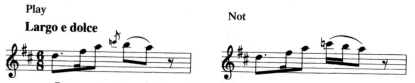

Grace notes Example 1a and Grace notes Example 1b. J. S. Bach, Sonata in B Minor, BWV 1030, second movement, measure 1

Exception 2: A grace note is always long except when it is placed on the shortest value of the piece. It is then played short and before the beat.

Grace notes Example 2a and 2b. J. S. Bach Sonata in B Minor, BWV 1030, second movement, measure 2

Play

Not

Grace notes Example 3a and 3b. J. S. Bach Sonata in E Major,
BWV 1035, first movement, measure 3

Play

Not

Grace notes Example 4a and 4b. J. S. Bach, Sonata in E Major,
BWV 1035, second movement, measure 1

Exception 3: A grace note is always long except when it is comprises an interval of a third or more. It is then played short or "filled in" by a *coulé* or *port-de-voix* in the case of an interval of a third.

Play   **Siciliano**

or

Not   **Siciliano**

Grace notes Example 5a, 5b and 5c. J. S. Bach, Sonata in E Major,
BWV 1035, third movement, measure 1

Play

Not

Grace notes Example 6a and 6b. J. S. Bach, Sonata in E Major,
BWV 1035, third movement, measures 4–5

Exception 4: A grace note is always long except when it is placed on repeated notes of the same name. It is then played short and before.

Play

But not

Grace notes Example 7a and 7b. Mozart Concerto in
G Major, K. 313, first movement

There is also a curiosity in baroque keyboard music: the *acciaccatura*[3] meaning "crush" or "squeeze" in Italian. Not only was the grace note short or very short, the two concerned notes were crushed together to create acute dissonance. Such an effect is beyond the possibilities of the flute, but it shows that not all grace notes were long.

Often the flexibility and imaginative character of baroque music were overlooked. For a long time (approximately 1850 to 1950) baroque grace notes were considered a purely decorative, if somewhat dry, embellishment. Then, as the baroque revival gained momentum, ornaments in general and grace notes in particular became the issue, to the extent that they sometimes appeared to be the tree hiding the forest. Always light and dry, or always long and loaded with historically correct baroque pathos? The truth, as usual, lies somewhere in between.

> *In a nutshell:*
>
> Grace notes are not always graceful. An appoggiatura reinforces harmonic tension. Sometimes ornaments serve as decoration of the line, but excesses in embellishment are the sign of decadence, as in flute romantics. Good taste is knowing how far ornamentation can go.

---

3. *Acciaccatura*: 1. A short accented *appoggiatura*. 2. A note on second above, and struck with the principal note, and instantly released (*Pocket Manual of Musical Terms* [New York: Schirmer, 1905]).

Please refer also to:

Freedom   Rubato
Hierarchy of Beats Tension
Interpreting Accents Style
Phrasing

HANDS

Flute stability is the prerequisite of healthy and efficient instrumental playing. Stability helps tone as well as virtuosity, legato as well as articulation, high range as well as low, dynamic control as well as intonation.

Primitive or sophisticated flutes of all ages and of all ethnic origins have one thing in common: they rest on the same point of the left hand—the first joint of the left forefinger,[1] halfway between the embouchure plate[2] and the right thumb.[3] From my instrumental playing perspective, total solidarity between the lip plate and the chin results from the isometric balance of forces between these fulcrums. These forces apply not to holding up the flute vertically, but rather on a horizontal plane, perpendicular to the flute.

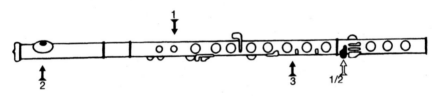

Hands Figure 1

The first teacher should be extremely patient and meticulous. Changing a faulty hand position after the first six months is very frustrating for student and professor.

One of the assets of the French system (open keys) is that it guides a beginner to a healthy hand position. A French-system flute, if it can be found, is the ideal starting instrument. Once a good position is established, the French system does not matter much anymore. It's a kind of fetish. If the offset G♯ is more comfortable, is should be the right choice.

1. Fulcrum no. 1.
2. Fulcrum no. 2.
3. Fulcrum no. 3.

Hands Figure 2

Left Hand

Up to a point, it could be said that the left hand is more indispensable than the right. It is possible to play half of the whole range of the flute with the left hand alone, using harmonic fingerings:

Hands Example 1

The right hand improves the intonation and the color of these notes, but they are already there, in some form, with the left hand. Whole passages can be played this way.

White notes are played as fingered; A♯/B♭ is fingered with the thumb B♭ key.

Hands Example 2. Ravel, *Daphnis et Chloé*, solo, beginning.
White notes as fingered. A# / Bb fingered with thumb Bb key

No amount of slamming with the right hand would help if the left-hand fingerings were not precise.

Another example of the usefulness of this stability for tone production: Attack *ff* a low G or G#: it may be a bit unsure. Now try the same thing while crossing over your right hand to hold the head-to-body joint bearing the brand name: security is much improved. For these notes also, if there is time, extra stability is welcome.

Hands Figure 3. (left pinky under G#)

The same idea applies in the high notes *pp*: solidarity between lip plate and chin provides an extra margin of control.

I have often wondered why so many teachers and methods require that the left wrist be "broken." It does not really help anything, but it can lead to pain in the hand or higher up the arm. The rationale is that it allows the left ring finger to reach the G key easily. If that were the case, an offset G (as in the original Boehm system and most beginner flutes) would do better than the in-line or French system.

I believe that one must be as comfortable as possible, without any tightness: therefore, morphology permitting, fingers should be flat and in alignment with the forearm. This implies that the left elbow should not be lifted far off the chest.

A simple idea for a good left hand and wrist position: stand as if you were waiting for the bus, arms alongside the body, flute in your right hand. Now, gently pinch your right earlobe between your left thumb and forefinger.

Hands Figure 4

Hands Figure 5

This gesture makes you bring up your arm, turn your head to the left a few degrees, and raise your elbow no more than necessary. Finally, bring your flute to your left hand: this is a natural position.

When you raise a small bottle to your lips with the left hand, your movement is totally natural. If your playing position is comparable, there is nothing to add.

When the wrist is at an excessive angle, the left thumb finds itself pushed up

Hands Figure 6

beyond the rods. Its lever is shorter, hence less efficient. With a relatively straight wrist, the fleshy part of the thumb operates the B and B♭ (Briccialdi) keys. The position is better and the action more flexible.

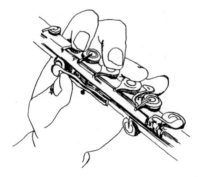

Hands Figure 7

Right Hand

The strong muscles of the left arm provide the main stabilizing effort. It is counterbalanced in great part by the transversal force of the right arm focused at the contact point of the right thumb.[4]

4. The only finger that is never involved in producing a note.

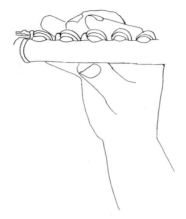

Hands Figure 8

The right thumb, steady by nature, must not uphold the flute's weight vertically. This aggravates grasping as well as slam-and-squeeze. Instead, it should
maintain the flute's position on a horizontal plane to allow the freest action of
the right-hand fingers. These fingers should, for the same reason, be as flat as is
comfortable. When a book or a flat object is picked up from a high shelf, fingers
are not pinching it, nor are they rounded out.

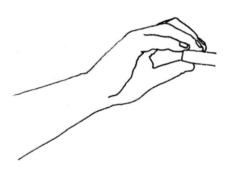

Hands Figure 9

The right wrist is in alignment with the fingers, which are almost flat. The
thumb's position is roughly opposite the space between the right forefinger and
the middle finger (depending on individual hand conformation.)The teacher
should not allow the thumb to stray under the B♭ lever. Sometimes the middle
finger must be slightly less flat than the others to compensate for its length. In
general, however, straight or flat fingers are preferable. If they were really
rounded out, as is often taught, they would pinch the flute. A greater effort is
necessary to lift a pinched finger than one lying flat. Pinching (or slam-and-

squeeze) slows down finger action. It can impose extra stress on the tendons and create tension all the way up the arm.

Sometimes young players actually hold the flute with the first joint of the right forefinger resting on the rod. While this does contribute to stability, it should be discouraged early on as an impairment of the hand's action in fast passages.

Even when they are not at work, these fingers should stay flat and close to the keys. The next drawing shows a negligent right hand (mine!). The fingers are too far from the keys. The thumb is too far forward. These fingers are going to slam-and-squeeze. The result will be less equality in finger phrasing and a noisier technique.

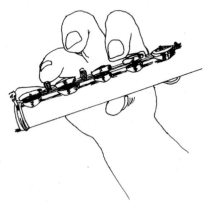

Hands Figure 10

This is one of the reasons that, providing there is no double jointing at the thumb level, the right thumb should be in alignment with the forearm. The right wrist should not be at an angle: force of any kind is better carried by a vector[5] than by a resultant.[6]

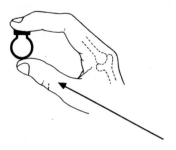

Hands Figure 11

5. A straight line animated by direction.
6. A force equal to two or more forces applied to the same point from different directions.

Today as yesterday, tradition teaches that the right pinky[7] should always be on the down position[8] except for D1 and D2.[9] The result is that we may see the whole right hand in an awkward position, with the pinky almost bent out of shape by enormous pressure. While it is at times a partial asset to stability, it would benefit many young players to get used to the fact that stability depends on fingers that do not make notes. My view is that the right pinky should not hold the flute, that one should "get rid of it" as often as possible because its blockage is an extremely common obstacle to right-hand dexterity.

Hands Example 3

A valid objection: "What if too much pressure is applied by either hand (or arm)?" This can happen indeed. However, we are talking about balance of both hands, as in carrying a bowl of hot soup: our innate reflexes regulate the mutual forces so that the liquid stays level. Spills happen, in flute playing too. Stability does not mean rigidity. The learning process starts with awareness of problems. Then comes education of our reflexes, so that strength applied at naturally stable places[10] cannot hamper the action of note-producing fingers, most notably the right pinky. In this sense, one can say that there cannot be too much stability.

> ### In a nutshell:
>
> Logic and comfort must be taught early. Bad habits are difficult to correct. They can hurt. They can stymie the development of young flutists, even hurt them. Use the strong arm muscles and fulcrums to avoid forceful and noisy finger movements.

7. Little devil no. 2.
8. I.e., venting the D♯/E♭ hole.
9. As well as some optional fingerings in the high range.
10. I.e., fulcrums.

> *Please refer also to:*
>
> Beginners   Muscles
> Fulcrums   Slam-and-Squeeze
> Little Devils   Stability

HIERARCHY OF BEATS

In 4/4 time, the first beat (downbeat) is usually the strongest. Then, in order of emphasis, comes the third beat, which is weaker than the first. The intermediate weak beat is the fourth, which serves as upbeat to the next phrase. The weakest is the second beat: it serves as release for the often-accentuated downbeat.

Hierarchy of beats Example 1. Schubert, Introduction and
Variations on "Ihr Blümlein Alle," op. 7

Letters in the hierarchy of beats examples represent the following: DB = downbeat; RB = release (weakest) beat; SB = secondary beat; uB = upbeat (weak); dDB = displaced downbeat.

Hierarchy of beats Example 2. Mozart, Concerto in G Major,
K. 313, first movement, beginning

In 3/4 time, it is more stylistically natural to erase somewhat the second beat instead of reinforcing the first:

Hierarchy of beats Example 3. Schubert-Bœhm,
Theme and Variations on *Le désir*, op. 21

Likewise, in 6/8, to ease up on the second eighth note of each beat:

Hierarchy of beats Example 4. J. S. Bach, Sonata no. 2 in Eb
Major, BWV 1031, second movement, Sicilienne

Siciliano

Hierarchy of beats Example 5. J. S. Bach, Sonata in E Major,
BWV 1035, third movement, Siciliano

There are of course exceptions—for instance, when the emphasis is intended
by the composer on a normally weak beat, creating a deliberate accent or syncopation:

Allegro

dDB = displaced downbeat

Hierarchy of beats Example 6. Beethoven, Trio in G Major for piano, flute,
and bassoon, first movement, beginning

Lentement

Hierarchy of beats Example 7. Marin Marais, *Les folies d'Espagne*

> ### In a nutshell:
>
> The rhythm of a phrase is not only a uniform beat. Like a spoken sentence, it has articles, verbs, and objects, as well as emphasis and release.
>
> ### Please refer also to:
>
> Interpretation   Style
> Phrasing   Upbeat

IMAGES

There is a technique of interpretation. Interpretation is not something that comes to your instincts and hormones out of a clear blue sky. It takes study and thought, but it should feel natural to you and to your listeners.

Interpretation should sound simple, because like culture, "It is what's left when you have forgotten everything."[1] But too often culture (and knowledge of interpretation) is like jam: the less one has, the more one spreads it around.

Music is sometimes descriptive. Titles are bestowed upon masterpieces after they have been composed. The "Moonlight" Sonata made Liberace very rich, but it can be listened to in broad daylight. The "New World" Symphony flatters America's idea of itself, but it is, first of all, a beautiful symphony. Debussy himself titled *La mer*, but it goes beyond the imitation of wind and seagulls.

A work of art should not represent anything but itself. The greatness of a painting is not in the likeness it gives of a landscape or of a face. Any good photograph can do that. Rather, it is a vision of the world through the mind, the heart and the hands of the artist. It is better than a faithful representation.

"The mission of art is not to copy nature, but to express it! . . . We have to seize the spirit, the soul, the face of things and beings."[2]

Did Vincent van Gogh just paint twisted Provençal landscapes under a mad sun, or does he move us by the scorch of his tormented soul? Does Claude Monet want us to see an endless series of water lilies, haystacks, and cathedrals at different times of day, or do they simply model his abstract search for the vibrations of light and color? The enigmatic half-smiles of Leonardo da Vinci are not just portraits of ladies and Madonnas. They are also a reflection of his own ambiguity and mysterious genius. Edward Hopper seems meticulously to paint everyday America, but his bland scenes are actually commentaries on the banality of daily life. Even abstract contemporary art, so criticized for not representing

1. Herriot.
2. Honoré de Balzac (1799–1850), in *The Unknown Masterpiece*.

or meaning anything, at least represents itself, as the expression and thoughts of the artist, who is always recognizable.

One can paint only what one feels. To be convincing, an interpretation needs to be sincere and heartfelt. How does this apply to music in general and flute performance in particular?

Interpretation can be analyzed and studied, but it must not be copied. The temptation to imitate the recordings and mannerisms of great players is great.

Now comes the inspiration offered by nature or art. If your imagination seems to have dried up, instead of listening to the CD for the tenth time, go outside and smell the air. Ask yourself if the music you are working on recalls feelings, even timeless images. Is it morning, is it night, is it calm, is it light or pompous, is it stormy, is it aloof or burning with passion, is it summer or winter, is it tormented or serene, does it have the freshness of spring or the flamboyant melancholy of autumn, is it a manicured classical garden, or the jungle, and so on?

Or look at paintings, and trace their moods as images for your interpretation: the light of Vermeer, the sensuality of Caravaggio, the opulence of Renoir, the cool elegance of Ingres, the homely charm of Pieter de Hooch, the fanatic symmetry of Mondrian, the deliberate ugliness of Picasso, the obsessive clutter of Jackson Pollock, the violence of Goya, and so on. All moods are ideas for us to put into our music.

Texts—poems or fiction—are also an inspiration, either because they are contemporary with the music we are playing or because they illustrate certain moods—mystery, heroism, love, compassion, and religious feeling—that are the source of our emotions. These can be expressed by our interpretation of music using technical means such as vibrato, virtuosity, dynamics, articulation, and so on. But if music is not a reflection of our thoughts and feelings, it is but an empty shell.

In the interpretation of a piece, we are the vehicle of someone else's mind and emotions. And yet, the same music does not ring the same way every time. A symphony can be molded differently, according to the meaning it has for different conductors. Even our familiar flute repertoire of Bach, Mozart, Debussy, and Prokofiev can feel different at different moments.

Technical solutions aside, most important is the quest for the author's intent and for what we ourselves intend to convey through it.

In a nutshell:

Examples are good. But don't just copy the latest CD, which is simply a moment in time. Developing your playing skills has a goal: interpreting the music of the composer and through it expressing your imagination, your thoughts, and your emotions.

Please refer also to:

Articulation	Interpretation
Dynamics	Vibrato
Freedom	Virtuosity

INTERPRETATION

Music is the mirror of our soul, itself the reflecting pool of our emotions that are fired up by music, and vice versa, ad infinitum. The more we are able to dwell on our emotions, the deeper will be our comprehension of music and of ourselves. Total grasp of music's secrets is an infinitely inaccessible goal, just like— as in *Alice in Wonderland*—the image on the other side of the mirror.

The question we have to ask ourselves is: What does this passage mean to me? Music is made of many moods. Is it peaceful, violent, mystic, tormented, happy, lazy, sad, passionate, patient, mysterious, urgent, inquisitive, positive? Does it speak of morning, of night, of fate, of hope? Does it smell like a spring rain or like the subway? Does it have the colors of autumn or the grays of dusk? Do I love it, like it, or loathe it, and what can I do to communicate my emotions?

In a way, our interpretation is similar to the painter's art: the subject is the same, Rembrandt's self-portraits or Monet's water lilies and cathedrals, but every picture is different. We must not be afraid of a certain spontaneity, as long as the basic musical grammar is understood.

I am constantly telling myself and my students to work at instrumental skills in scales and exercises, and to look every day at our reflection in the mirror of instrumental playing. Is that contradictory to imagination and emotion? Certainly not. There is music in the simplest of exercising patterns.

Practice as an artist: that is a constant. Neither the conquest of good instrumental playing nor the knowledge of certain interpretative ideas will make an artist out of a tree stump, but certainly lack of them makes the most gifted an invalid.

Literally speaking, the word *interpretation* has the meaning of *translation*, the performer or interpreter being the vehicle between the silent signs on the page and their coming alive as sound and music. Interpretation is also a personal and variable experience, an image of the composer's soul as seen through the prism of the interpreter's thoughts and emotions. Still, lest it be incongruous or incomprehensible, such a poetic endeavor must fall into certain objective patterns and tacit rules. They constitute style, just as grammar underlies languages, regardless of the aesthetic content.

For us musicians, the wrong approach to interpretation is to go right to the emotional content without pausing to assess stylistic and compositional elements implicit in the complete score of a work. A superficial practice of the flute part alone can alter or reduce music's meaning. Study of a sonata is incomplete without knowledge of the piano score.

Your chamber music part must be ready before the rehearsal, and you should have a good idea of what the others are playing, Working on the well-known excerpts is excellent, but they deserve to be studied in the orchestral context.

The following thoughts on interpretation are not meant to establish rigid rules, as would some of the editions of Mozart or J. S. Bach. Editors' metronome tempos, dynamics, and articulations are inflicted on the trusting student as if they were always the composer's wish. These reflections will try to lead the reader to personal re-creations stemming from the inner logic of the composition and to tap the imagination of the performer.

Interpretation comes from within the head and the heart of the performer, not from copying, affectation, and imitation.

What are the parameters? Character, tempo, mode and key, structure, perspective, and content.

Consider the character of the piece as much as the tempo indication (allegro, allegretto, andante, adagio, etc.).

Pride, joy, tenderness, torment, serenity, mystery, passion? You have the whole rainbow of human emotions at your fingertips.

If you are not sure, look up the meaning of the musical terms. Most of them are in Italian, and they are often poetic and picturesque: *capo* = head, *coda* = tail, *scherzo* = game, *aperto* = open, *assai* = very, and so on. German, French, and English are less common, but also evocative. Any indication by the composer is worth understanding.

Look at the time signature: 3/4, 4/4, 6/8, and so on. More importantly, find the pulse or tempo: do you feel it in one, in half notes, or subdivided?

Will you be able to play the fastest passages cleanly in this tempo?

Interpretation Example 1. Schubert, Theme and Variations on "Ihr Blümlein Alle," op. 160 Variation 1, second part, measure 17

All these parameters change with each subject.

Speed means nothing per se. The most brilliant allegro is not always the fastest.

One must have experience and a lot to say to play an adagio very slowly. Slower does not mean more expressive—usually the opposite!

In an accompanied solo or sonata with keyboard, the "soloist" can often be seen gesturing and stomping to mark his tempo and his dominance over the accompaniment. Yet, in many cases, a natural perception of the pulse can be found in the accompaniment, either in a seemingly unimportant pattern (for example, in the bass line of Bach's Sonata in E Minor, BWV 1034, second movement, *Allegro*, measures 40–47)

Interpretation Example 2

or in a simple rhythmic formula which pervades the piece (for example: the bass line in the introduction of Schubert's Introduction and Variations on "Ihr Blümlein Alle," op. 160: one long, two short, constant, through the first seven measures.

Interpretation Example 3

Another example is the first five measures of the accompaniment of Fauré's Fantaisie:[3]

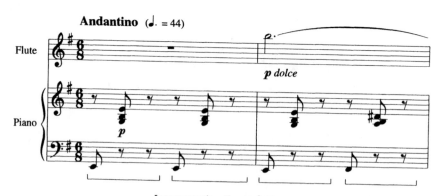

Interpretation Example 4

3. This type of formula is still called in France *mesures de café au lait* in orchestra jargon. In the cafés of old-time Paris, there was a small orchestra. Since the union break did not exist, the pianist would fill time while his colleagues would have their coffee-and-milk; the *café au lait* measures, repeated as many times as necessary for them to finish, would be the signal to go back to work.

Interpretation Example 4 (*continued*)

or a passage whose configuration shows that it cannot go over a certain speed (for example, *variation 6* of Schubert's *Introduction and Variations, op. 160*; in this case, because of the piano's left-hand octaves, the 3/8 cannot be played in one beat).

Interpretation Example 5

Interpretation Example 5 (*continued*)

In a group, even if the flute has the prime role, flutist should always be able to yield to the tempo of the mass instead of trying to convince by force. If there is merit to a musical idea or tempo, it will inspire an interpretation through persuasion better than through struggle.

Strings playing staccato or spiccato (here the second violins) give a workable tempo for the whole group.

Interpretation Example 6. Mozart, Concerto in C Major,
K. 299, third movement, beginning

Likewise, in the entrata of Beethoven's Serenade, op. 25, the spiccato violin and viola give a better pulse than the flute.

Interpretation Example 7

When there is no upbeat, the lead instrument gives the start, but tempo is established by the accompaniment, mostly by the instrument with the most notes, for example in the Adagio and Finale of Mozart's Quartet, K. 285 (see Interpretation exx. 8 and 9).

When an upbeat is present, the start is simpler, but the accompaniment still gives the pulse. For example: start of the finale of Beethoven's Sérénade, op. 25.

The score, considered as a whole, is the key. It helps to grasp whether rhythm or phrasing takes precedence, if the piece is a vivacious dance, an elegy, a light step, or a song, a poem, or a funeral march.

The listener can feel a certain uneasiness if this analysis has not been made. Either the piece is being played with too much rubato and without structure, or, conversely, the account is too stiff. It does not breathe or it lacks tension and release.

Adagio

Interpretation Example 8

Grammar of Interpretation

- Study with the complete score (piano for entire works, or orchestra for excerpts).
- Find the tempo from a passage that has a running flow of notes and a pulse, not just from the beginning of the piece.
- When the accompaniment has a rest of one beat or longer, the composer is allowing you to take time. If the accompaniment has a strict rhythmic pattern, the safe and musical thing to do is to follow it. An excellent pianist might follow you but an orchestra? Never.
- Music, like life itself, develops on tension and release. Find the places that have tension and take time for it to build. After the release that you should physically feel, don't linger. The score will help you. Examples:
- Appoggiaturas and harmonic accents (for instance, a leading tone from a dominant seventh resolving tonally).

Interpretation Example 9

Wide intervals (especially if they are dissonant).
A dynamic progression.
A written accent (*sfz, sfp*).

- A slow or fast passage in an even scale pattern is not usually loaded with intention. Some passages are purely ornamental. Even in Mozart, virtuosity plays a major part; one should not make an emotional issue out of every note.
- When two notes are slurred, it can generally be assumed that the second one is a release of the first. This means not that the first note is louder than the second, but that the second one is softer than the first. Technically, you can help this by not slapping the keys on the release and by keeping fingers close to the keys for phrasing.
- A wide interval is somewhat comparable. Consider the second note as the release, while playing the first one with tension.
- In Italian the suffix *-ndo* means "in the process of." Read "accelerando" as slow in the process of speeding up, "crescendo" as still soft in the process of growing louder, "diminuendo" as loud in the process of getting softer, and so on. Therefore, play your dynamics in the direction of the phrases—that is to say, do not systematically diminish long notes if you are in a crescendo line, for instance, or do not be already soft at the open end of a decrescendo line. A change in dynamics or tempo is most effective when held back and then executed with conviction.
- Be conscious of silence, before you start and at the end, when sound dissipates, but also in the course of the piece. Silence by Mozart is louder than many *ff*'s.
- Use colors.
- On repeated notes or patterns, change dynamics, vibrato, timbre. Here is where your imagination and knowledge come together. Don't always use a "big tone."
- Feel and taste the difference between major and minor, between D♯ and E♭.
- Do not play tempered:[4] play the tonality, the key, the mode, the happy D major, the somber E minor, the tragic C minor, the triumphant C major, the quizzical F minor, and so on. Scales and arpeggios will help you with that. Give them the color you like, as you will apply it in your interpretation.

Music speaks without words, changes our view of the world without graphic representation, disturbs without physical aggression, and seduces without caresses. But through immediate perception, it is the symbol of evidence unsaid.

---

4. Tempered: a scale where all the half steps of the chromatic scale are equal—i.e., they are all a little bit out of tune.

> ### *In a nutshell:*
>
> A musical composition is the fruit of thought, craft, and inspiration. Our interpretation must take the score apart through analysis, then put it together again in performance. Form precedes content, but it is a means to the end of expression and feeling. All our instrumental tools serve that purpose. Intelligence has never hurt emotion.
>
> ### *Please refer also to:*
>
> | | |
> |---|---|
> | Accompaniment | Rubato |
> | Dynamics | Tempo |
> | Images | Tension and Release |
> | Intonation, Intonations | Upbeat |
> | Phrasing | |

INTERPRETING ACCENTS

An accent is a punctual concentration of musical energy that highlights or stresses the tension of a moment. It can be of a different nature: acoustical, harmonic, or expressive.

Indicated *fp* or *ffp*, an accent is sometimes almost percussive, louder than the note:

Interpreting accents Example 1

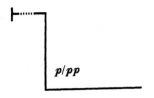

Interpreting accents Figure 1. Reproduced with the kind authorization of Alphonse Leduc publisher and owner of the world wide copyright—Paris, France

An *fp* or *ffp* requests a very fast drop, on one note, from the loud to the soft. It is as much an accent as an effect, frequently used since Beethoven. The flutist must go from a very sustained sound to nothing, as if the blowing had stopped. Played by the strings, it becomes visually explicit: the bow almost stops. The player must convey the impression that this note burns.

An *sf* (sforzando) must not be misread for an *fp*. It also affects one note only, or, more precisely, one sound: if the note is long or carried over bar lines with slurs, the "reinforcing" applies to the duration of that note. There can be many *sf* in a general *p*: the *sf* brings the prevailing dynamic to the next level (*p* to *mp*, *mf* to *f*, etc.).

The *fp* in measure 2 of the following example is not sustained, but the *sf* is.

Interpreting accents Example 2. Beethoven, Symphony no. 3, "Eroica," first movement

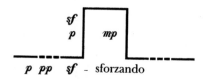

Interpreting accents Figure 2

An *sfp* is again different. Starting with a relatively soft tongue attack, the sudden surge is followed immediately by a fast diminuendo. Achieved, for flutists, by a sudden acceleration of the air speed, it is produced by pushing the air out with the abdomen, an action comparable to what happens when we sneeze. The strings increase and decrease the speed of the bow, along with its pressure. We should try to do the same with the air.

Interpreting accents Example 3. Beethoven, Symphony no. 3,
"Eroica," first movement, letter E

sfp-sforzando / piano

Interpreting accents Figure 3

A harmonic accent is normally not indicated; it results from tension in the harmony, or, in a single melodic line, from an interval, itself a reduction of the implicit harmonic environment.

Interpreting accents Example 4. J. S. Bach, Partita in A Minor, BWV 1013, Sarabande

Knowing where to place an accent is the groundwork of interpretation. Study the complete score, not just the flute part, to find the points where the music writing provides space to build up tension. Pacing requires patience to construct the tense moment. Once the climax is reached, release implies returning to tempo and to conclusion without systematically slowing down, as is so often done.[5]

The performer must track down the high points through analysis and intuition. Awkwardly placed accents affect interpretation in the same way comical foreign accents deform our own languages.

Harmonic accents are usually not indicated by signs in the score when they conform to implicit laws of style and agogic. For instance, the release of an accent is always less loud than the accent. If it occurs in two slurred notes, as in an appoggiatura, the second note must have less emphasis than the first. This does not necessarily mean that the first note is louder than the second, but that the second is softer than the first.

For an accent followed by a developed release, the note(s) bearing the accent should not be diminished, so that the first note of the resolution is not more intense than any part of the accent.

This is one of the great difficulties for pianists, who must somehow give the illusion that the release comes out of the accent's decay.

5. Unless the release is the conclusion of a piece.

Interpreting accents Example 5. Brahms, Symphony no. 4, Finale

Interpreting accents Example 6. Mozart, Concerto in G Major,
K. 313, second movement, measures 16–19

Interpreting accents Example 7. Mozart Concert in D Major,
K. 314, second movement, measures 19–22

Another example of an implicit law of style is that an upbeat placed on weak beat(s), or half beat(s), should be less intense than the strong beat(s) it leads to. When the latter is written in a less favorable range than the upbeat, one must control the agogic: the higher upbeat, in spite of its naturally brighter color, should not be louder than the downbeat.

Interpreting accents Example 8. J. S. Bach, Sonata in E Major,
BWV 1035, third movement, Siciliano

Syncopations[6] shift the accent from a strong part of the beat to a weak one. They need not be indicated because they have their own natural tension.

6. In romance languages, *syncope* is also used medically for "missing a heartbeat," i.e., a heart attack.

Interpreting accents Example 9. J. S. Bach, Sonata in B Minor,
BWV 1030, second movement, measures 13 to end

"The accent in syncopation is not my rule, it is the rule of life."[7]

On the other hand, when the composer wants an accent different from the implicit rule, he uses the sign > to give stronger emphasis to the unusual.

Finale Allegro Molto ♩ = 152

Interpreting accents Example 10. Reinecke, *Sonata Undine*, Finale

The sign ʌ indicates the need for a greater weight on one note. Here the sound spreads, for a brief moment, to alter time, space and dynamic.

In a group of notes, the sign > designates a passing inflexion. This went without saying in baroque interpretation at a time when accents were not indicated. It was left up to the "good taste" of the performer. Editions covered with dynamic and accent markings can be very misleading in this respect.

Before an accent, there is, as it were, an imaginary grace note of expectation or silence, of tension within the musical discourse, a fraction of suspended eternity, constructed and desired. This is true whatever the weight of the accent indicated by >, *sf*, or *fp*, and even more so when it affects a harmonic accent.

The upbeat to an accent should not be vibrated too much. Excessive vibrato weakens the implicit tension of the harmony. The accent and its release can be vibrated. The effect is comparable to the compression of a coil until it can accumulate no more tension, and then vibrates on release.

Adagio

Interpreting accents Example 11. Mozart Quartet in
D Major, K. 285, third movement, measure 12

7. Trevor Wye, *Marcel Moyse, an Extraordinary Man* (Cedar Falls, IA: Winzer Press, 1993).

In a nutshell:

Accentuation is like the features of a beautiful face. Underlining them enhances beauty, but exaggerated make-up deforms it. Venus becomes a clown. An accent must be understood, constructed, felt, reached, and released.

Please refer also to:

Agogic	Baroque
Appoggiatura	Silence
Air Speed	Vibrato

INTERVALS

I do not understand why tone is practiced as a separate entity any more than technique or tonguing. Instrumental playing is the sum of it all: listen to your sound in rapid passages, mind your intonation during staccato, smooth out your finger movements during phrasing, do not slam-and-squeeze in an interval (or anywhere else), and so on.

The tension on the first note of an interval is like the action on a trigger: progressive and imperceptible. If the squeezing is too brutal, the rifle moves and the target is missed.[8] The effort needed for an interval does not come on the change, but just before it. The actual interval is like a release.

In my way of playing, intervals should be practiced without lipping. If you should indulge in jawboning during a performance, fine. Music is the issue. But in a practice situation, you are trying to educate the basic tone production and control. Since you are not going to have time to work your chin on every note of an arpeggio in *Peter and the Wolf* or Mozart concertos, or any fast movement, you might as well keep your basic mouthpiece position and support. This is what you practice on intervals.

I do agree that for a shift or interval of more than an octave, some lipping is practically inevitable. The question is: do we really live constantly with wide jumps? Conservatively, intervals of an octave or less make up 99 percent of flute music. For example, out of thousands of notes:

- Ibert, Concerto: in the first movement, the separation of any two notes by more than an octave occurs eight times (only three slurred); in the second movement, none; in the third movement, seventeen intervals are wider than an octave (three staccato).

---

8. The only time I fired anything was under orders by the French Army, many, many years ago.

- Mozart, Concerto in D Major, K. 314: in the first movement, twenty-six intervals wider than the octave (all separated or staccato); in the andante, none; in the finale, none.
- Ravel, *Daphnis et Chloé, Second Suite:* First flute, two intervals wider than an octave (separated). Second flute, two notes wider than an octave (separated).

Therefore, the intervals that I advise for daily practice are all within the range of the octave or less:

Intervals 1

Intervals 1 deals with half steps and octaves.[9]
   Average vibrato, stable dynamic without crescendo or diminuendo

Intervals Example 1

Continue until the lowest note (B or C), then octaves up:

Intervals Example 2

And so on until the highest note, then:

Intervals Example 3

Go back in half steps until the starting note.

Intervals Example 4

9. Derived from Marcel Moyse, *De la sonorité: Art et technique* (Paris: Alphonse Leduc, 1934), but without swells or dovetails.

Intervals 2

Intervals 2 addresses minor and major thirds as well as their inversions, minor and major sixths, to be animated with a feeling for movement.

Average vibrato, stable dynamic without crescendo or diminuendo

Intervals Example 5. Average vibrato—stable dynamic without crescendo or diminuendo

Avoid slam-and-squeeze and continue to the lowest note (B or C):

Intervals Example 6

And so on until the highest note, then:

Intervals Example 7

Go back in thirds until you reach the starting note.

Intervals 3

Intervals 3 work at steadying and tuning perfect fourths and perfect fifths.

Shift using the center of gravity and air speed without jawboning and with average vibrato. Slur with the fingers. Sing the second note.

Intervals Example 8

Avoid slam-and-squeeze and continue to the lowest note (B or C), then up in fifths. Use stable dynamics without crescendo or diminuendo.

Intervals Example 9

And so on until the highest note:

Intervals Example 10

Then go back in fourths until you reach the starting note.

Intervals Example 11

Since the sum of the intervals is always an octave, these exercises have the same duration. Descending chromatics take longer than ascending octaves. The same for descending thirds and ascending sixths (or vice versa), and so on. The only missing intervals are augmented fourths (diminished fifths), which can be readily devised at will.

Before attempting dynamic changes, sing the interval *mf* at full sustained tone. I have long thought that controlling tone in one dynamic is more productive than swells on every note. Try also *pp* and *ff*, but the most basic is *mf*. You may change the dynamic of any interval, as long as the intensity of both notes of the interval is as equal as possible.

Timing Intervals

Have some kind of feeling for the beat. It will serve as a common denominator. At the passing of the interval, every intent must be to synchronize fingers, air speed, and shifting of the center of gravity.

Tuning intervals

The necessary development of your tone will also help train your ear. Upon playing Intervals 3, for instance, sing the second note internally while playing the first. If you must use a tuner, this exercise is the best, especially if your machine is of the relatively old type, which does not follow every sound you make. The ancient stroboscope, part of the furniture in band rooms, and the first electronic tuners showed one note at a time but responded to all multiples of the basic frequency, thereby telling you about the tempered intonation of the octave (second partial), fifth (third partial),[10] and so forth.

Let us consider now what happens when a slurred interval is not smooth. The critical moment is when the acoustically vibrating pattern of the sound (not to be confused with vibrato) is leaving the first note and the second note is being fingered. A millisecond of eternity . . .

An octave is usually smoother than a somewhat smaller interval because it is the second partial (harmonic) and uses, for the most part, the same basic fingering, except for the extreme high or low notes.

Even for apparently simple patterns such as the following, there can be a problem with smoothness. The fingering of the first note fingering is in black, and the fingering changes for the second note are in gray.

Intervals Figure 1. First-note fingering in black,
second-note fingering changes in gray

Intervals Figure 2

Left-hand finger lifts off just before right ring finger lands.

When, to form the second note, some fingers come down as others lift, we tend to slam the downward ones. Things are smoother when the upward fingers are the most deliberate.

But do not slam on the downward fingers. Instead, synchronize the movements of fingers with the shift of the air speed.

Our equivalent for the octave key of other woodwinds is the C key. When it is

10. Partials used to be called "harmonics."

involved, it is the one that should move first, because it is little devil no. 1. It is vital because it vents different harmonics (partials) of our schema, yet it is a lazy finger because of its awkward position. It wants to stay down on Eb/D#, a common mischief.

When the second note consists of fingers moving in opposite directions, it is safe to say that, since the down movement is more automatic than the liftoff, we should pay more attention to the fingers coming up than to those going down.

Finally, when an interval needs to be smoothed out, before trying to lip it, we should imagine a seamless track of air going from one note to next. From my experience, the most vital key in the shift between two notes is the one that vents or closes the hole closest to the embouchure, where sound originates. While the left-hand keys in general and the octave (C) key most often work that closest hole, the trill-key holes, when involved, are even closer. All fingers of the left hand, at one time or another, can be viewed as agents of the closest hole. In the high range, the trill keys become that closest tone hole.

To improve the synchronization of fingers in intervals, it is a good idea to time the shift by counting so that the fingers, air speed, support, and the inevitable slight facial movement all happen together and smoothly at the same split second. That is why I (and my students) play, as practice, metered intervals within the octave, instead of the proverbial and soporific long tones.

I am not against reading light material while doing these exercises, such as a weekly newsmagazine. Shame on me! My reasoning is that our actual playing involves two concurrent activities: reading or recalling (the music) and playing (the flute). Even as we read, we hear and control our playing. Many of our activities are twofold in this manner. As an orchestra member, you are always conscious of the conductor's motions without taking your eyes off the score; you can drive and speak or listen to the radio; as I write this, I am aware of some Schubert songs in the background; their beauty actually helps me to think.

In a nutshell:

Treat intervals as a cultivation of your fingers as much as tone. Think of the tone holes involved and vent the one closest to the mouthpiece first. Avoid most lipping. Tone work is as technical as finger twisters are. It is also the expression of soul.

Please refer also to:

Air Speed   Finger Phrasing
Finger Antagonisms   Jawboning
Center of Gravity   Intonation, Intonations

INTONATION, INTONATIONS

It is an inexhaustible subject. Many people have certitudes about it; they are dangerous, be they flutists, conductors, or instrument makers. Tom Nyfenger, with his sardonic humor, used the term "outonation."[11] Concern for intonation is the first of civilities toward partners with whom music is performed.

Tonal beauty, of course! Bright tone, clear tone, dark tone, ethereal tone, bravo! But often, the flutist, in his rapture about tone, gives it priority over intonation. One gets used to everything, including playing out of tune.

Intonation concerns act as a negative: it seems natural and beyond comment that an instrumentalist or a group play in tune. The listener does not even think of it. But if the intonation is defective, it is the first thing that is noticed, even by nonmusicians. A feeling of aural discomfort negates any perception of an expressive nature. Listen to the greatest pianist playing on an out-of-tune piano: the first thing you hear is the honky-tonk sound.

I have always regretted not having perfect pitch, and I succeed (hopefully) at playing somewhat in tune by referring to other pitches. Yet I am always ready to modify my playing to match other musicians, to the constantly changing harmonic environment, or to playing modes incompatible with our modern concepts.

Thus, when we say: " The modern flute is more perfect than the pre-Boehm traverso," we commit the sin of arrogance as well as a mistake, which often go hand in hand. Our modern criterion is equality in all ranges and on all the degrees of the chromatic scale. It is also what I try to teach in order to achieve instrumental playing as reliable as possible. However, for the flute players of yesteryear, it was not the main concern. "Intonation is a bourgeois luxury."[12] Colors changing with the keys, uneven timbre, even defects in intonation were elements of instrumental playing. They contributed to expression and to the character of their music. Boehm was criticized more for the "insensitivity" of his flute than for the imperfection of its mechanism. The lover's eyes change into virtues the beloved's defects.

Still, today, thank Heaven, each flute has its shortcomings, its own color, and each flutist has his own personal tastes and preferences.

In spite of what the experts (who are often salespersons) say, perfection is not of this world. Only the angels play in tune. Trouble is, nobody has ever heard them.

How's the weather among the gentle souls of the hereafter?
Have the musicians at last found the A?[13]

11. *Music and the Flute* (published by the author, 1986). Nyfenger was a well-known flutist in New York until his tragic death in 1990. He taught at Yale and Oberlin.
12. Pierre Séchet, current professor of baroque flute at the Paris Conservatory.
13. Georges Brassens (1921–1981), French minstrel in "Mon vieux Léon," a song about a deceased musician friend.

Since there is no absolute truth, the other instruments being what they are and styles being so personal, there can be no ensemble playing, and ultimately no music, without everyone being willing to adapt and to bow to the common good.

Relative Intonation

Intonation should be practiced in a harmonic context, or at least a tonal one. Even atonal and serial music must sound in tune. The traditional Western major scale derives from the Pythagorean[14] scale (also called the just scale).

One can strive to play with a well-tuned piano. That is a first approximation.

One can purchase an electronic tuner. This should be used in homeopathic doses because tuning isolated notes is only part of the answer. That is the second approximation.

During daily practice, play very tonal and melodic arpeggios such as no. 2 and no. 4 in *Sept exercices journaliers*, by M. A. Reichert,[15] slurred and free in a phrased sort of way, insisting sometimes on the widest intervals, sometimes on the leading notes and semitones. By all means disregard the ridiculous tempo markings, which try to make these musical exercises a mere test of speed. Reichert's exercise no. 4 is based on the perfect major and minor chords and their inversions.

Intonation, intonations Example 1. Reichert no. 4

Reichert's exercise no. 2 uses the same plus their connections with dominant seventh chords.

They are music and should be treated as such. For intonation practice, select one note and listen to it throughout the current exercise to understand how its

14. Pythagoras (572–497 BC), a Greek mathematician who first described the phenomenon of sound: a string (or a tube) resonates first in a fundamental frequency, then in overtones (harmonics) that have a frequency of n times the fundamental. Reduced to the fundamental, the first four partials form a perfect major chord. Take C1 as fundamental: the first harmonic is C2, the second G2, the third C3, and the fourth E4. Brought back to the fundamental, they form C–E–G, the basis of Western tonal music. Note: more and more the term "partial" replaces the term "harmonic." The fundamental is the first partial, the second harmonic is the second partial, and so on.

15. Mainz: Schott Editions, 1873; Paris: Alphonse Leduc, 1950.

Intonation, intonations Example 2. Reichert no. 2

life evolves from the onset to the end of phrase, to a higher or lower placement within the sequence, and with or without vibrato. You can do the same thing with a tuner, preferably one with a fixed-note function. Following a crazy needle all over the dial is like a dog chasing his own tail.

One must keep in mind that, in any given key, the sum of an interval and its inversion is always a perfect octave. This truism needs to be reaffirmed when practicing intonation.

My Intervals 2 and 3 can be used in this perspective. They cover in about a week the most frequently heard intervals inside the octave.[16] They are excellent training for tone and for educating the ear. Hear and sing the interval internally before fingering it.

So, let us assume that your flute is basically in agreement with a well-tuned piano or with a tuner:

- Your chromatic scale will conform to equal temperament, that is, the octave's twelve semitones will all be equal, theoretically. One can always dream. . . .
- With respect to the Pythagorean scale:

The perfect fourth and fifth will be . . . perfect (almost). If your tuner responds to octaves and fifths (two and three times the frequency of the fundamental), you have a valid intonation-training tool.
The major third will be a little wide and the minor sixth a little narrow.
The minor third will be a little narrow and the minor sixth a little wide.
The major second will be very slightly narrow and the minor seventh very slightly wide.
The major seventh (to the leading tone) will be a little narrow.

Thus, assuming your flute were perfectly tuned to equal temperament, and assuming, as in a dream, that the instruments surrounding you were also, then your intonation would be quite acceptable. You could, as a luxury, try to play along the same lines as string players, closer to the Pythagorean scale, whereby

16. Ninety-five percent of slurred intervals in pieces are within the octave. It is strenuous and unprofitable to work at huge intervals with facial contortions and great jaw strain.

a C♯ is not a D♭, F♯ is not G♭, and so on, because a diatonic[17] semitone differs by only one comma[18] from a chromatic[19] semitone. For instance, A is four commas higher than G♯, and A♭ five commas lower than A. Thirds can be tuned, but not always in the expected direction: major thirds flatter, minor thirds sharper. Strings have a tendency to play flats lower than we do, whereas our sharps and naturals tend to go sharp and blend better with theirs.

Intonation, intonations Example 3. Mozart, Quartet in C Major, K. 285c, Variation 4

Intonation, intonations Example 4

17. Involving two notes proper to a given key.
18. The smallest difference in pitch easily perceptible by the human ear.
19. Involving two notes not belonging to a diatonic key.

Our G♭, in unison with the viola, is always sharp because violists "feel" it flat. From a sensual point of view, this narrow minor third has a very poetic color. Usually, however, a compromise is welcome: "String player, my friend, don't 'Pythagorize' too much, and I will try to go in your direction. Let's meet somewhere in between. . . . But what pleasure when we do meet."

In the orchestra, the first flute often plays one octave above the first oboe.

Intonation, intonations Example 5. Beethoven, Symphony no. 7,
end of first movement, Introduction

To sound in tune here, the flutist must play a little flatter than he or she would alone. In fact, when they do come out alone from a chord, flutists should raise their pitch slightly to avoid sounding flat. Perhaps this is due to the fact that other instruments' timbre masks certain of the flute partials. I am not sure of the exact reason, but I have often noticed this phenomenon.

Ghost Tones

"What is more out of tune than a flute? Two flutes playing together."[20] This unfortunate statement has been widely quoted. No musical reviewer can resist this teenager's jest. And since music writers find their inspiration in each other's books, we are always taken to task.

Yet Mozart was right, as usual. When flutes hold an interval or a chord "in the open," a strange interference occurs. It sounds as if an extra flutist were in the room. These ghost tones[21] amplify the uncertainty of the intonation, especially

20. Mozart in a letter to his father.
21. Also known as difference tones.

in the ledger notes. We have often experienced this in duets or flute ensembles. It happens also in the orchestra.

Intonation, intonations Example 6. Richard Strauss, Ein Heldenleben, final chords

The truth of the intonation is affected by the faint presence of a tone whose frequency is equal to the difference between the frequencies of the two notes actually being played.

Often this uninvited guest is welcome. It results in a sort of fundamental, one or two octaves below.

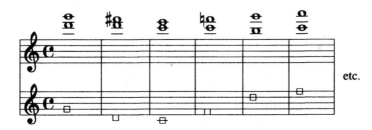

Intonation, intonations Example 7

Unfortunately, this ghost tone is not always compatible either with the harmonic environment or with the interval desired: you hear beats. It needs to be tuned by altering the pitch of one of the two "real" notes. Sometimes one pitch has to be lowered in an unexpected direction to raise the ghost, and vice versa. By making the played interval narrower or wider, the difference (ghost) tone can be brought into "just intonation," and the interval is tuned naturally. Remember that the smaller the interval (major and minor thirds), the lower the ghost tone, because its frequency is the difference between that of the two "real" notes. Tuning difference tones in an unexpected direction is an excellent exercise for the ear: "Learning to play intervals in tune by listening to the placement of the difference tone trains the ear to hear and adjust for very subtle pitch differences. This aural technique contrasts with the primarily visual aid of the tuner and is very beneficial to ensemble playing where one has to adjust quickly by ear to another player's pitch."[22]

It must be added that this phenomenon does not occur as noticeably with other wind instruments. The flute sound is poor in overtones, which is not the case with the other woodwinds.

In a nutshell:

Intonation is a matter of being flexible, of listening and working with others. No machine can replace that. Nobody is right or wrong if the music suffers. Use your ears more than the tuner.

Please refer also to:

Tuning	Intervals 2
Intervals 1	Intervals 3

ISOMETRICS

Flute playing involves a great deal of "muscle action developing tension while the muscle is prevented from contracting."[23] This is simpler than it seems: equilibrium is achieved when forces involved in a system are evenly distributed and balance each other. Weightlessness, for instance, is an isometric[24] state in which the centrifugal force generated by the speed of a space object is exactly equal to gravitation.[25]

How does this affect flute playing?

Comfortable posture is a case in point. When we wait for the bus or read a bulletin board, we are not conscious of any effort. The leg and foot muscles instinctively correct any imbalance. Yet if we were to lean one way or another, an instinctive reflex would come into play, as isometrics would be affected. While playing, there is no reason why we should produce any effort just to stand or sit.

---

22. Frances Lapp Averitt, professor at Shenandoah College, Winchester, W.Va., in "Tuning with Difference Tones," *Flute Talk* (April 1986). Averitt's article is more detailed than the passage here. She has also written a treatise, "An Intonation Method for Flutists Based on the Use of Difference Tones" (available from the author).

23. *The Concise Oxford Dictionary* (New York: Oxford University Press, 1990).

24. From the Greek *iso-* (same) *-metric* (measure).

25. The National Flute Association's *Flutist Quarterly* (Summer 1993) showed astronaut Ellen Ochoa playing her flute in outer space during her flight on the shuttle *Discovery*.

The contact between the chin and the lip plate is also an isometric point of stability. The directional force sustained by the left arm balances with the resistance of the mandibles. Exaggerate one, and the other must compensate.

Holding the flute as stably as possible reflects tridirectional isometric forces. One comes from the first joint of the left hand on one vector (1), counterbalanced by the tip of the right thumb and the chin on two parallel vectors (2, 3). It is important to remember that these forces act on a transversal plane and not on a vertical one. To be stable the flute should be held not "up," but "across," as it were.

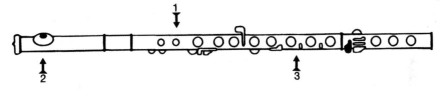

Isometrics Figure 1

When the flute is isometrically balanced in this manner, the fingers need not squeeze the keys, especially in the right hand.

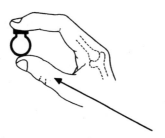

Isometrics Figure 2

Breath Control

Breath control is also an area where conflicting forces must find equilibrium: breath support by the abdominal belt is vital, but without the ability to control the air flow, the chest would deflate unchecked like a child's balloon.

Appoggio is isometrics in action. The chest muscles, acting as if to negate the collapse of the chest, contain the energy generated from the cough point. This state of controlled balance is the isometrics of air management.

Head Posture

In a relaxed and effortless position, such as reading at eye level, the head is subject to opposing directional forces meeting at an isometric resting point (Figure 3), which is the head's center of gravity, roughly at the cervical vertebrae.[26] But if the chin is jutted (Figure 4) or dropped for any length of time, the equilibrium is displaced, with consequent fatigue, pain, and eventual injury.

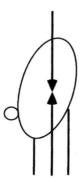

Isometrics Figure 3

Isometrics Figure 4

In a nutshell:

Isometrics are an essential part of comfort and efficiency in flute playing. They affect balance between vertical forces in posture, between lateral fulcrums in the flute's position, and between muscle pressure in the air column.

Please refer also to:

Appoggio   Muscles
Cough Point, Sneeze Point   Posture
Fulcrums   *Tenuto, Sostenuto, Ritenuto*

---

26. Atlas-axis. Atlas: the first cervical vertebra, named after the mythological Titan, whose curse was to bear the weight of the world. Axis: the second cervical vertebra, providing lateral movements of the head.

JAWBONING

There has always been more than one school of tone production, in any instrument. However great the difference in the level of noise, we have more affinity with brass than with reed instruments. For one, neither a horn nor a flute can blame their problems on the reed.

I remember an illuminating discussion with my schoolmate Maurice André, one of the rare trumpeters of our generation to have had a dazzling solo career. He told me that he used very little lip or chin movement. He relied almost exclusively on the abdominal belt and a low center of gravity.

Must flutists believe facial gymnastics and systematic jawboning help constitute a productive and reliable way of playing?

By jawboning, I mean constant change in the angle of the airflow into the embouchure. Playing intervals of more than a third (for example, changing from the lower to the middle range), they seem to need a different thrust of the chin and/or an alteration of the shape of the lip aperture.[1] My contention is that this practice is neither logical nor totally reliable. If we slur a slow chromatic scale down from, say, middle F♯ (the exact middle point of the flute's entire range) to low F♯, there is no perceptible lip or chin movement.

Andante ♩ = 84

Jawboning Example 1

Likewise, if we were to go chromatically the other way, but in an identical manner, from the same F♯, we would arrive at D above the staff without any noticeable jaw or lip change.

Jawboning Example 2

The movement is smooth; there is no need for adjustment. On a bad day, if we have only one good note in the middle range of the flute, by proximity and without messing around with the embouchure, we should be able to extend this qual-

1. The air brush.

ity over at least an octave. Our ears are our best (and cheapest) professors. Boehm advises starting on a different note, C2.[2] "While sounding the C with a beautiful, clear and pure tone, close the C key[3] by a quick motion [of the thumb], yet without altering the embouchure or the force of the wind. The B thus obtained should remain unaltered in quality and purity of tone. Then sound the B alone, and, after breathing again, proceed to B♭. Continuing in this way and with the least possible alteration of the embouchure, gradually, certainly and without exertion proceed to the lower tones and in similar manner, practice the tones from C2 upward to the highest. Since each tone is always developed out of the preceding tone, which is as perfect as possible, all of the tones will remain perfect in quality, strength and purity."[4] The only slight correction we might be led to make is for intonation, not for the actual tone production of each note.

Why then is it necessary to use these facial movements to go from the high note to the low or vice versa? Granted, intervals wider than an octave must often be helped, but 99 percent of the intervals we have to play in actual music are within the octave. The octaves, for the most part, can be played without jawboning, in a manner that I will describe below.

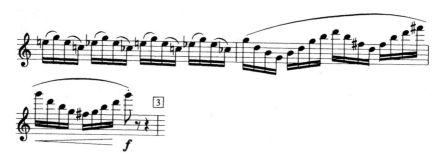

Jawboning Example 3. Prokofiev, *Peter and the Wolf*, beginning

On the other hand, let us play a rapid succession of intervals, an arpeggio over two octaves:

Remember: the tempo is indicated as quarter = 176!

Or attempt the end of "Lux Aeterna" in Verdi's Requiem:

There is just no time (and no need) for jawboning. What is necessary is:

• Support as low as possible.
• Smooth phrasing with the fingers.
• Great stability of the lip plate on the chin.

2. Which he calls c4.

3. Actually the B thumb key.

4. Theobald Boehm in *The Flute and Flute-Playing in Acoustical, Technical, and Artistic Aspects*, trans. and annotated Dayton C. Miller (Cleveland: Savage Press, 1908).

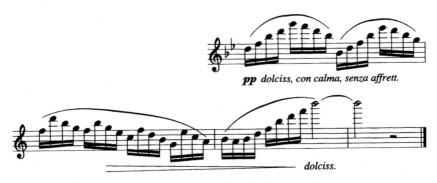

pp dolciss, con calma, senza affrett.

dolciss.

Jawboning Example 4. Verdi, Requiem, *Lux Æterna*

It is almost like a scientific equation: lip pressure + left arm support (stability) + air speed = tone. Change any parameter, and you must compensate with another parameter.

To create an isometric point of focus at the lip aperture or air brush, you could use more lip pressure and less left arm support; or you could leave the lips alone and compensate with the stability generated by the left arm. If you produce a lot of effort with the lips, you risk fatigue and imprecision under stress. If you use less facial action, then you must rely on the left arm to bring in the flute.

Therefore, my way of playing emphasizes the action of strong muscles (arms, especially the left arm, abdominals, even leg muscles) for support, leaving control to weaker ones (lip, finger and intercostal [chest] muscles).

Comfortable and efficient playing is impossible without flexibility (*souplesse* in French). But *souplesse* requires that fragile muscles work as freely as possible. Don't produce the sound or the phrase with the lips. Don't systematically play intervals with the chin. Don't balance the flute by holding it with the fingers that form notes.

You could try pulling a semi trailer with a garden tractor. It might be possible, but under great strain and with drastic consequences for the motor. *Souplesse* is getting the same result with a powerful and smooth engine, never working at more than half its possibilities.

Constant jawboning and forcefulness in technique, like slamming the keys, contribute to pain in playing. They are not recommended in cases of RSI,[5] carpal tunnel syndrome, TMJ[6] syndrome, writer's cramp, focal dystonia, tennis elbow[7], and many other horrors. I have been fortunate enough to avoid them, by luck no doubt. I have always avoided playing with pain. I have tried to use the simplest means, thinking about the physical as well as the aesthetic aspects of music making and listening to my body as much as to my soul.

5. Repetitive strain injury.
6. Temporomandibular joint.
7. Epicondylitis.

"Very well," say the jawboning advocates. "But how do you get the shift in air speed and angle that generates a wide interval?"

First, obsessed as we are with our tone and embouchure, we fail to see that often fingers, even one finger, are responsible for many a broken interval. For example:

Andante

Jawboning Example 5. Mozart, Concerto in D Major, K. 314, second movement

Andante ♩ = 56

Jawboning Example 6

Good technique does not only imply playing fast and loud. Smooth phrasing with the hands is also an effect of good playing. Rough fingers affect musicality and efficiency.

The shifting of the air speed for wide intervals must be generated by the abdominal belt (support), at the cough or sneeze point, below the navel. The leg muscles, in the standing position, or the lower back muscles, when sitting, contribute to a low center of gravity, as do low shoulders that help open the throat.

To reach for a high note while in the middle range, think first of lifting left hand fingers instead of slamming the right-hand ones. Then lower your shoulders, push on your legs, feel as if you are sinking into the ground, and jut your belt out (not your chin!). After a while, you will see this is more reliable and smoother than a mandibular movement and a big slap of the right-hand fingers.

The Chastain Maneuver

Now let's try the Chastain maneuver, playing octaves in the pattern described in Intervals 1 (quarter note = 60). Starting from a sitting position, count two or three beats and stand up at the bar line. This action brings the center of gravity into play almost without your being conscious of your lips. It shows that jawboning is most of the time unnecessary.

Jawboning is still necessary to correct intonation, especially to taper off a long note. There are two elements that are sometimes overlooked in this matter:

If the flute is held too loosely, intonation control must rely exclusively on lipping and jawboning, with varied results. The more stability is achieved, the more intonation can be corrected with the hands. For instance, the B♭ lever can help, without affecting the "real" fingering, by providing that extra little balance to turn the flute in or out.[8]

Jawboning Example 7

Most long notes don't have a printed diminuendo, but we are tempted to do one anyway. The tone should not be throttled on a diminuendo. The air speed must be maintained to keep the intonation from falling. Bringing up the chin is also helpful for this, but not as the only means.

For intonation in f or ff, lowering one's center of gravity, playing with low shoulders, opening one's throat, and, as a last resort, rolling in the flute all contribute to controlling sharpness.

In conclusion, I do think that jawboning can be helpful, but it should be one of many options. I am convinced by any style of playing if it works under stress and does not threaten flutists' health. If it works, do it. But do not block out any experiment or any new idea. There should be no taboos, only the great joy of making music.

> ### In a nutshell:
>
> Jawboning does not have only advantages. It is useful for correcting intonation. It quickly becomes a mannerism if used constantly. Ninety-five percent of intervals in our repertoire are under the octave. They require the involvement of the whole body, not just the mouth and chin.

8. All these notes can be played with the right forefinger on the B♭ lever for balance. There are other combinations.

Please refer also to:

Center of Gravity   Little Devils
Dynamics   Finger Phrasing
Fulcrums   Silent Keys
Intervals

KEYS

Silent Keys

I rarely mention the word technique. I am not naturally inclined to technical things, and I am afraid, if not resentful, of machines. We are expected to blindly respect CDs, edited to so-called perfection, tape recorders that sound either too awful or too good, breathing contraptions that simulate life, tuners to have perfect ears, metronomes to have perfect rhythm. . . . It's all for sale.

Having said this, I must admit that I am writing on a word processor. The ASPCA no longer tolerates plucking geese to make quills, and my fountain pen is reserved for checks and love letters.

Instrumental playing includes all the aspects of our dear flute: tone, fingers, articulation, slurring, pitch, vibrato, breath. . . . One may feel weaker in one area or another, but working on one without thinking about the others leads nowhere. Not even interpretation is instinctual. It involves thought and practical solutions. There is a technique of phrasing just as there is a musical approach to instrumental problems.

Even when the tone is beautiful in one area, shifts in range or articulation, clumsy attacks, and faulty slurs can ruin a perfectly good musical intention. Let us use as an example the first part, the andantino, of the Fauré Fantaisie. There are many more illustrations, but this piece is well known to flutists of all levels. Besides, it is one of those things that look deceptively simple. The allegro is scary, with its runs and rapid tonguing. But after two lines of the andantino, everyone has a good idea of how you play, and this innocent-looking phrase is not as easy as you thought.

A flexible embouchure depends on the flute's stability, and stability is achieved by the way the flute is held. The more fingers are on the instrument at any given time, the more reliability will be felt at the embouchure. The easiest notes are middle D or D$\sharp$: both hands are on the flute. Outside the extremely high and low ranges, the most difficult attacks are on notes with few fingers holding the instrument: C, C$\sharp$, and B above the staff.

There is a solution: using one of the right hand fingers as stabilizer. This is what I mean by "silent" keys.

Silent keys Example 1

Silent keys Figure1

The bridge between the low and middle registers is always problematic, especially in slow movements, for the same reason: between C and D, we switch from very few to all fingers, and back.

Silent keys Example 2

Silent keys Figure 2a

Silent keys Figure 2b

Silent keys Figure 2c

A note held only with the left hand, such as the A in measure 5, is more comfortable and focused if one finger of the right hand serves as a silent key (non–note forming stabilizer). Again, the passing of the bridge is smoother between D and C (and vice versa) when the right pinky is not used on the C, and the flute is stabilized instead with the right ring finger.

Silent keys Example 3

Silent keys Figure 3

The temptation is great, for a big jump such as that at the end of measure 18, to force it out with considerable facial movements, when in fact it needs a stable preparation for the low D♯. This is achieved by putting down the right ring finger as a silent key. Since D♯ follows, the right pinky stays.

Silent keys Example 4

The same fingering stabilizes the octave at measure 25:

Silent keys Example 5

Silent keys Figure 4

Low notes are often in desperate need of focus and stability. If time permits, as in measure19, the left pinky (little devil no. 3) can be placed directly on the tube and immediately below the G♯ key, without touching it, of course. This is not strictly a silent key. Let us compare it to that and call it a silent finger:

Note: For all the notes of this passage, you can keep the left pinky resting on the tube, under the G♯ key.

This recreates to some extent the left-hand position of the original Boehm system (open G♯), where all left-hand fingers including the pinky were on the flute

Silent keys Example 6

Silent keys Figure 5

Silent keys Figure 6

for the low notes. It provided an extra sense of stability and reliability for the sound in attacks and staccato and for the focus in general.

Preparing the fingers and getting rid of little devil no. 2 does not hamper the playing of the low C mechanism. It will help this difficult note at little expense. Once again, it is not an embouchure problem; it is a stability issue, where tone meets technique.

Silent keys Example 7

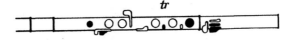

Silent keys Figure 7

When you work at your phrasing, plan your silent keys until they become second nature. Your sound control needs your hands as much as your technique needs your tone.

Small Keys

The B♭ lever—also called the B♭ side key—is a mechanism that long puzzled me. Were three fingerings for B♭ necessary? Why not use the "real" fingering (i.e., the right forefinger) and forget the others?

I currently use five or six fingerings for low and middle B♭, plus three for top B♭. I was taught that there were "good" and "bad" fingerings. I soon realized that bourgeois morality and ethics had nothing to do with fingerings and that musicality was the issue, because "good" can be unmusical and "bad" more fun. (Flutists of the world, unite!) "Good" applies to rules laid down by books, teachers, and parents and is deemed indisputable. But if a certain way to play the flute feels easier, gives you more pleasure, and stems from the imagination, chances are the books, teachers, and so on will tell you it's "bad."

Coming back to our B♭ fingerings, I use the "real" one (right forefinger) very little, because after sixty-odd (sometimes very odd) years of practicing the flute, it still flaps about, especially between G (or F♯) and B♭ (or A♯). Examples abound: you will find them in anything in flats or in five or more sharps.

The reason for this is the difficulty of simultaneous action between fingers of the two hands working in opposite directions.

Most pros and teachers use mainly the so-called Briccialdi key,[1] one of the very few keys invented over 150 years to improve the Boehm design. It is the most practical, although they sometimes forbid their students to use it (do as I say, but don't do as I do). It allows free-flowing patterns for the four first keys in flats on the first two octaves. But then, as anybody knows, the high G♭ cannot be played with the thumb B♭ down, because it is a natural harmonic of the C♭ (or B♮).

For the keys in sharps containing A♯–B patterns, the B♭ lever comes in handy, because you can hold it down between G♯ and A♯.

It does require a bit of practice (that's "good"!) to pass freely from thumb B♭ to B♮ and some mental work (that's even better!) not to hold the thumb too tightly on the Briccialdi[2] key. If bassoonists commonly work from six to ten adjoining keys with the same finger (the left thumb), why can't we juggle two?

Some passages will work better with the B♭ side key.

It takes cares of the G–B♭ flap and releases smoothly for the B♮.

Use your imagination for fingerings: color, ease, pitch, reliability, dynamics, comfort, pleasure; they are "alternate," perhaps, but "good" or "bad"? The issue is music, not morality.

---

1. Left thumb B♭.
2. Guilio Briccialdi (1818–1881), Italian flute virtuoso, who invented the B♭ thumb key. Boehm's system had the B above the B♭.

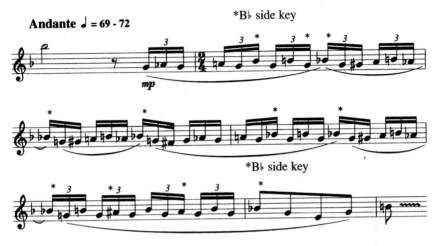

Silent keys Example 8

Key Clicks

In general, a noisy technique is a bad technique. However, contemporary composers sometimes require key clicks or key percussions for special effect. One key is snapped to set the air-column in motion without actual tone production. The best key for that purpose is the G, activated by the left ring finger.

Finger Tonguing

This is the opposite of snapping. The key closest to a difficult note is imperceptibly hit on an attack without using the tongue. For the lowest notes, this facilitates the onset of the vibration within the tube.

> ### In a nutshell:
>
> Go for the best musical configuration. Don't worry about the moral aspect of fingerings. Use silent keys and silent fingers, B♭ side key, B♭ thumb key, and right hand ring finger for the bridge. Anticipate your fingerings. As soon as possible, get rid of the right pinky. It's vital for only six notes.
>
> ### Please refer also to:
>
> | | |
> |---|---|
> | Boehm System | Little Devils |
> | Bridge | Low Register |
> | Finger Antagonisms | Stability |
> | Finger Tonguing | Trills |

LIPS

Lips are too often considered the most important part of flute playing, because it is at their level that air becomes musical sound. The lips are not the only element to produce the tone. It is the air brought by the air column breaking upon the outer edge of the embouchure hole that creates a sound.

Many players think about their lips (their "chops," in musicians' jargon) and only that: they are forever touching them, looking at them, trying new head joints and warming up with long tones. They are like drivers who consider the steering wheel the most important part of an automobile. Actually, it provides essential direction, but no effort. The air column produces the energy of playing; the lips provide control and direction, but not force.

There is no ideal lip position. Teachers who constantly try to change their students' lip formation are actually doing them a disfavor. Symmetry has nothing to do with it, since the flute is played in an asymmetric position. Each lip morphology is unique in shape, thickness, size, and firmness. More important is the way the lips are used, as a guide. Comfort is the issue, within reasonable proportions. If it works, do it!

The character of anybody's tone is in what they hear and how the air column resonates inside and out of the flute player. "You can only reproduce the tone that you hear inside of yourself. Embouchure technique comes from what you want to hear, not the other way around."[1]

By striving to constantly shape tone with the lips, weak muscles become overworked and fatigued. A dead end is reached, even, in the worst cases, a form of paralyzing psychosis. Actually, the lips should not produce any effort. Their mission is to lead the air brush to the breaking edge,[2] but the energy of the air (speed and pressure) comes from many factors, but not from the lips. Air inside the lungs, the mouth cavity and the sinuses resonates, as does the acoustical environment, but not the lips.

A lip technique that works in practice, without stress, but is unreliable under stress is counterproductive. What is expected of a technique is that it respond to the needs of music under unfavorable circumstances, not that it conform to a laboratory theory.

The lips should stay practically still and flexible, in the same general position, whatever may be the range, the dynamics, and the intonation or delivery problem. In the old French methods,[3] it was taught that the lips should have the position they have when trying to evacuate (spit) a fig seed or a tea leaf from the tip

1. Adolph Herseth, principal trumpet of the Chicago Symphony Orchestra, in Jim Doherty, *Smithsonian Magazine*, September 1994, "For All Who Crave a Horn That Thrills, this Bud's for You": 94–103.

2. The outer rim of the embouchure plate hole.

3. Henry Altès, *Célèbre méthode de flûte*, facsimile ed. by Jean-Pierre Rampal and Alain Marion (Paris: Allo Music Editions).

of the tongue. It is simple, and it is still valid: the lips should be moderately pinched in a half smile to conduct the air brush effectively and effortlessly. The sound's energy comes from elsewhere. The fashion of a completely loose embouchure, with mouth corners drooping, gives a false impression of relaxation: it does not help control, it produces "turbo-sound" and, through its instability, it increases stress. Conversely, pinching the lips for high notes and wide intervals leads to fatigue and a "gas-leak" sound. In the presence of stress, the throttling of the tone cause more stress: a vicious circle.

Even though I might run against prevailing ideas, I believe:

- That lip gymnastics are harmful,
- That a comfortable lip position in the medium range applies to all registers.
- That sound is not generated by the lips, but by fulcrum no. 1[4] and support from the cough point.

To be sure, slight lip movements are almost inevitable when changing registers, especially in conditions of stress during public performance and auditions. In this case, anything is permissible: give free rein to music and to your creative imagination. However, during daily practice away from stress, arpeggios, intervals, thorough study of repertoire, even problems of articulation and virtuosity should be dealt with through instrumental stability and lip flexibility. No facial movements to fish out this low note, no pursing to reach this high note.

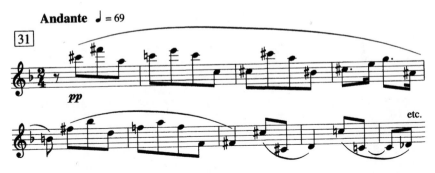

Lips Example 1. Prokofiev, Sonata in D Major, op. 94, third movement, end

For this passage and for a thousand others, don't think of your lips. Sink into the ground. Use your center of gravity on your feet (if you stand) and on your kidneys (if you sit).

---

4. The first joint of the left forefinger.

In a nutshell:

The lips should not produce any effort. They act as guide and control. Without any stress, and with very little movement, one can play the whole range of the flute chromatically without moving the lips. Why should it be different in arpeggios and intervals? Since we cannot move the lips on every note during fast passages, there is no reason to do so in slow phrases.

Please refer also to:

Air Column	Jawboning
Air Speed	Muscles, Strong and Weak
Arpeggio	Stability
Center of Gravity	Warm-Ups
Fulcrums	

LITTLE DEVILS

The three little devils are:

- the left forefinger (little devil no. 1), which operates our octave key.
- the right little finger or right pinky (little devil no. 2).
- the left little finger or left pinky (little devil no. 3).

For various reasons that we shall explore, they are responsible for many of our troubles.

Little Devil No. 1 (Left Forefinger)

This is our octave key. It comes into play to connect middle D and E♭ to practically all the notes from G inside the staff to D in the ledger lines. It is also the center of balance of the flute, almost exactly halfway down the tube. Closed and unobtrusive in most of the lower range, it starts acting up for middle D and E♭: how many flute students have had trouble with closed E♭, especially in descending scales? Flutists and teachers must nip this little devil in the bud, for it is very hard to get rid of this habit later.

Our little devil no. 1 really becomes a nuisance in the medium and upper ranges. Many broken slurs come from it. Examples:

The quality of the wide slur depends on little devil no. 1.

Little devil no. 2 is useless here, but watch little devil no. 1.

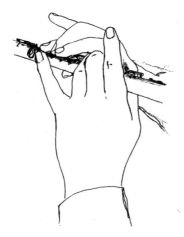

Little devils Figure 1

Little devils Example 1. Poulenc, Sonata, first movement
Copyright Chester Music, London

Little devils Example 2. Mozart, Concerto in G Major,
K. 313, second movement, last measure

These passages, among many more, show the perfidy of little devil no. 1. They seem simple, but we must dominate their actions before resorting to jawboning.

If you often miss slurs or intervals above the staff that you thought were easy, instead of jawboning them, think of our little devil no. 1. Strangely enough, its crooked position makes it harder to close, contrary to other fingers that are harder to lift than to put down. In fact, the left forefinger is essential as an octave key, for finger stability as well as for focus of the sound. It is the fulcrum of technique and articulation.

Little Devil No. 2 (Right Pinky)

Its evil spells are due mainly to the fact that it must rise as the others come down. We have been taught to keep it open at all times except for Ds. We are used to holding the flute with it, so much so that we often see a right pinky almost bent back by squeezing. The consequence is that little devil no. 2 sometimes refuses to come back up when told, thus slowing down a whole run.

Little devils Example 3. Mozart, Concerto in G Major, K. 313, third movement, measures 208–9

For this passage, do not use the right pinky at all.

At the risk of sounding heretical, I advise not considering the D♯/E♭ key as a major holding point. Instead, the flute should be stabilized at three points of support, the fulcrums, none of which are used for fingering notes: the first joint of the left forefinger, the tip of the right thumb, and of course, the lip plate. In other words, the flute should be held first and foremost by those fingers that don't make notes. Consequently, I often tell my students (and myself): "When you are going down to low D, get rid of little devil no. 2 as soon as you can."

Little devils Example 4

Little devils Example 5

Little devils Example 6

You absolutely must have little devil no. 2 down for only six notes of the flute range (excepting the extreme low and high notes).

Little Devil No. 3 (Left Pinky)

Like little devil no. 2, its action is contrary: it must be lifted while the others come down. In the original Boehm system, the little finger would close the G♯ key instead of opening it. Even today this system (called open G♯) is in use in Russia and by some excellent players in England. It actually makes more sense, because all the fingers of the left hand move in the same direction, and the hold on the flute is more stable in the low range. In our prevalent French system flute, in the high range (E♭, A♭), if we are a bit nervous, we have a tendency to tense up on the fingers, and . . . enters little devil no. 3. For no apparent reason, except this tension, an innocent little run that worked fine at home will not work under stress. The reason is that little devil no. 3 refuses to leave the A♭/G♯ key. It must be kept under surveillance like the others.

As usual, both systems have their advantages and inconveniences, as well as fanatics and adamant opponents.

If we can help it, our hands should be a help, not a hindrance. More than just practicing blindly, it takes thinking and changing our conventional approach to fingerings. There are no "good" and "bad" fingerings, as some puritans would have it. If you find five different ways to play something, bravo. Some fingerings serve the music better. That's the most important. If, on top of that, they are easier and give us more pleasure, why resist? After more than fifty years of flute playing, I still find that an innocent-looking slow passage is difficult to play—to play well, that is.

Why? Must be those little devils.

Little devils Figure 2

In a nutshell:

The left forefinger is our octave key: its awkward action breaks many slurs. The right pinky's motion hinders the low range and the bridge: except for six notes, we can keep it out of the way. The left pinky's contrary action affects high notes: let us not hold it too tightly. Let us think about our music and adapt our playing to that goal, not to some hypothetical fingering correctness.

Please refer also to:

Finger Antagonisms	Fulcrums
Boehm System	Hands
Bridge	Intervals
Finger Phrasing	Slam-and-Squeeze
French System	Stability

MEMORY

Even as computers become more and more sophisticated and their capabilities more far-reaching, the human brain is still the most amazing of all. There is no limit to its possibilities. Its memory is boundless. The more you learn, the more you can learn. Our brain does not fill up. When you speak a language or two, the next one is easier to learn, and so on.

In the realm of music, memory affects not only the acquisition of the text, but also the playing skills. The latter is the subject of an article in *Science*.[1] Researchers used scientific sensors that measure blood flow to different parts of the brain and electric impulses to and from muscles. The term "motor task" corresponds to actual movements, whereas "internal model" (IM) refers to the acquired cerebral pattern that drives the performance of the skill.

How does all this affect flute playing?

Gaston Crunelle taught me during my days at the Paris Conservatoire to prepare difficult passages very slowly, breaking them into very brief rhythms. This is a well-known process, but the important part, said Crunelle, was to avoid trying them immediately up to tempo, or worse yet, to increase the metronome beat progressively, which would destroy the previous patient work. This has worked very well for me over the years, and I advise my students to do the same. I am not always sure they are convinced at first, or if they do it. If they don't need this procedure and succeed, I leave them alone. But I don't know of any difficulty that resists such a thorough approach.

Intuitively, Crunelle's advice corresponds precisely to the scientific research published in *Science*. "We've shown that time itself is a very powerful component of learning," says Henry H. Holcomb. "It is not enough to simply practice something. You have to allow time for the brain to encode the new skill. As one practices a motor task, movements become smoother, and the muscle activations reflect a reliance on an internal model (IM) that anticipates the requirements of the

---

1. Reza Shadmer and Henry H. Holcomb, "Neural Correlates of Motor Memory Consolidation," *Science,* August 1997: 821–25.

task. A single session of practice with a novel mechanical system may lead to long-term storage of an IM in the brain. However, when practice ends, a functional property of the IM continues to develop. Within five/six hours, the recently acquired IM gradually becomes resistant to behavioral interference, that is, it consolidates." This explains why certain skills are acquired forever, illness and trauma notwithstanding: riding a bicycle, swimming, manual activity. Endurance and efficiency need to be developed anew, but the basic skill is there.

This is also true of flute playing. Let me speak of a personal experience. Just after graduation, I was called to Algeria by the French Army, a duty not unlike Vietnam for American boys. I spent more than two years without touching my flute. When I was finally discharged safe and sound, I thought my musical life was ruined. An old friend told me: "You don't forget that. . . . It's like riding a bicycle!" He was right. Within a month I was back in shape to where I was before, or even better, because such events have a deeply maturing effect.

The researchers in *Science* concluded that it takes five to six hours for the memory of a new skill to move from a temporary storage site in the front of the brain to a permanent storage site at the back, in the cortex.[2] "Results on learning control of novel mechanical systems suggest that the representation of an IM in humans is most fragile soon after it has been acquired."

Once a difficult passage has been practiced slowly, don't try it right away. Just as with academic homework, sleep on it. Practice something different or engage in another activity. The next day, try to play the passage at tempo. If it still resists, practice it slowly again, in the same manner.

Other interesting conclusions stem from this study.

If your brain stores a good IM, unfortunately it equally remembers a bad habit that, as everyone knows, takes more time to eradicate and relearn.

The earlier you prepare for a lesson or a performance, the more solid your instrumental knowledge will be. Conversely, last-minute preparation is totally counterproductive: what you hastily prepare at the last minute will actually interfere with your performance. I have noticed that sometimes the first reading works better than repetitions because hang-ups have not set in.

When I hear, "I need one more day for my lesson," I usually say nothing, but I think, "Too early to play, too late to practice."

Memorizing

Memorizing is a technique like tone, scales, or breathing. It must be studied and practiced a half hour per day in the bus, on the plane, or in the bathroom. It does not matter where, and it does not make noise.

Don't forget that the human mind never fills up. The more you learn, the more you can learn. Knowledge of music has no limits. Don't forget that another expression for memorizing is learning by heart.

2. Gray matter.

Melodic Memory

This is a very repetitive and time-consuming practice. It has to be maintained constantly. Any distraction in the hall, in your accompaniment, or in your head can throw you off. It is therefore unreliable for competitions and high stress performances. Worse, it relies on sequences of right notes and melodic patterns. If a wrong note happens, you can be misled.

Photographic Memory

Photographic memory[3] is not as vulnerable to stress as is melodic memory. It stays with you practically for life. And it leads to note perfection, which worries us so much.

Of course, these two methods are not mutually exclusive. An intimate knowledge of the music, both of the flute part and of the full score, is essential. The ideal is to mix all of your mental idiosyncrasies to produce a good performance.

1. Look at the music, at its layout, at its graphism.
2. Analyze it, phrase it, build it, take it apart, and build it again.
3. Take two bars, or ten, or whatever, starting with the beginning even if you know it.
4. Look at this passage as long as you like, and read it like a difficult and fascinating book that you want to understand thoroughly.
5. Look up and "see" this passage. Speak the notes out loud. "Paint" them in the air. Everything must be there:

All dynamics.
All articulations.
All notes to perfection.
All tempo markings.
All bar lines.
Even the place on the page needs to be memorized.

6. Repeat this process until you can paint this phrase in the air without the flute. Remember: Any mistake now will also be memorized.
7. Write it out. No mistakes. Paint it again! Check. Compare. If it is perfect, go have a drink! If not, repeat the previous procedure. Don't just correct the mistake!
8. Next phrase or passage, and so on.

When the piece is finished phrase by phrase, start again with two phrases together, then sections, then movements, finally all the way through. Always apply the same process. Never move on until it is completed. During the "painting" process, don't play this piece; only play through when the memorizing is com-

3. Uwe Grodd, professor of flute, developed this method with great success at the University of Auckland, New Zealand. All his students play from memory and feel safe.

pleted. While playing, "see" all the elements. If you can't or have to stop, you have gone too fast.

The speed of the process is not important, since once you have conquered it, the piece will be there for life just like 2 + 2 = 4.

At first it will take about one hour for a short passage of a few bars. But three months later, a passage of the same length will take ten minutes. And the next year, no problem at all. After two or three years you will be so secure that you will be able to play anywhere because, if you make a mistake, you will know immediately where you are on the page and in the development of the piece. You will be able to continue easily, whatever happens.

In a nutshell:

You cannot wear out your memory. The more you know, the more you learn. The brain needs time to process skills and knowledge. If you play a practiced or a memorized piece right away, you destroy the temporary memory. It needs until the next day to be stored.

Please refer also to:

Finger Antagonisms   Reichert
Arpeggio   Sight-Reading
Études   Warm-Ups
Practicing

MUSCLE GROUPS

The human hand is an amazing machine. There are an incredible number of muscles of all shapes and sizes, interwoven, working at times in the same direction, sometimes in contrary or antagonistic motion.

The muscles that activate the fingers involved in playing the flute are mostly in the forearm. Without intending to be exhaustive or competing with the medical experts, we can have a direct perspective of these muscles' action.

Wear a short-sleeved shirt or a T-shirt so that you can glance at your left forearm while playing. Pick up your flute and play a simple pattern:

Muscle groups Example 1

The action is basically the same for the right arm, in spite of a different position, but it is difficult for you to see it yourself out of the corner of your eye. You may instead look at yourself in the mirror while you play, which is always a good idea.

On the outside of your left arm, you can see muscles rippling under the skin surface. These are the extensors. They lift the fingers upward and allow them to release whatever they were holding.

If you could look at the underside of your forearm, you would see similar movements. Here are located the flexors. They activate the downward or seizing motion of the fingers.[4]

Although oversimplified and fragmentary, given the complexity of the hands' anatomy, this describes the process from a flute player's point of view.

The most restful position for the hands is when, with the wrist resting on a flat surface like a table, the fingers are also in contact with the surface, without pressing down. The arm muscles are inactive. As soon as we try to lift a finger, a slight effort is perceptible, increased with each lifting finger: the extensors are at work.

Imagine now that we are really pressing down hard on the surface with all our fingertips and that we try to lift one or two of them: the effort of both the flexors and extensors is huge. It generates tension up and down our hands and arms.

When we transpose this experience onto the flute, we find the main reason for cramped playing, painful shoulders, tendinitis, and many ailments that plague flute players. Add to that constant jawboning, and you have a catalog of miseries. One can hardly say that the flute position is ideal: the neck is slightly bent to the right and turned to the left. Compared to the violin, however, it seems quite natural.

Shoulders and elbows held high are not the best position for the neck. The prevailing opinion is that tension initiates in the neck area[5] and affects nerves, tendons and muscles all the way down the arm to the wrist and hand. The theory is that by working to relax the neck and shoulders through excellent disciplines such as Alexander, Feldenkrais, or yoga, we can find the panacea for all our aches and pains.

I believe the process works in the opposite direction. Tension starts at our fingertips. When we slam-and-squeeze on the keys, as if to conquer a problem by force, and when our finger technique is noisy, it is a sign that we are using too much pressure. We are brutalizing the flute. In turn, the extensors must fight to counteract the force of the flexors to lift the fingers, thus producing tension that radiates back up through the tendons, arms, and shoulders. It is like pedaling uphill with the brakes on.

Flute players have been told to relax so many times that they forgo all the stability of the instrument-holding posture and end up doing lip acrobatics and straining the weak facial muscles. Facial muscles are not meant to do that. When

4. Anatomical explanation courtesy of Paul Matus, M.D., Lorain county coroner.
5. Atlas-axis vertebrae.

playing with a loose flute and slapping fingers, we are not calling into action the strong leg muscles or the abdominal and arm muscles (biceps.) These have been called the energy muscles. We use them without thinking to stand, walk, run, push, lift, and so on. They are well within their power when we play the flute, and for this reason they do not generate tension and problems of overuse.

On a practical level, what can be done to play more easily and efficiently? There is no overnight cure, but here are a few solutions:

- Do not slam-and-squeeze, that is, do not use force on the downward movements on the keys. Avoiding slam-and-squeeze improves many problems: less key noise, less mechanical harm to the padding, better slurring, musical connection in phrasing, and more reliable attacks and articulation.
- Use your energy to lift the fingers instead of bearing down on the keys.
- Stay close to the keys. The solution is in scales played smoothly at a comfortable tempo, and in intervals.
- Remember that if your mechanics are noisy, you must be slamming your fingers down too hard from too high.
- Above all, do not hold the flute with fingers that form notes. The more stable you are with the fulcrums, the less force you will need to hold the flute.
- Little devil no. 2, especially, should not be bearing down. It should be an adjunct to stability, not a hindrance to virtuosity. The fulcrums, acting on a horizontal plane, can exercise a certain stabilizing force precisely for the reason that they are working in one direction only, activated by the strong arm muscles.

Consider an engine lacking in power: it has no flexibility. When too much is demanded of it, it wears out fast, because it has to operate at full potential. When used sparingly, our muscles' strength is a source of flexibility and ease, not of struggle and stress.

> *In a nutshell:*
>
> Play lightly with the strong arm muscles instead of violently with the weak finger muscles. A noisy technique is an unsophisticated and unmusical way of playing the flute. Stabilize the flute with non-note-producing fingers. Strength equals flexibility. Brutality equals weakness. The way you use your muscles influences tone as much as finger ease.

Please refer also to:

Finger Antagonisms	Scales .
Fulcrums	Stability
Hands	Stress Control
Intervals	Warm-Ups
Phrasing	

MUSCLES, STRONG AND WEAK

A weak motor has no flexibility; under constant stress, it tires quickly. To pull a load, it must always work at maximum output. It will soon end up in the repair shop.

There is an analogy with every facet of flute playing: if there exists a choice between weak and strong muscles, the latter must in general be called into action; they are more flexible because they do not operate at full power and therefore tire less. Let us take a few examples.

Breathing (Inhalation)

The strong abdominal muscles provide the most important action by releasing the belt and creating a vacuum in the chest cavity. The pectoral and intercostal muscles also come into play. They are weaker, but most of all, their action is in a flat direction and for that reason slower. They must heave the chest and shoulders, which is necessary for a full apnea[6] but inefficient and tiresome for normal breathing, as well as constricting for the throat.

Blowing (Exhalation)

This too calls the abdominal muscles into action to push air out. If the pectoral and intercostal muscles were generating pressure at this time, it would be very strenuous and inefficient. Instead, they counteract the energy generated in the abdomen through isometrics.[7] In apnea, they actually prevent the collapse of the shoulders and chest that would empty the lungs under the pressure of abdominal support. It is a sort of passive resistance that they provide (appoggio), much more suited to their nature and essential for air management.

---

6. Apnea: a full blocked inhalation as performed by a deep-sea diver.
7. Isometrics: action of muscles working against others.

Support

The powerful thigh muscles enhance support. When we push a stalled car or try to lift a heavy load, most of our vertical force comes from the legs. The automatic tightening of the legs contributes to air support. The strongest muscles are used for standing, walking, running . . . and flute playing. Play from the ground up, or, according to my metaphor: "Play with your feet!" This also applies when sitting: support comes from abdominal muscles and the lower back.[8] Even then pushing on your feet will give you added support.

Tonguing

It is often the case of misused effort. It is of little consequence to me where the tongue is placed. There is not one fixed position. Our ears should tell us. If it works for you, do it! Misunderstanding comes from the fact that if we are playing a loud staccato, we tend to use the tongue more than in soft passages. It must be remembered that a loud staccato needs no more movement than if it is played *piano*. Quite to the contrary: a soft staccato lacks the natural energy of the loud tone and a more precise tonguing would be in order. Regardless of dynamics, the tongue action is about equivalent.

The tongue is a strong muscle, but articulation is not its primary function. It is merely a valve that opens and closes an opening, just as in our internal combustion engine. The tongue does not produce tone. If it produces noise, it's certainly bad.

Tone Production

This requires a lot of stability. If we rely only on the embouchure (sphincter or orbicular muscles), we have the very example of putting stress on weak muscles. Most of the energy for producing tone comes from support—everyone agrees to that. But the fulcrums, especially the powerful muscles of the left arm, counterbalancing the right thumb and chin, allow us to travel the different ranges of the flute smoothly. To use our automotive comparison, the leg and abdominal muscles are the motor, the arm muscles the chassis. The lips are the gearbox or the steering wheel, only transmitting power or providing direction without effort. When the tone is visibly produced with the face, danger looms. Warm-ups are a good way to loosen up. However, they should concern not only the lips, but the total playing apparatus, from head to toe.

8. Which can recline against a low seatback.

> ### *In a nutshell:*
>
> Economy of effort is not laziness. Put to use your strong muscles (abdomen, arms, legs) in every area, and give your weak muscles (lips, chest, even fingers) a rest. Do not mistake the effort you make for the finished product. You need more strength to speak softly than to bellow. Give your heart musically, but don't hurt yourself physically.
>
> ### *Please refer also to:*
>
> | | |
> |---|---|
> | Air Management | *Tenuto, Sostenuto, Ritenuto* |
> | Fulcrums | Throat |
> | Intervals | Tonguing |
> | Lips | Warm-Ups |
> | Stability | |

NOTES

One of our obsessions is playing the notes, or rather not missing too many of them. It even seems to be the only concern among some teachers and orchestra personnel managers. It is hard to disagree, of course. Yet it would be interesting if all the parameters of flute playing had the same importance. Sound comes in conjunction with notes. The notes are not an entity in themselves; rather, the musical content is spoken through the notes.

We should practice instrumental playing as a whole. Style, phrasing, articulation, intonation, and notes must all be seen as a total experience.

Solfège

Germanic musicians use the alphabetical system to name notes, with the peculiarity that B is sometimes called H.[1] English musicians and those of the British sphere (e.g., Australia and New Zealand) use the "pure" alphabetical system.

Americans, due to the variety of their musical influences, use both systems, mostly the alphabetical system, but also solfège in areas where musical institutions were influenced by the Italian, French, and Spanish cultures.

An Italian monk, Guido d'Arezzo, initiated *solfège* in the tenth century. For the

1. E.g., J. S. Bach, Messe H-moll in German, B Minor Mass in English; Suite in H moll in German, Suite in B Minor in English.

purpose of using syllables compatible with singing, he chose the first syllable of the verses of a hymn: *ut, re, mi, fa, sol, la, si.* In the seventeenth century, *do,* which is a little more melodic, replaced *ut,* which is still used in theoretical works.[2]

This system is in fact practical for singing because it enhances the voice. The consonant provides the onset, and the vowel carries the sound.

I was taught at the Paris Conservatoire to ripple off all the notes of a piece in solfège at top speed. I do find it useful for sight-reading, articulating, and memorizing. But pushed to the extreme it becomes a technical exercise with no musical meaning.

In a nutshell:

The notes are very important. I am ready to forgive an occasional slip but less the constant disregard for instrumental playing and phrasing.

Please refer also to:

Articulation	Practicing
Instrumental Playing	Sight-Reading

PAIN AND PLEASURE

If you hurt when you play (lips, jaws, arms, back, or heaven knows what), it is likely that you have not cultivated a good and comfortable relationship with instrumental playing. Sooner or later, the cause of these problems must be confronted.

Flute playing is, or should be, a source of pleasure—for the listener, no doubt, but first of all for the flutist. "Charity well rendered starts with oneself."[1]

It is not as selfish as it sounds. How can you help others when you cannot help yourself? How can you bring enjoyment to your listeners when you hurt and suffer? How can you love anything when you hate yourself?

Practice is not so much a way to deal with our guilt feelings as a path to happiness and pleasure. This hedonistic philosophy might not be popular in the Puritan work ethic of "no pain, no gain." However, pleasure in its deepest meaning requires sensitivity, patience, kindness, and self-knowledge, rather than greed,

---

2. *Clef d'ut* = tenor clef.

---

1. "Charité bien ordonnée commence par soi-même" (French proverb).

gluttony, or lust. Hours face to face with my flute brings me pleasure, musical fulfillment, and happiness.

Comfortable and efficient playing is impossible without flexibility. Flexibility requires that fragile muscles work with as little strain as possible: don't produce the sound and phrase with the lips, don't systematically play intervals with the chin, and don't balance the flute by holding it with the fingers creating the notes. Constant jawboning and forcefulness in technique, like slamming the keys, contribute to pain in playing. Shoulders and elbows held high are not the best position for the neck.

From my experience on the flute, I find the reason for many ailments that plague flute players is cramped playing: painful shoulders and spine, tendinitis and RSI (repetitive strain injury, also known as overuse syndrome), although this is not the only cause of RSI.[2]

Listen to yourself. Taste your sound like a savory dish. Enjoy the fluidity of your fingers. Feel the balance of your body. Play well just as you would speak well. Draw lines in space, always new and always repeated; give color to the ephemeral notes that stop time; find rest after tension. All that is the flutist's drug.

It is thought and said that instrumental playing is the labor of the material domain, while music and interpretation soar to the lofty summits of the spiritual realm. Many teachers will not stoop to offer instrumental solutions, and many college-age students find it beneath them to approach anything instrumental. "I did not come to college to play exercises," I was told a few times.

The pleasure of instrumental playing and the joy of recreating music do not conflict. Serving music is the ultimate goal, of course. However, I am no longer ashamed to confess that the pleasure of playing the flute, before anything else, is the motive of my life's dedication to music.

I have always tried to think of working on the flute as "playful playing pleasure." It is the best way for me to foil time and its hourglass, those old spoilsports. Why make flute playing complicated when you can make it simple? Why not play a simple tune with simplicity, instead of loading it with pathos and buzz? Musical quality is my first concern, but my mottos are:

- If it does not hurt the music and it works for you, do it!
- If there is an easier solution to a problem and if it does not hurt the music, do it!
- If it does not hurt the music and it feels better, indulge, enjoy, and do it!

But if your playing does not work and gives you no physical pleasure or leads to pain, you must think about yourself. Never play with pain. Don't force yourself to practice if you hurt. It will only intensify your problems, sometimes irreparably.

2. Richard Wolkomir, "When Work You Do Ends Up Costing You an Arm and a Leg," *Smithsonian*, 1994: 90–101.

This quest concerns all aspects of flute playing:

1. *Breathing*. Three-fourths of our breathings are perfectly normal. Breathe as you would do for a simple spoken phrase. You don't have to breathe like a whale if you are a goldfish on the shelf; just open your mouth and breathe enough to tell your flute, "I love you, most of the time."

    If you want to take a deep breath, try something pleasant: the next time you yawn, watch how wide open your throat is and how relaxed your shoulders and tummy are.

2. *Embouchure position*. Who says that your embouchure has to be dead center, at right angles with the flute? Pythagoras? Archimedes? If your position works (even if it's as crooked as mine), keep it there. Don't confuse logic and symmetry with ease and comfort; they are not necessarily roommates.

3. *Vibrato*. It does not come from the diaphragm, wherever that is, or from the lips, so it must be from somewhere in between. How about from your heart? Listen to what moves you and just do it.

4. *Dynamics*. The natural tendency of flute dynamics, called agogic, is to increase with the rise of the musical design (ascending scale or arpeggio) and diminish with the fall in range (descending pattern.) Of course, you have to learn how to play loudly in the lower register and softly in the high octave. I will address this elsewhere in this book. But your interpretation feels and sounds more natural if you follow the agogic than if you fight it.

    Likewise, articulation has an impact on dynamics: logically, the shorter the note, the less sound it has; so you are helping yourself (and the music) if you use a bowed style of tonguing to play louder and a more pointed staccato to play softer:

    When you want to play softly or freely, go to the score and check the musical environment. If it's crowded, don't fight it. Wait until the composer has left you alone: he is extending an invitation to be free and play with imagination.

    As soon as the accompaniment occupies the terrain again, the easiest and most efficient way to play is to adapt instead of fighting. This implies that you practice your interpretation with a good pattern of the score in your head.

5. *Tonguing*. On one side of the Atlantic, young flutists are taught, "Never tongue between your lips"; on the other side, "Always tongue between your lips." Why make a religion out of it? In any given situation, try everything, and if one way works better for you, do it!

6. *Finger position*. Why demand of young flute players that their fingers be rounded out like "little hammers"? That is a very uncomfortable way of holding anything. When you pick something off a shelf, the most natural way is the best: flat fingers and no pinching, even with the so-called French system (open hole), because it is the least cramped position.

7. *Diaphragm*. Forget about it; it is not an entity in itself. Like Timothy Tim's ten pink toes, they go with him wherever he goes, up and down, down and up.

The best way to breathe is the most natural: when you read a poster, you don't raise your shoulders or tighten your belly, do you? Stand the same way in front of your music, raise you arms, breathe normally, and do it!

8. *Fingerings*. There is a kind of puritanical taboo about doing the "right" fingering (i.e., the hardest)—good against evil, that sort of thing you know. . . . But if your final execution is musically better with a "different" fingering because it is easier and you are happier in spite of your guilt, then, do it!

The old method from which I learned[3] started giving fingerings around lesson five, calling them *sensible*, which in French means "sensitive." Among others:

- B♭ thumb key. Most pros do it, because it is easier, even if they teach you otherwise. Learn to slip your thumb on and off. Bassoons have a handful[4] of huge keys under the left thumb. Why can't we deal with two?
- F♯ played with middle finger in all three registers. You don't have to be systematic. It is an option in fast scales and runs. In a slow phrase, the "good" fingering is better (and not more difficult.)
- Getting rid of the right pinky (except for E and E♭) if it improves a slur, a run, or low register staccato.
- Trill or harmonic fingerings in the third octave played with the left hand only contribute to making things smoother and, therefore, the music better.
- Try finding your own "intonation" fingerings that help to tune certain notes. They are extremely useful for orchestral playing, especially for the piccolo. All the pros do it, but some don't like to share their trade secrets.

Playing with facilitating ideas does not imply cutting corners. Practicing in a less mechanical way and thinking about different solutions increase your own pleasure. Enjoy as much as possible instead of banging your head against "correct" patterns and finger twisters.

Supreme ease and comfort are results of good instrumental playing. They bring pleasure and freedom, but they require love and thought. They mean two hours of practice a day and as much time using your ears, your head, and your heart. Mastering a hard piece takes hours. Knowing yourself takes years.

In a nutshell:

Always play for pleasure: it is the reward of thoughtful practice. The simplest patterns, exercises, deserve to be as beautiful as repertoire. Ease and comfort come with good instrumental playing. Interpretation is impossible without it.

---

3. Henry Altès, *Célèbre méthode de flûte*, facsimile ed. by Jean-Pierre Rampal and Alain Marion (Paris: Allo Music, 1977).

4. Up to nine, even eleven on the Heckel bassoon.

Please refer also to:

Comfort	Slam-and-Squeeze
Instrumental Playing	Stability
Practicing	Yawning

PARIS CONSERVATOIRE AND FRENCH SCHOOL

Although in the 1970s the French republic created another Conservatoire National Supérieur de Musique in Lyon, on an equal standing with Paris, the model
for most musical institutions of Europe was the Paris Conservatoire. Founded in
1784 as École Royale de Musique, in 1795 it assumed its present title.

Past directors include Luigi Cherubini, Ambroise Thomas, Theodore Dubois,
Gabriel Fauré, and Marcel Dupré. Among its professors were Hector Berlioz,
Anton Reicha, Paul Dukas, Jules Massenet, Charles-Marie Widor, Charles Tour-
nemire, Marcel Dupré, Olivier Messiaen, and Nadia Boulanger. Until 1977, there
was only one flute class. Paul Taffanel, Philippe Gaubert, Marcel Moyse, and
Jean-Pierre Rampal were some of its professors. Adolphe Hennebains and Crunelle, although not as highly profiled or as well known, also left their mark, as did
William Kincaid, Joseph Mariano, and Julius Baker in the United States. There are
no private lessons with the professor. All teaching is done in front of the whole
class, who must in theory attend twelve hours of master classes a week. Private
lessons are the responsibility of the associate professor.[5]

Like most education in France, the Conservatoire has free tuition, even for
non-French applicants. This explains why the entrance exam is extremely competitive. The auditions are live,[6] held during a three-day first round in the spring,
where about 150 candidates choose two pieces from a list of six. One out of ten
qualifies for the last round. Its program is announced three weeks before. It is the
same for all, and performed with piano. Usually five to ten flutists are admitted,
depending on the year.

The curriculum is strictly musical, lasting a minimum of three years. It used to
be possible to compete for a prize after only one year. Rampal and Maxence Lar-
rieu, among others, successfully did just that in their time. The minimum re-
quirement was then moved to two years, then three. It is no longer possible to
compete at the Concours des Prix without having completed a certain level of
solfège and theory.

Once one is in the Conservatoire, nonmusical matters are set aside in favor of
intense practice, music, more practice, theory, sight-reading, orchestra, and en-

---

5. Raymond Guiot during Alain Marion's professorship, Kathleen Chastain during mine.
6. Which implies that applicants from far away may be deterred from appearing in person.

semble music. Students' schedules are not cluttered with nonmusical topics—endless papers to write and so forth. The philosophy is that if you want to develop your mind and your culture, you will do that anyway once you have made your choices and found your place in the world. But the discipline of learning music as a real professional will not present itself again. As in sports, there are skills that will be learned only with great difficulty after the age of twenty. Some researchers claim that the best "window" for learning music is before ten years of age. Maturity comes later. It needs time, like good wine. But for playing skills, it's later than you think.

Furthermore, the French grading system is based on achievement in auditions and not on progress or seniority.

The advantage of a liberal arts system is that you know a little bit about many things. You can shop around for your education. But you have to be very gifted (and lucky) to excel in two or three fields simultaneously.

The quality of a school is reflected in the talent of its best students, but also in the fact that everybody has a certain level, a certain professionalism guaranteed by the *Premier Prix* or *Second Prix*. There is more than one of each every year, because they are awarded when the jury judges that they are deserved, not by strictly competitive ranking.

I used to think that this purely musical curriculum was not making enough room for academic education. I changed my mind when I became part of the American college scene. There are so many topics required or available that students just do not spend enough time working on their playing. I always feel that in a curious mind, culture can be deepened almost at any age if the desire exists.

The main reason, in my mind, for the excellence of the Paris Conservatoire is the quality of the students: even second-rate professors produce first-rate students, and second-rate students are taught by first-rate professors.

A wide network of specialized provincial conservatoires supports the Paris Conservatoire. They prepare aspiring musicians for Paris. Thus there is a certain common root in musical education. In the case of the flute, the French school is little else than a discipline of musical education and dedicated practice. There are as many French schools as there are French flutists. Their affinity is not in some secret of tone color or virtuosity, but simply in a basic way of practicing and playing. Tradition does not die (but people do, and as my father used to say, "Cemeteries are full of irreplaceable flutists").

A tradition that does not evolve is not alive. We live in our time, and we learn from tradition as much as from innovation, which will be the next tradition. A "school" of playing is the transmitted expression of imagination and novelty, not some kind of deep-frozen scripture. Art, and music, are in constant mutation, and not always for the worse.

No one flutist can confiscate the French school, or any school, and claim rights to its tradition. "Tradition is innovation that has succeeded."[7]

---

7. Jean d'Ormesson, contemporary French writer and essayist.

Yet it is obvious than the professor of the Conservatoire has a great influence on a generation. There used to be only one class for each wind instrument.[8] The Concours des Prix is the big event, at the end of the academic year in June. It is a sort of sporting event where all flute aficionados gather. It is open to the public, and the jury is made up of famous flutists from all over the world. The tradition, for the past hundred years, was that a new work would be commissioned just for this purpose, published in great secret one month before the Concours, premiered and played from memory by the contestants. Thus were born many well-known works of the flute repertoire[9] during the first half of the 1900s. More recently Ibert, Dutilleux, Messiaen, and Jolivet contributed important pieces without which our repertoire would not be what it is. Inevitably, some lemons fell through the cracks and gave credence to the saying that "they were not worth the paper they were printed on."[10]

Many non-French attend the Conservatoire de Paris, under the same free and competitive conditions—in the past, American,[11] Canadian, Spanish, Italian, German, Japanese, Korean, Scandinavian, and of course British. One of them, who became very famous, was constantly disagreeing and bickering with Crunelle. He later complained that Crunelle would read the paper during the lesson. I asked my old professor why. He said that since his advice was not being followed, he did not see the point in arguing. What the student disliked, in fact, was that Crunelle had found the right attitude: the student wanted to be listened to. Some people are wounded more by indifference than by antagonism.

In a sense, the sign of a good teacher or school is when even the less gifted students play well. String students of the Galamian or Gingold or DeLay violin schools or the Parisot or Starker cello schools might not all be new Heifetzes, but they have a common methodology, one that is evident in American orchestras. Crunelle had that persistence: everybody came to the end of the year playing the best they would ever be able to do. Concours pieces were performed from memory, and nobody said it was impossible.

For me, the secret of the French School is a methodical approach to playing and practicing. It is different from warm-ups. When an element of your playing is giving you trouble, take it apart and practice it; then put it back together. Too often people want ready-made solutions. "How is fast tonguing done?" "How can my speed be increased?" "How is vibrato produced?" A few perfunctory long tones or casual warm-ups won't do it. It is simple: one has to work at it, not on pieces but on exercises. For every musical problem, there is a technical solution; for every technical problem, musical ones.

The Société des Concerts du Conservatoire,[12] founded in 1828, was originally

8. Owing to the popularity of the flute, there are now two: Sophie Cherrier and Pierre-Yves Artaud.

9. *Flute Music by French Composers*, edited L. Moyse (New York: Schirmers).

10. Robert Dick.

11. Recently Linda Chesis and Dionne Hansen (winner of the 1991 Flute Talk Competition).

12. Now Orchestre de Paris.

staffed with the professors and best students of the Conservatoire. For a century, it was associated with the school only in name. To this day, the Paris Conservatoire has very high standards, but the history of French orchestras, unfortunately, has not, for many reasons, lived up to the reputation of one of the world's best music schools.

In a nutshell:

Tradition is not the opposite of innovation. Styles of playing evolve under the tutelage of great musical institutions and eminent professors.

Please refer also to:

Instrumental Playing	Repertoire
Practicing	Warm-Ups

PHRASING

A musical phrase is similar to a spoken sentence. It is an attempt to organize sounds and syllables to give them a direction, a meaning that will make their intellectual, spiritual, and emotional content intelligible. Phrasing is a relationship between freedom and constraint, tension and release, intensity and repose—between time and space, and between sound and silence.

It is impossible to load every single syllable of a speech with drama: it becomes quickly emphatic and boring. "The pursuit of the extraordinary is the character of mediocrity. When one despairs of doing a beautiful, simple, and natural thing, he attempts a weird one."[13] Likewise in music. If all the notes of a passage are highlighted, it becomes a hysterical interpretation that often disfigures masterpieces. Somehow, it reminds me of a sandwich advertised "with everything on it: five meats, three cheeses, lettuce, tomato, mayonnaise, mustard. . . ." The works![14]

A musical phrase or motif exists in itself. Harmony, however, is implicit. To simplify matters, let us say that when the harmony is consonant (major or minor triads and their inversions), the phrasing flows without tension. On the other hand, dissonant harmony denotes tension and build-up. A line containing sevenths or augmented fourths (called tritones) or diminished fifths (which are in fact part of seventh chords) requires more tension.

---

13. Denis Diderot (1713–1784), philosopher and encyclopedist in *Salons*.
14. Subway Restaurants.

The science of phrasing resides in the expression of harmonic tension and release and on grammatical familiarity with the various elements:

- the beginning (upbeats).
- the development.
- the progression.
- the appoggiaturas.
- the culmination.
- the resolution and end of the phrase.

This quickly becomes second nature. It is like speaking a language from childhood and deepening its knowledge through study and love.

Upbeats

An upbeat[15] is like an article or a pronoun in a spoken sentence: rarely is it reinforced except to purposefully emphasize: I will, we want, my flute, and so on. No part of an upbeat (1) should be louder than the downbeat (2) following it.

Phrasing Example 1. Poulenc, Sonata, first movement

Even if the upbeat is short, it should in general be lighter than the phrase it announces. Crunelle taught us that our upbeat symbolized, for the phrase it introduced, its tempo, its character, even its key.

Some upbeats are so famous that hearing the first notes is enough to recognize the national tunes.

Phrasing Example 2

15. Also called "anacrusis" or "pickup."

Even if the attack is difficult, the music requires enough control to avoid forcing the upbeat.

Phrasing Example 3. Beethoven, Symphony no. 3, "Eroica," second movement

An upbeat can be drawn out (1) and lead to a climax (2), but there again, it should not culminate too soon, lest it lose energy prematurely.

Phrasing Example 4. Gluck, *Orfeo ed Euridice*, Dance of the Blessed Spirits

An anacrusis (1), unless otherwise requested by the composer (or the conductor), should be in the same color and character as the line to which it leads (2); when it follows a long note (3) it should take up its dynamic and feeling. Your ears tell you that. This procedure allows you to hide your breath better (4) by balancing your tone on either side of the breathing break (5).

Phrasing Example 5. Verdi, *La forza del destino*

Pacing

The physical shape of a musical phrase gives an indication of the harmonic tension: scale patterns are usually tonal, even if they modulate, and need not be overly expressive. Wait until the intervals widen (1), which is an indication of tension, as is the presence of a leading note (2).

Phrasing Example 6. J. S. Bach, Partita in A Minor for Flute,
BWV 1013, Sarabande, end of first part

Tension can come from rhythm:

Phrasing Example 7. Beethoven Symphony no. 7, Marche funèbre

The insistence on the dactylic rhythm (one long, two short) contributes to a fateful feeling. We have the same effect, symbolizing a beating heart in the introduction of Schubert's *op. 160*, the Introduction and Variations on "Ihr Blumlein alle."

More often the flow of a phrase wants to escape the prison bars of the metronome: no two notes have exactly the same value in an expressive phrase. They are in the same basic tempo, but they are leading us somewhere, toward (1) the accents (2) or away (3) from them. They are *parlando* ("spoken") or rubato.[16]

Even as we strive to sound spontaneous in our interpretations, the development of phrases follows certain patterns. Long notes should reflect the direction of the phrase. Work on agogic,[17] either to moderate or to make use of it. Don't system-

16. "Stolen": take some here, give it back there.
17. The natural tendency of performance, either musical (long notes decay, fast runs rush . . .), or instrumental (higher is brighter, staccato is softer . . .).

Andande (teneramente, molto cantabile, con espressione)

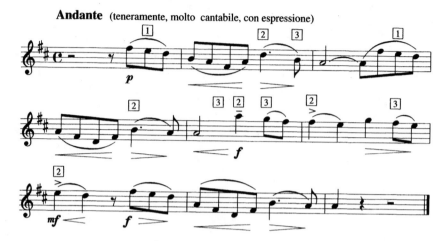

Phrasing Example 8. Tchaikovsky, Symphonie no. 6, "Pathétique"

atically decay long notes. In a phrase whose intensity is ascending through a simple incremental progression (1) or a harmonic march (2), the part of a long note (3) that has the most energy[18] is the moment immediately preceding the next note (4); the long note should not decay below the level of the notes following it.

Phrasing Example 9. Mozart, Clarinet Concerto in A Major, K. 622, second movement

Conversely, in a descending phrase, each new note should be less intense than the previous one, regardless of its natural color or the location of breaths. One should play these phrases with mental binoculars to see where they must land.

18. Not necessarily the loudest dynamic.

Phrasing Example 10. Mozart, Concerto in C Major, K. 299, second movement

This motif (1) (indicated *f* by Mozart) will have a natural tendency to diminish. In order to keep it alive, conserve energy until the temporary resolution (4). The sixteenth notes (1') are scale patterns leading to an appogiatura (2), where the second note is less intense than the first and prepares for the next group. The last appoggiatura (3) must still have energy so that the last note of this sequence (4') is the least active in this context.

When an identical pattern is repeated[19] more than once, it is a good idea, in general, to vary the intensity:

Progressive	1. Least	2. More	3. Most
Regressive	1. Most	2. Less	3. Least
Echo	1. Most	2. Least	3. Most
Mirror	1. Dynamic A	2. Dynamic Z	3. Dynamic A
Or	1. Dynamic Z	2. Dynamic A	3. Dynamic Z

Changes in dynamic level have to be deliberate, almost exaggerated to be well perceived. Do not be literal about dynamics. They are an indication of relative strength more than an untouchable and frozen command. (See Phrasing ex. 11, page 182.)

Let us use dynamic indications without being their blind slaves. In the build-up of an accent, the crescendo (4) actually means *p*, the softest part of that progression, whereas diminuendo (5) means *mf*. It is an indication of a louder motif in the process of being dampened. (See Phrasing ex. 12, page 183.)

Shaping a musical phrase before playing means finding its structure and grammar. Where are the appoggiaturas (1), the reiterations (repeats) (2), the upbeats (3), the culmination of a crescendo (4), the length of a diminuendo (5), the questions (6), the answers (7), the suspension marks (8), the silences (9)?

I compare the line of a phrase to a bird's flight. I do not mean the flight of a group, during migration. Then the flight is linear; the goal is far; nothing can distract it from its trajectory. These great autumn moves are magical. I am thinking instead of a swallow's flight, on a summer evening. The line is never straight, but

19. Iterated; reiterated.

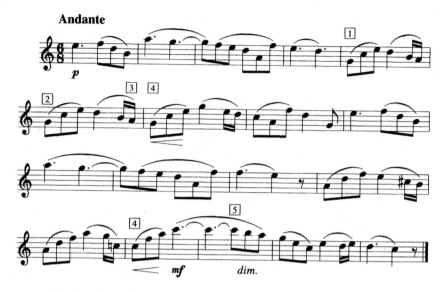

Phrasing Example 11. Mendelssohn, Violin Concerto, second movement

one guesses it, anticipates it, and follows it. Our brief breathing is the bird that closes its wings as we bat an eyelid. Musical punctuation is the tree that hides the bird for an instant. We know where the line will start again; the flight is not broken. A rest is the cloud that suspends the trajectory for a moment. But we find it soon, at once similar and different.

Without being too precisely descriptive, a phrase can reflect the stages of life, or the minutes of a day. To each day its path, its joy, its pain, its labor: daybreak (an introduction), sunrise (a crescendo), an intense moment, midday upon the sea (a climax), the emotion of the dying sun (a diminuendo), the appeasement of twilight (a held note), night, a storm, torments, peace. . . . There are points of tension, moments of rest, meditation, calls, shrieks, and chatter. Imagination guides us.

Once grammatical analysis is done, it allows us to "speak" the music, as much as to speak with music. The hidden sense and poetic content become more apparent. It is then up to our imagination and sensitivity to infuse meaning and life into our universal language, to give our art "the inflections of dear silenced voices."[20]

20. Paul Verlaine (1844–1896), in "Le rêve familier" (The Familiar Dream).

Phrasing Example 12. Gluck, *Orfeo ed Euridice*, Dance of the Blessed Spirits

In a nutshell:

Phrasing is a transposition of language. Refining one's understanding and means of expression will ultimately blossom into an interpretation as spontaneous as a native tongue. Phrasing must come from within, not from outside through imitation. Learning how phrases work has never destroyed anyone's imagination. Knowledge is not the opposite of feeling.

Please refer also to:

Accents	Rubato
Attacks	Slam-and-Squeeze
Appoggiatura	Tempo
Breathing	Tension and Release
Dynamics	Vibrato
Finger Phrasing	

POSTURE

Even before the end of the first phrase, the spectator notices outright a flutist's awkward posture. I do not condone standing at attention—high chin or high elbows. High shoulders, especially, strangle the throat and the tone. Stand naturally and just bring the flute to your lips.

Posture Figure 1

Posture Figure 2

Shoulders should stay aligned with elbows and vice versa. The head will be turned thirty degrees to the left, but this is better than pulling the right elbow out of alignment with the right shoulder.

I advise the use of the legs to activate support. When we lift a large weight, we feel strongly the action of the leg muscles. Less evident is the contraction of the abdominal muscles that we use for support. In actual playing posture, it is good to stand or sit with feet firmly in contact with the ground, to feel our own weight and to have the impression that we are pushing the ground away, as it were. A bit of hip swinging and graceful footwork can highlight a performance and ease some nervous tension. We must, however, try to be always conscious of gravity, even in animated passages.

Likewise for the sitting position: low elbows, low shoulders. Knees should be spread about ten to twelve inches. Ladies who find this ungraceful should not wear a short skirt. Ask cellists or harpists—trousers can be elegant.

The correct attire is simple, especially for a public presentation. A concert is not a fashion show. For whatever gender, nothing we wear should distract the listener from the music. Extravagance is just as out of place as sloppiness.

Sitting in an ensemble, the chair should not be at a right angle to the stand but slightly oriented to the right so that the head is turned toward the left elbow. This way the right elbow is also comfortable. It is the flute that must face the audience, not the buns or the chair. Slouching is of course wrong, but supporting the lower spine on the back of the chair is more comfortable and saves your energy. However, not every chair is appropriate.

No movement of the head should try to fetch the embouchure as if it were an object foreign to the body. It is the instrument that comes to the lips without our having to change the bearing of the head. The chin is the resting place; there must be firm contact at all times, provided by the left forearm muscles via the first joint of the left forefinger. Optimistically, our comfort and efficiency of playing has, for its essential foundation, our own body equilibrium.[21]

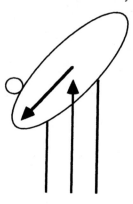

Posture Figure 3

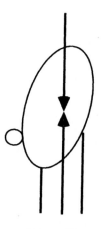

Posture Figure 4

"The position of singing must remain throughout the act of singing. 'Sing in the position of breathing—breathe in the position of singing' expresses the postural attitude. Posture need not be altered for the renewal of the breath."[22] Replace the word "singing" with "playing the flute" and you will have a good approximation. Think of how you blow more than of how you breathe. Breathe noiselessly as you would lying down or reading a poster or just waiting for the bus.

21. "A state in which the energy in a system is evenly distributed, and forces balance each other"; *The Concise Oxford Dictionary* (New York: Oxford University Press, 1990).
22. Richard Miller, *The Structure of Singing: System and Art in Vocal Technique* (New York: Schirmer Books, 1986).

<blockquote>

In a nutshell:

Use the legs when standing to provide support. When sitting, try reclining the kidneys gently against the lower part of the chair back, pushing the tummy *out* for support. Always have a sense of gravity. Avoid jutting the chin to fetch notes; use that for correcting pitch.

Please refer also to:

Comfort	Practicing
Fulcrums	Stability
Muscles	Support

</blockquote>

PRACTICING

When I was a child, my mother laid down the law. There were two vital things I had to do before turning in for the night: brush my teeth and say my prayers. To this day, I have not figured out which was the most important. I still have my own teeth, and I hope I am not yet on my way to a flutist's hell.

Practicing has some of that ambiguity. Some feel guilty if they have not done their "long tooones." Others have a thing about warm-ups. I confess that I am partial to the Scale Game.

Most musicians feel that insufficient practice time is an explanation or an excuse for not performing up to standards. Some say: "I practice four or five [or more] hours a day," and yet the result leaves something to be desired. The quality of the work is more important than the time spent. The clock gives us an alibi with which to pacify our guilt machine.

"It worked perfectly during practice." Actually, in practice you are not so conscious of your flaws, because you are not under stress, whereas on stage or at your lesson, you blow the slightest imperfection out of proportion. For example, listen to friends and colleagues: with or without stress, they sound to you about the same as they always do. Hence, the same with you; it is the nervous perception that, in your mind, exacerbates your shortcomings.

My symbolic practice schedule is an attempt to make the best use of time. But first, a few common-sense principles:

- Be realistic about what you can do, regardless of your level; don't assign yourself goals that you are quite sure you will not pursue reasonably—for instance, two études a week plus finger twisters. These make you upset and angry with yourself. Pretty soon you drop them altogether.

- For daily practice, choose instead things you can play relatively easily, but play them perfectly. There is no excuse for playing something easy imperfectly in practice; you progress better on easy perfection than on inevitable disaster.
- Always play musically: scales, arpeggios, and études are all music; they are boring if we consider and make them so.
- Practice what is most useful for instrumental playing. A disproportionate amount of our repertoire is made up of scales and arpeggio passages. "The Taffanel-Gaubert *Daily Exercises* calisthenics catalog these basic formulas very well and constitute a Bible of technique for the conscientious flutist."[23]
- Don't practice speed without a feeling for line, or tone without comfortable posture and fingers.
- Much of our practice time for études and pieces is wasted on things we have not even read properly.
- Do not practice with your metronome clicking all the time. I am going to sound heretical, but I think it counterproductive to practice "difficult" passages with a slow beat and then to increase the speed one notch at a time. Instead, break up the difficulty. Use very short and snappy rhythms, always staccato, at a slow tempo to isolate your finger reflexes, "stop-and-go." The "stop" part can be long, but the "go" is like a trigger releasing an interval:

Practicing Example 1a. Ibert, Concerto, beginning.
Reproduced with the kind permission of Alphonse Leduc publisher
and owner of the worldwide rights—Paris-France

Practicing Example 1b

Practicing Example 1c

23. John Krell, *Kincaidiana: A Flute Player's Notebook* (Culver City, Calif.: Trio Associates, 1973).

Practicing Example 2a. Ibert, Concerto, Finale. Reproduced with the kind permission of Alphonse Leduc publisher and owner of the world rights—Paris-France

Practicing Example 2b

- Then leave it alone. Don't try to get it up to speed, or you will destroy all your patient work. Scientific studies have shown that motor skills need five or six hours to be stored in the brain.[24]
- Sleep on it, and when you next pick up your flute the following day, check it out without warming up.
- Instead of warming up, get yourself used to play what you are working on at the drop of a hat, in the worst conditions: play the week's program through and through at tempo, after running around the block or up a flight of stairs. This emulates the effect of stress on your breath and your nerves.

Shortness of breath is for me the most noticeable effect of stage fright or stress: all my wonderful resolutions about long phrases are shot.

Sight-Reading

Learn to read and sight-read: apply your concentration immediately, see at a glance tonalities, time, subdivisions, rhythms, and patterns and their changes. All this you do before looking at the runs and licks.

There is almost no secret for good sight-reading besides doing it. Find a flutist friend of your strength, or preferably stronger, fish out a duet, look at it for one minute, and away you go.

Do not stop. This is the only secret for sight-reading. If you do, it means that your head is in the past, however recent, whereas your eyes and thoughts should turn forward. Silence your guilt machine: everybody makes mistakes. The only sin is to stop.

24. *Science*, August 1997.

A Practice Schedule

1. Inventory (5–10 percent of practice time.)

   When you start, without preparation other than mental, without warming up, play everything you are practicing that week except daily exercises (scales, tone exercises, and arpeggios): étude, orchestral excepts, and repertoire. Do not stop; do not look back; do not replay. For the time being, just remember what went wrong. Circle it on your part as soon as the movement is over. It might not be what you expected. Remember: difficult is what does not work in performance.

2. Review (5 percent of practice time)

   Think and write down what went wrong, and why.

3. Basics: Scales, Arpeggios (10–20 percent of practice time)

   My preferred basics are Taffanel-Gaubert daily exercise no. 4; Debost's Scale-Game, as it is called—flutistic daily jogging with the beauty but without the pain, on some thirty to sixty different articulations; and for arpeggios, Reichert daily exercises no. 2 and no. 4, played slowly and freely.

4. Tone Exercises and Intervals (5–10 percent of practice time)

   Do whatever your teacher says, with an emphasis on posture, breathing, vibrato, stability, smooth fingers, and the least possible jawboning.

5. Rest and Enjoy (5 percent of practice time)

6. Mending the Disasters (20–30 percent of practice time)

   Fix what went wrong in 1. Inventory. Work with slow, broken rhythms.

7. Repertoire, Excerpts, and Étude (20–30 percent of practice time)

   As necessity and enjoyment command.

8. Sight-Reading as Much as Possible.

The only place where you cannot tolerate your imperfections is in your practice room. On the stage, in performance, at the audition, your thorough work will pay off. You will pull out all the stops and think about music and expression first. Worry about the wrong notes ahead, not the ones you did back there. Casualties are counted after the battle. Remember, the most important elements of your playing are not your lips, or your fingers, but your head and heart. Using them will work wonders.

The will to win is not nearly as important as the will to prepare to win.

In a nutshell:

The purpose of daily practice is to improve you for the long term. Don't reduce it to long tones and pieces. Choose easy basics, but play them perfectly. There is no stress so there is no excuse for poor practice. Leave finger twisters and huge intervals aside. Daily practice is for working on yourself as much as on repertoire. Today's practice is next year's warm-ups.

> ### *Please refer also to:*
>
> | | |
> |---|---|
> | Finger Antagonisms | Scale Game |
> | Arpeggios | Sight-Reading |
> | Études | Stress Control |
> | Intervals | Warm-Ups |
> | Memory | |

PROGRAMS

Choosing a program for our recitals is often agonizing. To this day, it is a problem for me. The following ideas need not be always followed (I am sure they won't be), but they are the fruit of my experience as a player, as a professor, and as a listener.

Most Flute Recitals Are Too Long

A "professional" program of an hour and a half, including intermission, often stretches to two hours. A senior recital (normally one hour) goes to an hour and a half, or more. A junior recital that should be a half-hour concert drags on to an hour. This is due to the five-minute late start, moving on and off stage between pieces, and the huge round of applause that will no doubt salute our performances. A good idea is to time ourselves to 10 percent short of the allotted time.

When we start thinking about a concert, we have, first of all, to set our priorities.

The last thing we want is to have the audience yearn to leave. They should be thinking that we did not play enough. If our program is too short, they will rarely blame us for laziness. But if they are bored. . . .

We want to be liked, loved, and adored, and not sound academic or snobbish. We want to please more than convince. We want to show our qualities, not our political correctness. We want to be beautiful but not at the expense of comfort. We want to be compatible with our musical partners.

Most Flute Recitals Are Drawn Up with Other Flute Players in Mind

We have in our head a super performance on CD by one of the great flute players of the time. But no live performance can duplicate that. Technicians take care of balance and mistakes. Dynamics and projection of the flute sound are tailored without stress. That is why so many of our young colleagues are disappointed with the live concerts of the great.

We are playing for the other flutists in the audience. We are afraid of the beady ears of our professor (in my case, of my students) wondering: "Gosh, what will they think?" Chances are, whatever we do, they won't like it anyway. So why worry? For all this, Barry Green's *Inner Game of Music*[25] makes very good reading.

Besides, your audience is made mostly of people who have the good fortune not to be addicted to flute playing. They know nothing about the fake fingering you used on that F♯ and do not hold it against you for messing up a little. So play for them, and for yourself.

Most Flute Programs Want to Prove Too Much

You will not be able to play all the great pieces in a hundred minutes. It would be very trying physically. It would not be a good idea musically either. They would destroy each other and you with them. Even Poulenc asked me not to play his Sonata and Prokofiev's back to back.

Accept the fact that your interpretation might not be as interesting as you think. Play pieces that fit you, even if they are not always the most meaningful to you. Remember that flashy romantic and modern pieces show off your qualities, whereas the well-known classics show off your defects. Everyone complains about one's own technique; almost no one worries about one's own interpretation.

Don't think that a piece with many notes is harder than a slow movement. For me, difficult is what does not work in concert. Upon starting a recital, unexpected problems of breath, intonation, and attack are more often the issue than fingers.

In a professional audition, give preference to an experienced and older pianist over a person in your age group, even though the pro might not be able to afford a lot of time. When performance time comes, your friend the inexperienced accompanist, who was unconcerned at rehearsal, suddenly becomes just as scared as you.

Most Flute Concerts Are Not Varied Enough

The flute repertoire sometimes lacks depth, but most periods are represented:

Baroque (Bach, Vivaldi, Telemann)
Classical (Mozart, Gluck, Beethoven, Haydn)
Early romantic (Kuhlau, Weber, Hummel, Schubert)
Late romantic (Saint-Saëns, Widor, Fauré, Reinecke)
Corny romantic (Boehm, Demerssemann, Genin, Doppler)
Sweet romantic (Chaminade, Godard, Borne, Griffes)
Art Nouveau (Debussy, "French music," Conservatoire pieces)
Twentieth-century modern (Hindemith, Jolivet, Martinu, Schuloff, Poulenc, Martin, Prokofiev, Ibert, Roussel)

25. Barry Green, *The Inner Game of Music* (Garden City, N.Y.: Anchor Press, 1986).

American twentieth century (Copland, Muczynski, Burton, Foss, Bernstein)
Twentieth-century contemporary (Dutilleux, Sancan, Berio, Dick, Messiaen,
Boulez)

In my view, there should not be more than one piece from each period unless
it is a group of short pieces gathered in a set. Playing Martinu and Hindemith or
Fantaisie Pastorale Hongrivise and *Carmen* back to back is not a good idea. If a
harpsichord cannot be procured, a set of unaccompanied pieces will create variety.

In general, unless it is compulsory, orchestra reductions should be avoided. If
all the tuttis are played, it's interminable and hard for the pianist; if they are cut,
the proportions of the concerto are disfigured. There are exceptions—for example, the Frank Martin *Ballade*, the Griffes *Poem*, the Chaminade Concertino,
the Mozart Andante, and so on.

Most Flute Concerts Are Not Well Paced

Let us consider a recital of ninety minutes: a maximum of sixty minutes of music
including a late start of five minutes plus an intermission of fifteen to twenty
minutes.

The first piece should be relatively short (five to ten minutes), not slow and not
problematic for breath (this is where nerves hit first!)—for example, baroque
(Telemann, Handel, Hasse, C. P. E. Bach, and Blavet, but not J. S. Bach, since he
is always difficult for air, among other things), or a Conservatoire piece (the
Georges Hue Fantaisie, Ganne, the Gaubert Fantaisie, the Perilhou *Ballade*, etc.).

The second piece should find you less stressed out and ready to tackle an important work, because your fright is almost gone and your endurance is still intact—for example, J. S. Bach, Hindemith, Muczynski, Reinecke, Widor, Dutilleux, and so on.

Just before intermission comes your flashy piece, your *pièce de resistance*. On it
depends whether your friends (and competitors) and critics will come back after
the break! You are hot and enjoying this, so go for it—for example, the Prokofiev
Sonata, the Schubert Variations, the Martin *Ballade*, Demerssemann, the Widor
Suite, the Copland Duo, the Jolivet *Chant de Linos*, and so on.

The first half should be slightly more substantial than the second. The intermission has had everyone buzzing about your "awesome" performance. Now is
the time to play something for yourself. It's the blue moment. Or maybe you
want to make a statement, modern or political—for example, the Schuman
Three Romances, the Gluck Dance of the Blessed Spirits, Debussy's *Syrinx*, the
Griffes *Poem*, Joplin's *Rags*, Fukushima's *Mëi*, Varese's *Density 21.5*, Messiaen's *Le
merle noir*, Berio's *Sequenza*, Robert Dick's *Flying Lessons*, the Boulez Sonatine, the
Liebermann Sonata, the Schulhoff Sonata, and so on.

Another idea for this slot is transcriptions of favorite songs or opera arias, or a
group by special-interest composers, such as women composers, American com-

posers, Jewish composers, minority composers, French composers, Art Nouveau composers, flute music by organist composers, and so on.

The last of the program would be well-known crowd pleasers—for example, the Poulenc Sonata, Borne's *Carmen Fantaisie*, the Martinu Sonata, Bartók's *Hungarian Peasant Suite*, or the Hindemith Sonata.

For encores, if need be, short and cute nothings. Or why don't you whip out your tin whistle or your bagpipe?

In any culture, a festive meal is a ceremony. And a concert is a festive occasion. Even if it sounds trivial, maybe your program could be constructed like a menu. It does not have to be in an expensive restaurant, but it can be a place that serves what you like or what is good for you (not always the same thing!). It could also be different from your regular fare, exotic or ethnic.

> *Hors d'oeuvres*
> *Fish or fowl, with rice*
> *Salads or raw vegetables*
> *Roast and stews, with potatoes*
> *Desserts*
> *After-dinner sweets or cheeses*

Because it actually helps to build a program, let me use, half in jest, an old English wedding tradition to ensure good luck for the couple:

Something old:	Baroque or romantic
Something new:	Twentieth century or contemporary
Something borrowed:	A transcription from voice, violin, or folk
Something blue:	Your "soul piece"

In a nutshell:

Don't throw all your favorite pieces into one program. Don't start with the slowest; don't finish with the hardest. Enjoy yourself and avoid being boring.

Please refer also to:

Blowing	Memory
Breathing	Style

QUODLIBET

A certain number of edicts prevailing in the flute playing world have been transmitted and deformed through oral tradition, much like tribal taboos. My purpose is to poke fun at them, with no desire to offend anyone. Most of these axioms refer, like many canons of morality, to deceased prophets who cannot disagree: the gospel according to Gaubert, to Taffanel, to Kincaid, to Barrère, to Moyse, or to Tabuteau (for oboists). Modern-day gurus such as Rampal, Nicolet, Baker, Jaunet, Kujala, Gilbert, and others would be very amused by the final misinterpretations of their teachings.

Anybody is entitled to say today the opposite of what they stated yesterday. Politicians, conductors, and students do it, so why should professors be exempt? Nobody is infallible, especially not the writer of these lines.

I dedicate this to the memory of my predecessor at Oberlin, Tom Nyfenger, whose book[1] made fun of flutistic mannerisms[2] and whose fundamental self-doubts brought about his own tragic end, ten years ago.

Questions and . . . Answers

Posture and Position

A flute player must stand at attention, elbows and shoulders high, chin up?

What is this? A Marine honor guard? Don't slouch, but stand like a civilized human being. Do you raise your shoulders when you read a bulletin board?

A flute player must practice standing, not sitting?

This belongs in the category of: "Do it the hard way, it's good for the soul." And "no pain, no gain." The Puritan ethic does not always apply. Do what feels the most comfortable. If you are lucky enough to play in an orchestra, you will have to sit, so don't be ashamed to try. You might notice that your tone sounds different, even better, sometimes.

A flute-player must sit with a straight back at the edge of the chair, knees closed, elbows raised, like a bird on a branch ready to take off?

There is nothing wrong with resting the lower part of your spine and feeling the back of the seat when your feet are flat on the floor. Imagine that you are conversing socially on a chair, not pigging out on the sofa.

1. *Music and the Flute* (published by the author, 1986). This book is now out of print.
2. Such as "Twenty-Five Perversions of Syrinx."

A flute player must stand with feet apart like a fencer
or a sumo champion?

Why not stand normally, as when you wait for the bus?

The flute embouchure must be exactly centered
under the nose and at a right angle to the vertical
plain of the face?

The flute is asymmetrical in essence, and the right angle does not exist in nature. If your embouchure feels good and works for you, don't change it. You will be in the same boat as many of your excellent peers of all ages. Your sound is not created by angles, but by your ears and heart.

Fingers

Fingers must be rounded?

The last thing you want for your finger speed is to pinch the flute like a lobster claws its prey. The flatter your fingers are, the more easily you can lift them.

The left wrist must be bent?

This is a source of many cramps and pains. Tendons and muscles work best when pulling in a straight line. Try pinching your right earlobe with your left hand. Are you bending your wrist?

Slapping the keys makes notes come out better?

Except for some contemporary pieces, the keys should not make any noise. Hold the flute mostly with the points that don't produce notes.[3] Don't bear down on the right pinky. The secret of a smooth technique is lifting fingers smoothly and not slapping or pinching the flute when they come down.

Jawboning

You must have a different chin position for practically
every note?

With nerves and stress, those precise movements risk being for the birds. Besides, if you have a beautiful tone on middle G, you can do a slow chromatic scale down to low C or up to high C with no embouchure change. On the other hand, when you play a fast arpeggio, you are not going to have time to do all the gym-

---

3. The first joint of the forefinger of the left hand, and the right thumb.

nastics that some people think will correct intonation even before the note is played. Try and make as little chin movement as possible. Play with your ears, not your jaws.

Vibrato

Your cheeks have to flap about with your vibrato?

It might give you the impression that you are relaxed, but once you have lost power in the low range, control in the high notes, and all precision in articulation, how relaxed will you be?

Practice

You don't need to practice scales and exercises, because you find them in your solos?

This is like saying, "I don't train for my sport because I will work out during the game."

You had never made this mistake during practice?

Most probably you had ignored it, hoping it would go away in performance, like a bad dream.

Your practice is a mess, but you will concentrate during your lesson (concert, performance, exam, audition)?

The only place where playing badly is inexcusable is during practice: there is no stress, you are comfortable, and you are your only public.

You practiced four (five, six) hours?

That is three, or four, or five too many if you did not think, listen, and concentrate. Clock time is just an alibi you use to deal with guilt, like running to offset guilty calories.

You don't like "difficult" exercises?

Nobody does: they are frustrating and stressful. It is more fruitful to play "easy" patterns perfectly than finger twisters with hate in your heart. "No pain, no gain" is Puritan rubbish. Love and pleasure go further.

A great technique means playing fast?

You cannot separate AT&T (see following) from tone and interpretation. Fingers must be musical; sloppy phrasing comes as much from fingers as from tone.

*A slow movement in a Bach Sonata is easier than the
Ibert Concerto?*

Ibert takes weeks; Bach takes years. "Difficult" is what does not work in concert or under stress: breathing, staccato, high notes *pp,* and low notes *ff.*

Breathing and Blowing

Always breathe to the fullest?

If you want to say "Good morning," don't breathe for a Shakespearean mono-logue. Breathe like a fish in a bowl, without stopping, instead of like a whale.

*A huge breath and a big volume of blown air will
produce an enormous tone?*

It will give you turbo tone: a lot of air in the sound, shortness of breath, and no control over dynamics or articulation, which only work with good focus.

Breathe and blow with the diaphragm?

If you did not do that, flute or no flute, you would have choked long ago. The poor thing just goes up and down without our control. Still, the abdominal mus-cles can help.

"Circular" breathing?

Instead, try circular blowing , which does not stop, and breathing in short gasps.

Intonation

*The scale of your new flute guarantees that you will
play in tune?*

In spite of manufacturers' claims, only your ears and mind (and luck) will help you play reasonably in tune.

Never tune with vibrato?

What's wrong with tuning the way you are going to play?

Tuners are the answer to intonation problems?

If that were true, oboists and band conductors would always be right. An A# and a B♭ are not the same note: one is the leading note of B major, the other the mode generator of G minor. The poor stupid tuner does not know any different.

Fix the intonation of each note separately and you will be in tune?

Fine, your music will sound as poetic as computerized messages. Feel intonation melodically and harmonically, with your senses, not with a machine.

Metronome

You've spent your practice time with the metronome?

Wonderful, but machines like it (tuners, tape recorders, CD players, etc.) cannot replace the human mind, heart, and ears, lest humans want to become machines too. (Some people actually do.)

Rhythm

Rhythm and tempo are the same thing?

They are different by nature: rhythm comes from within; it relates to your pulse and to your emotions. On the other hand, tempo stems from a machine, be it a clock or a metronome. Check your tempo with the machine, but cultivate and live with your rhythm.

Dynamics

To get a "big tone" you have to blow a lot? To play soft, very little?

This is a vast subject. The bases of the two are totally different: it is twice as tiring to play soft as loud. Why? Because to project your sound loudly you have to relax everything, lower your shoulders, and open all your air cavities, whereas soft playing requires you to be more stable, to support for control of intonation, to withhold for air control, and to vibrate more so that the tone stays animated. Remember *Tenuto* (stable embouchure), *Sostenuto* (support), *Ritenuto* (withheld).

AT&T (Articulation, Tonguing, and Technique)

There must be a trick for AT&T?

There is: play Taffanel-Gaubert daily exercise no. 4 with the Debost Scale Game for a few years.

MCI (Musicality, Charm, Interpretation)

You are unhappy with your AT&T, but satisfied with your MCI?

People always complain about their money, never about their personality.

Interpretation

Every note in a piece must be loaded and "meaningful?"

It sounds like the fast food down the road: "Five meats, three cheeses, and everything on it." Simplicity is the issue, not pathos.

Phrasing

You want to play espressivo?

Allow harmonic tension to build up through the dissonant chords, appoggiaturas, wide intervals. Without rushing and once a high point is reached, release and let the tension ease without slowing down. But don't try to do too much.

All long notes at the end of a phrase or before a breath should be tapered?

This makes for such predictable phrasing. If the long note is in ascending-phrase mode, it should ascend also. The tone on either side of the breath should be matched to give the feeling of an uninterrupted line. If the last note does not have a decrescendo, let it diminish naturally with support. Don't risk having to do embouchure gymnastics to keep it in tune.

Challenge established truths. Do it for yourself and by yourself, especially if they are hand-me downs three or four times removed: "Gaubert or Kincaid told my great-uncle. . . ." However, when a conductor or a professor asks you to do something, give it a try instead of discarding it offhand. Everybody will feel better. There won't be any fights, and you will have acquired something: the ability to do what does not come naturally to you. Your ability to grow comes from your ability to reassess what you believe, as well as the ways and means to do so.

REPERTOIRE

"Why practice the basics (scales and daily exercises) when pieces contain patterns that can serve as practice? Since flute repertoire and orchestral works are the only things people will listen to us play, why bother with anything but that, aside from some perfunctory warm-ups?"

There is quite a lot to say about this often-heard opinion. But let us look at repertoire as a practice issue.

The flute repertoire has an important list of works, but we must acknowledge the fact that only about twenty possess a high status through the fame of their composers. To avoid hurting anybody's taste or feelings, we will stop the roll call at Mozart, Bach, Schubert and Debussy. Does that mean that we should only play these and a few others, and disregard everything else? Quite to the contrary. There are some wonderful works by lesser-known composers that are excellent material and do not dwarf the student.

No piece resists being played over and over again. The danger, though, is burnout. Constant repetition only aggravates and solidifies defects that are difficult to shed. I remember struggling through Handel's Sonata in G; it was fifty-odd years ago, but to this day I cannot play the second movement without stuttering the staccato.

The choice of repertoire is also crucial. A piece from *Flute Music by French Composers*[1] displays more notes but requires fewer basic qualities and less maturity than a Bach adagio. Yet it is hard to convince young flutists of this. One young lady auditioned one day at Oberlin with her own choice of repertoire: Bach. When I asked for something less lofty, she replied: "I like Bach; he has always served me well." Her sight-reading and basic skills, need I say, did not serve her so well.

If you must practice Bach, why not use the best études of all, the Bach cantata obbligatos?[2] They are not transcriptions, and they will provide you with a wealth of beautiful music and ideas you can apply to any repertoire, including the poor, overused Bach sonatas.

More often than not, technically challenging twentieth-century works turn out better in performance. I believe that the major works of the flute repertoire should not be assigned too early on. As with many things in life, there is only one first time, and spontaneity is a great part of our joy.

"Gaubert takes weeks, but Mozart takes years."[3] Years of what? This is what I would like to try to explain.

At any given time, a properly rehearsed performance of any given repertoire will be a photograph of the accomplishments of the student or artist at that moment in time. Outside of correcting a few wrong notes, it will not be much bet-

---

1. Louis Moyse (New York: Schirmer, 1967).
2. *Bach Cantata Obbligatos Assembled in the original text*, Franz Vester (London: Universal, 1972).
3. Gaston Crunelle (1898–1991), in his lessons at the Paris Conservatoire.

ter the next day or week. Instead of rehashing a piece until it is "nailed" or "perfect," whatever that means, general playing ability must be improved first, or at least simultaneously.

A great element of worry in repertoire and études is not always an intrinsic difficulty. It is often a reading problem, even in works we know, a psychological block on an amount of flats or sharps (C♭ or B, F♭ or E, key of D♭ or C♯ major; the same fingerings, but one comes easier than the other), or thirty-second notes looking more fierce than eighth notes at double time.

Here is the practice schedule I followed at the Paris Conservatoire, as Crunelle advised. However, students will and should alter it to fit their own needs.

The proportions may seem unusual:

Scales	½ hour
Tone and intervals	½ hour
Sight-reading	½ hour
Daily exercises	1 hour
Étude and repertoire	1 hour
Total	3 ½ hours

(Actual practice time; indispensable rest periods not included)[4]

Some professors, and certainly most students, would feel that the repertoire part is disproportionately small. After all, repertoire—pieces and orchestral excerpts—is the most public and obvious part of our activity. It is the tip of the iceberg, and the works are the most beautiful, gleaming (we hope) moments of our lives. True, but they would not exist without the hidden part, the practice, the self-doubts, the maturing, the hopes and failures. We have all had them.

Let us say before we go further that being a musician is a means to an end: serving music and composers. Mindless technical practice is a dead-end street. The ultimate goal is performance and content, meaning and beauty. But what is a beautiful idea expressed in a clumsy fashion, a lofty thought worded in an incomprehensible tongue, a feeling conveyed in the vocabulary of the gutter?

For us, that means applying musicality to instrumental playing, creating the tools that will help us express our own hearts and minds while serving music and beauty.

Likewise, we can work at our finger virtuosity without losing a feeling for tonal quality. We must think about our sound without disregarding the role of fingers in phrasing. We should worry about articulation without sacrificing the sense of the phrase.

"Mr. Kincaid did not spend much time on solo repertoire (at least with me) because he believed that if you learned the essentials of musicianship and learned to control the instrument, you would know how to approach the repertoire on your own."[5] So we must develop, as much as our poor overworked repertoire and excerpts, our instrumental playing: sight-reading and basics.

4. This time spread should be reduced or augmented accordingly for workdays of ninety minutes or six hours.

5. Robert Cole, "William M. Kincaid," in *Flutist Quarterly* (Fall 1995): 44–48.

Sight-Reading

As much as possible, sight-reading must be developed, alone or not.

Take one movement at a time, about two pages. Give yourself one minute before playing to survey the task at hand, and decide that you are not going to stop. The act of stopping shows that your head is in the recent past, whereas, whatever happens, you must be thinking about the very near future. Don't be ashamed, don't apologize, and don't use audible foul language. Nobody's perfect; just keep going.

Here are four or five principles to systematize sight-reading, which I like to call *prima vista* (first sight). They may seem obvious, but try them.

Rapidly, before trying the fast passages, check:

1. The key and its changes
2. The beat and its changes
3. The slowest notes and the fastest run
4. The tempo of the beat and its changes
5. How it starts and if there are suspensions, fermatas or cadenzas

Only now can you look at all the little black monsters. Remember, accidents don't always happen in the "difficult" passages, but often in the least obvious places like slow counting. Never mind; don't look back, and keep going.

Étude and Repertoire

Études are a kind of super sight-reading. Their aim is to cultivate, for about a week each, the ability to read ahead, willpower, and concentration. I have never been able to play a perfect étude, so I don't demand it from my students. Once a day, preferably upon starting your daily practice, try out your étude and your repertoire at full tempo, without stopping. Make a mental or written note of what was not satisfactory, but don't practice it right away. After working at the basics, you can come back and rework the deficient parts of both étude and repertoire.

Before practicing repertoire, read everything well, accompaniment included. It seems evident, but many mistakes come from lack of careful reading.

To study a difficult run—for example, the opening of the Ibert concerto—isolate it according to broken rhythms.

Very snappy slow rhythms will educate your reflexes, if you stay slow and don't try them at an accelerated tempo. If you must practice with the metronome, do not speed it up. Yielding to this temptation destroys all the reflexes you have just patiently built in. Instead, put off the trial run until your next practice session, preferably the next day.

Being methodical does not mean being boring. A Roman poet said: "Mens sana in corpore sano."[6] A spontaneous heart expresses itself through "a sound mind in a sound body."

6. Juvenal, c. 60 A.D.–c.140 A.D. in *Satires*.

In a nutshell:

Practice instrumental playing while thinking about repertoire, not the other way around. Sight-read as much as
you can. Hone your skills humbly as a good craftsman
would, and keep your interpretations out of the freezer.

Please refer also to:

Instrumental Playing	Scale Game
Metronome	Sight-Reading
Practicing	Warm-Ups

RESONANCE

Resonance is the acoustical essence of sound.

Flute tone, like all sound phenomena, is a vibration implemented into a
medium, usually air. It is called a sound wave.

Sound is a vibration of the medium, but it is not vibrato. Sound cannot be produced in a vacuum. It needs a medium—in most cases air, but it can be lighter
than air (such as helium), making the pitch sharper, or heavier (such as carbon
dioxide), turning the pitch flatter.

You can experiment with this phenomenon if you play right after having a car-
bonated drink. Should an accidental return of the gas occur, your tone suddenly
goes very flat, for a second, then comes back up to pitch. The greater density of
carbon dioxide (CO_2) is the reason.

The temperature inside the flute also influences resonance. Cold air is denser
than hot; therefore, it resonates at a lower frequency.

There can be no sound in a vacuum. Correlatively, any air particle in contact
with the sound source enters into vibration with it.

The volume of air where you are playing resonates, but so do all the cavities inside your body: chest, mouth, throat, sinuses, even bones. They contribute to
give each of us a distinctive sound. A cold is unpleasant because the head cavities do not resonate.

Our tone of voice is a direct result of the component resonance of our facial
spaces. It is the constant emphasis of good voice teachers, and it is mine, for I
think the voice is the best example of tone production for flutists.

If no respiratory problem affects you, open your throat, breathe and blow as in
a yawn. Your tone opens up too.

Try to open your nostrils. The pharynx opens even more, and the head's hollow cavities enter into sympathetic resonance, amplifying your tone and giving it

timbre. Singers, our models, are well aware of this phenomenon: they call resonators the internal volumes of the face (mask).

The acoustical return of the space where you are playing, even if is acoustically dead, gives you a different, more objective view of your sound. Listen to the resonance of your flute. "Another idea is to practice facing a corner of the room so that the sound is equally deflected into each ear."[7]

In other words, play the room as much as you do your flute. Analyze the tone you produce as if you were listening to yourself from a few feet away, not only according to what you are doing: "I am blowing hard, therefore my tone is loud," or "I am barely blowing, but the conductor asks me to play softer." (Another interesting one is: "I must be in tune, because my tuner shows that my pitch is right.")

Also try the following experiment: since you cannot cup your ears (you will need your hands to play!), have someone hold up a piece of cardboard in front of each ear while you play. Your perception of your own sound will be noticeably altered.

Practice your tone on intervals, especially on Intervals 3. When you play octaves and ascending fifths, whose frequencies are multiples of the fundamental, you perceive an enhancement of the resonance—if your intonation is true, that is. You may find thus a pleasant way of improving tone, resonance, and intonation.

If one plays a sound into the lid of an open grand piano, all the harmonics of that note respond. They hum for a long time after the source has stopped, providing the dampers are off the strings. It creates a magical effect, somewhat like the iridescence of the rainbow after the rain.

The space in which we play, however large, also resonates with our music. I always suggest playing not only your flute but also the room, all the more if you don't like its acoustics. Don't complain constantly about it or boast about your latest miracle embouchure by Sears and Wal-Mart. Play and listen to what comes back to you from the room to your ears, which are, after all, your best (and cheapest!) teachers.

There is no such thing as a perfect instrument, any more than there are perfect jobs or perfect couples. Providing you have found a reasonably manageable head joint, live with it for a year or two. Then see if a new mate will be better than the former one, or better yet, if you are more livable yourself.

When someone tells you, "Your flute has a great sound!" you have to take that as the greatest compliment: it is the result of your own resonance. All the great flutists I admire have great flutes, but strangely enough, not all great flutes I know have great flutists.

Scientists say that only the shape and length of the tube influence the resonance of the flute. Never mind about wood, plastic, pewter, or platinum—

7. John Krell, *Kincaidiana: A Flute Player's Notebook* (Culver City, Calif.: Trio Publications, 1973).

science says it is all the same. But acoustics is not an exact science. We can be grateful that, in the last resort, human invention has the last word.

Here is a totally unscientific opinion: a flute that is made to resonate by its owner becomes better with age. On the other hand, I have loaned my flutes to colleagues or students, and when the instrument was returned after a month or so, it had, on certain notes, the characteristics of the borrower: this D♭ is sharper than before, this E♭ deader, or it has a more wide-open upper range or a stuffier low register. Pure paranoia on my part, no doubt. But why should I not be entitled to my neuroses like anybody else? If there is any truth to this opinion, resonance must have something to do with the response of the tube's material.

Sympathetic resonance is the vibration of a medium or a space in affinity to sound, but it should not be mistaken for vibrato.

There is often confusion in flute players' minds: some tell me that having their cheeks flap about gives them a better vibrato and a heightened resonance. If it works for them, fine, but I don't advise it because it seems to me that it reduces the focus and control of the air stream. As far as articulation and tonguing are concerned, forget it.

Don't complain about the acoustics—you cannot change them—or about your embouchure—you are stuck with it for a while. Play and listen to what comes back to your ears, your best teachers.

Open your throat and your nose, relax your embouchure, drop your shoulders, and don't try to produce all of the tone with your lips.

In a nutshell:

Use the resonance of the flute and of the space. Do not judge your playing only by what you are doing, but also by what you are hearing. Play the room. Listen to your sound as if from a distance.

Please refer also to:

Acoustics	Intervals
Flutes	Vibrato

RITUALS

"The worst deafness is refusing to hear."[8] When a habit is well ingrained, it is like a neurosis. The first step toward a cure is accepting the fact that there is a problem, a dependency, on alcohol, on tobacco, on pills, or on flute mannerisms. I am not addicted to most of them, but concerning the latter, I am not so sure.

After playing the flute for more than fifty years, I should not be enjoying it so much anymore, but the urge still tickles me. That's my neurosis and I love it.

Let us look at a few flutisms, just for fun.

Starting and Playing Rituals

We all have our rituals. This one blows hard through the tube as if to flush the cobwebs that have accumulated since the last time she practiced. The other aims from the head joint down as through the sight of a shotgun. This other wipes the lip plate three times with a cloth. This powerful fellow takes the stance of a Japanese wrestler. That one cannot start a piece without a sweep of the flute even if he is alone, and so on.

Once under way, the gyrations start. Passion pervades the most innocent line. Even a held note deserves wiggling and tossing. We genuflect or rise on our toes. One foot affirms character with a stomp, the other beats time.

If it helps, let's do it, without forgetting that the most important is still the playing and that our neurotic movements can actually hinder our performance.

The Sacrosanct Long Tones

"I always start with my long toooones." They are often a way to assume we are practicing without using our brain or ears. They don't require concentration, we think, and anything where we don't have to move the fingers is considered easy. Why don't we play something that involves tone, fingers, intonation, breathing, tone (again,) tonality, articulation, and tone (always?) Yes, you got it: scales. Instrumental playing is not a dresser with one drawer for technique, one for tone, one for tonguing, one for pitch control, and so on. They all work together hopefully, to serve music.

Who has ever heard of a flute or head joint maker who did not claim that out of his shop comes the final flute marvel of the century? That's normal; business is business. The strange thing is that we believe it; we are constantly searching for the magical instrument. We are not alone: Adolph Herseth, the legendary principal trumpet of the Chicago Symphony Orchestra, confessed to having "hundreds of mouthpieces."[9] He alone knows which one he is playing, but we hear Herseth.

8. "Il n'y a pas plus sourd que celui qui ne veut pas entendre" (old French saying).
9. *Smithsonian*, September 1994.

We must have brand new flutes, with the latest scale, perfectly in tune, of course. Julius Baker played on many flutes, but it is he who has set the standard so high. Conversely, we might be holding on for dear life to our old head joint as to our alter ego.[10] I played for twenty-five years on a Louis Lot flute made in 1862. I thought I could not live without it. It was out of tune, like most flutes, or, shall we say, all flutists, but not more. I sold it to Michie and William Bennett. In England, the fashion is Louis Lot; they would not think of blowing one of these spanking new yellow American or Japanese flutes.

Our flute is our fetish, an extension of our being. And so be it, if we feel happier for it. Still, the flute is but a piece of sophisticated plumbing, and until machines take over, the flute player and his art are the ultimate answer.

Machines

Tuners, metronomes, and CD players are our servants, not our masters. Even after tuning, let us listen to ourselves and to others and find a common ground. The machine gives a starting measurement of pitch, nothing more.

Metronome

Let us feel the pulse and the throb of life before the inhuman beat of the metronome. The metronome is so dry and rigid that it has no reality. If only we still had the old pyramid with the visible pendulum. It was invented by Johann Nepomuk Maelzel[11] and used profusely by Beethoven. The problem is that the tempi indicated by Beethoven (and by others after him) are a source of great puzzlement to present-day conductors. Even composers I know who are alive today disagree with the metronome markings they wrote themselves. When performers try to follow the metronome markings, their interpretation is far from convincing. The critics love it but the public, which has little regard for this maniacal concern, is usually annoyed or turned off.

I still like the old pyramid. Most of the time it has a limp to it. I have to listen and adapt to it. I prefer the nostalgic click-clack to the mindless accuracy of electronic ticking.

Some modern metronomes have a one-in-two or one-in-three function that is useful for people who have a problem with rhythm. The hierarchy of beats is implicit in music and is in itself a slight alteration of the steady beat.

If the machine nonetheless helps to verify the tempo and control our slowing or rushing, let us use it. Let us not play with the metronome but against it. Phrasing and pacing are a way to bend and stretch the predictability of the hourglass. In music as in life, there are seconds that are longer than hours and stay with us forever.

10. The other self.
11. 1772–1838.

Let us look at the score to decipher the magic of a composition before rushing to recording and metronomes. CDs and tapes are designed primarily to bring music to the nonmusician, not to fabricate intelligence and feeling for the musician.

Of course, all these inventions are an asset. However, we do not toil for them; they work with us.

Big Tone and Air

I am blowing like crazy, so I must be playing *ff.* A well-placed, focused sound carries better while requiring less air. Focus is created by an uncramped smile and a stable position on the chin.

Vibrato and Tuning

Should one use vibrato while tuning?

We might be in accordance with the tuner, that ghastly machine. But chances are our beautiful tuning will not be right in actual playing. Tuning is always an approximation and involves an eagerness to adapt to others.

If we are to play with vibrato, then let us tune with vibrato. Is it better to be slightly off with the machine and true in actual playing, or the other way around?

Fingerings

If an alternate fingering easily produces the same or a better quality of music, let's do it. The road to hell is paved with good intentions. I don't think that no pain is no gain; more comfort is more pleasure.

Tradition

Are teachers and elders always right?

We wish. Even if they are wrong, our effort to execute what they ask gives us the knowledge and character to do our own thing. The best conductors are those who are capable of making us do things we do not agree with or that we think we are incapable of doing. Dead conductors and professors of the past are the best: at least they can't protest when their interpretations and ideas are twisted around.

In a nutshell:

Do not take any habits for granted, especially your own. Experiment with new concepts and question the old rules. Make up you own mind. A valid idea will prevail even when challenged. When the time comes, new options will have to be explored with an open mind. Don't blindly trust seemingly infallible machines. Respect for elders stems from persuasion, not rules.

Please refer also to:

Air	Machines
Blowing	Scale Game
Flutes	Tuning
Instrumental Playing	Vibrato
Intonation, Intonations	Warm-Ups

REST

Bicycle racers know how to rest "in the pack": they eat, converse, play pranks, relax, even relieve themselves, all the while going at speeds unthinkable to laypersons.

It is possible for us to rest while playing a piece. There is almost always a passage where "the flute plays by itself," where the music speaks effortlessly. Without losing concentration, one can rest a bit, come to terms with stress, and repair one's health to a certain extent.

Tension(s) can be alleviated by different kinds of rest:

- Nervous tension, when there is no special problem of fingers or tone production.
- Respiratory fatigue, when rests and articulation of the musical discourse allow many small pauses for breathing.
- Musical tension, when the character and content of the music require neither toil nor torment.

One misunderstanding about interpretation would tend to make every note meaningful. Good idea, but meaningful does not mean overbearing. On the contrary, for my taste in interpretation, less is more.

Actually, as a listener and an orchestral player, I often feel that some conductors tend to do too much. Places where the orchestra plays loud and straight, for instance, need not be conducted. Loudness expresses superficial passion, but passion is more often release than tension. Sweat and histrionics do not mean depth and artistic expression. Conductors show their worth when tension grows out of the implications in the musical text, harmony, pacing, and imagination.

Flutists, on the other hand, should not have to highlight every phrase. Predictable points like perfect cadences need not be overstated; they can be rest areas for listener and player.

Scale and arpeggio patterns come naturally to flutists who are on top of their instrumental playing. Dynamic levels of f and ff require no effort for us. We can actually let go while playing loud, but we cannot rest during soft dynamics.

Learn from the score where tension (musical and instrumental) builds; live with it, feel it, taste it. Then, when the music reaches release, rest both physically and emotionally. This happens many times in the course of one movement.

At times a half rest is enough to pause and restore one's health. It reminds me of a pit stop in a Formula 1 Grand Prix, where, in a flash, a racecar has a full tank and four new tires.

In a nutshell:

Expressive playing is an alternation of tension and release. Constant passion is tiring for everyone: the musician, the listener, and the music. Learn how to rest for musical and physical reasons. Rest and silence are inseparable from music.

Please refer also to:

Concentration	Score
Instrumental Playing	Stress Control
Scale Game	Tension and Release

RUBATO

Rubato means what it says: stolen. But in music, it implies stolen . . . and returned. Tempo remains steady within a given measure so that the musical delivery may be more or less early or late with respect to the basic pulse. One steals time from time. This creates a certain tension comparable to the inflections of a spoken phrase, whose release is never completely regular, unlike those in so many soporific speeches.

The metronome cannot discipline rubato, except in that it symbolizes the pulse of the fatal clock, whose bondage we, poor humans, try to defeat by stretching and compressing musical space. This conflict between tension and release is the essence of rubato, of phrasing, and of musical expression in general. Thanks to freedom and rubato, music can become ageless. Minutes seem eternal, time suspends its flight, the moment is almost sacred: "Du holde Kunst, ich danke dir" (Thou tender Art, I thank thee; Schober, set to music by Schubert).

In fact, if you use the metronome systematically, you should consider yourself its equal, not its slave. Practice with the metronome, by all means; but most of all play *against* the metronome.

The accompaniment of a phrase serves this same principle. Often the flutist is trying to tell his accompanist or his partners in chamber music, the time he or she wants to take here, this breath there, this spoken effect, that suspension toward an accent, and so on. Yet the accompaniment plays the role of a counterweight to rubato in the melodic line, in such a way that liberties taken by the leading line are structured and framed.

The great conductor Carlo-Maria Giulini said in a rehearsal of a Mozart opera in Aix-en-Provence that the foundation of the classical orchestra was to be found in the second violins and violas, which represent the pulse and to which the whole edifice should refer.

Rubato is almost an order given to us by the composer when he leaves us alone. For example:

Rubato Example 1. Mozart, Concerto in G Major, K. 313, second movement

Rubato Example 2. J. S. Bach, Sonata in E Minor, BWV 1034, third movement

As soon as the accompaniment reappears, the phrasing must express itself according to a regular pulse.

Yet sometimes this pulse is not even compatible with the rhythm of the leading line, as in Variation 3 of Schubert's Introduction and Variations on "Ihr Blumlein Alle," op. 160, or in the first movement of Georges Enesco's Cantabile et Presto. A binary pulse in one part conflicting with a ternary rhythm in an other indicates a sort of preprogrammed rubato. If it is together, in the sense of simultaneous, it is not right.

Yet our musical ancestors of the eighteenth century, who played very freely, would always refer as a last resort to *le bon goût* (good taste), a set of many unspoken rules and oral traditions subject themselves to interpretation. Where does it end?

Rubato is not welcome everywhere. Like all liberties, rubato has limits. When the listener starts to notice it, it's probably too much—hence the excess of certain "romantic" interpretations. Rubato is in fact a way to resort to devices in bad taste without the listener noticing.

In general, one must take time in the elements of harmonic tension (seventh chords, diminished fifth chords, dissonant chords), represented in the flute part by either wide intervals or leading notes:

Rubato Example 3. Mozart, Quartet in D Major, K. 285, second movement

Chromatic figures or leading notes also highlight the expressive character:

Rubato Example 4. Brahms, Symphony no. 4, Finale

Rubato Example 4. Brahms, Symphony no. 4, Finale (*continued*)

In this case, tension builds up with successive leading tones, reaches its climax through two consecutive fourths, then dissolves again with half-tone sighs. Build-up requires patience, tension wants time; but as soon as the expressive accent has peaked, time and tempo claim their due. Because of its natural character, rubato underlines musical meaning. But if there is no particular reason, it is unnecessary to systematically slow down the end of a phrase,[12] because it usually is, in itself, a release from harmonic tension. Likewise, a scale pattern in a phrase is a statement of tonality or a conduit of passing notes and does not have to be rattled by rubato it is not intended to have. It is like requesting a ticket for the bus as if you were begging your date for a kiss.

No doubt one must feel the ambiguous relationship between time and space, between tension and release, between yearning and fulfillment; this is musical instinct tempered by style.

In a nutshell:

Musical discourse has the inflexions of speech. Rubato gives time back to time after borrowing it. Too much unevenness in the tempo is as bad as too much stiffness. It is the alchemy of the performer. Tension must be highlighted, but it must not fall into caricature.

Please refer also to:

Accompaniment	Phrasing
Appoggiatura	Score
Freedom	Tempo

---

12. Except in most final cadences.

SCALE GAME

Gamme Game

The Scale Game[1] has been devised out of *exercise no. 4* in *Dix-sept grands exercices journaliers de mécanisme de flûte* by Paul Taffanel and Philippe Gaubert. Paul Taffanel taught them at the Conservatoire National de Paris at the turn of the twentieth century. They were formalized by Gaubert and published in 1923.[2]

Scales are the essential part of daily instrumental practice, as much as or more than tone exercises, because tone is always present in them. For greatest profit, they should be considered as music, which, in truth, they are. The transition that concludes each scale and introduces the new one through modulation serves as relaxation, as reassessment of the sound, as an ever more refined intonation and flavor of the various keys' color. Therefore, regardless of the tempo of the previous articulation, or of the next, this beautiful transition should always be played slowly and freely, slurred, phrased with the fingers as much as with the tone, with no precise reference to tempo.

Structural breaths are mandatory and are placed after each low and high tonic. The tempo can then be suspended to perform noiselessly a good inhalation with the "hhaah" sound. This is the time to open your tone and reposition your instrumental playing. The tonic of the new key should be repeated.

Emergency breaths are optional and caused by necessity. They can be taken at any time, provided that they are quick (without suspension of the tempo) and barely audible, and that the sound is balanced with the same dynamic on either side of the interruption. I prefer to place these "911 breaths" after the first note of a group of four, or after a strong beat instead of before.

It is better not to start every day with the same key. I suggest starting with C major, then Eb major the following day, then Gb major the next, and finally with A major before starting the cycle again with C major, and so on. It is not profitable to repeat one scale until it is "perfect." Monotony creates boredom, which, more than difficulty, is an obstacle to concentration. It is better to run calmly through all keys on every practice day.

The Scale Game is intended as "play" in its meaning of "game," not as a challenge. Comfort, not speed, is the issue. The tempo indications are mere suggestions. If a different one, faster or slower, works better, by all means, it must be used. The metronome should definitely not be adjusted for each scale. Remember: the modulations should be always slurred, slow, and sensual.

After a few days the tempo perspectives will come naturally. The metronome should be a help, not a dictator. Speed will come in due time.

Choose the dynamics at will, as long as the same level prevails for any given

1. *Gamme* is the French word for scale.
2. By Alphonse Leduc, in Paris.

key. Dynamics do not mean swells. Quite to the contrary, a scale started in one dynamic should be developed at the same level until the next modulation.

To practice the high range in all articulations, six keys can be repeated *ad 8va*. They are C major, C minor, D♭ major, C♯ minor, D major, and D minor. In this case, a simple scale replaces the modulating bridge.

At the average rate of thirty seconds per scale, and taking into account the nec-

Scale Game Example 1

essary stops and rests, a complete cycle of keys and articulations requires barely half an hour. In my view, this Scale Game should be played daily.

If time permits, a second thirty-key cycle can be accomplished each day using extra articulations. These are devised for variety and versatility. Each example will sooner or later turn up in repertoire (tonguing, concerto scales, off-balance runs, etc.). Each player should then select what is relevant to the repertoire or material currently being worked on. It is always interesting and rewarding to relate the Scale Game to musical reality.

Suggested Tempo for Each Group of Notes

| Medium fast = ± 80 | Slow = ± 60 | Very slow = ± 52 |
| Flowing fast =± 84 | Fast = ± 120 | Very fast = ± 144 |

Explanations

42. Dactylic rhythm

Scale Game Example 2

43. Anapestic rhythm

ti ki ti ti ki ti ti ki ti ti ki ti   ti   ki ti ti ki ti ti ki ti ti ki ti   ti ki ti

Scale Game Example 3

44. Trumpet-style rhythm

ti ti ki ti ti ti ki ti ti   ti ki ti   (option)   ti ti ki ti ti ti

Scale Game Example 4

45. Trumpet-style rhythm

ti ki ti ti   ti ki ti ti   (option)   ti ti ki ti ti ti ki ti

Scale Game Example 5

50. Concerto scale, slurred and staccato

Scale Game Example 6

51. Concerto scale, slurred and staccato

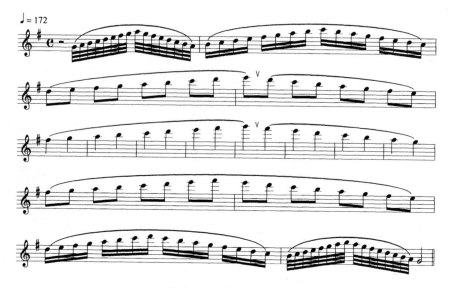

Scale Game Example 7

Scale Game Grid

Scale Game: Articulation, Speed, Dynamic

1. Slurred, flowing, medium fast, *mf*
2. Slurred, fast, *mf*
3. Slurred, medium fast, *p*
4. Single tongue, medium fast, *mf*
5. Ha ha ha, no tongue, medium fast, *mf*
6. Single tongue, fast, *mf*
7. Double tongue, same tempo as no. 6, *mf*
8. Double tongue, very fast, *mf*
9. Ki ki ki ki, slow, *mf*
10. 1 single, 3 slurred, medium fast, *f*
11. 3 slurred, 1 *staccato*, flowing,, *mf*
12. Doubling each note, slow, *mf*
13. Tripling each note, slow *mf*
14. Slurred by 2, fast, *mf*
15. Slurred by 4, accented, very fast, *ff*
16. 2 slurred, 2 single, medium fast, *mf*
17. 2 slurred, 2 double, fast, *mf*

Scale Game: Articulation, Speed, Dynamic

18. 2 slurred, 6 double, fast, *mf*
19. 1 staccato, then slurred by 2, fast, *mp*
20. 2 slow, 6 fast, flowing, *mf*
21. 2 slow, 6 fast, single, *mf*
22. 2 slow, 6 fast, double, *mf*
23. 2 slow, 6 fast, triple, *mf*
24. 2 slow, 6 double/triple, *mf*
25. 8 slurred +1, rest, very fast, *f*
26. 8 staccato +1, rest, very fast, *f*
27. 1 long, 7 slurred, fast, *f*
28. 1 long, 7 staccato, fast, *f*
29. 1 short + rest, 7 slurred, fast, *f*
30. 1 short + rest, 7 staccato, fast, *f*
31. "American legato" (da da da da)
32. Single tongue, fast, *pp*

Scale Game: Articulation, Speed, Dynamic

33. Single tongue, very staccato, very slow, *ff*
34. Ti di ti di *or* ti ri ti ri (baroque *inégal*) *mf*
35. Ki ti ki ti, inverted double, medium fast, *mf*
36. Quintuplets slurred, slow, *mf* ♫♫♫
37. Quintuplets staccato, slow, *mf* ♫♫♫
38. Septuplets slurred, slow, *mf* ♫♫
39. Septuplets staccato, slow, *mf* ♫♫
40. 1 single, 3 double, fast, *mf* ♫♫♫♫
41. 3 double, 1 staccato, flowing, *mf* ♫♫♫♫
42. Dactylic: 1 eighth, 2 sixteenths or anapestic: 2 sixteenths, 1 eighth, *f*
43. Trumpet style: 1 eighth, 3 sixteenths in triplets or 3 sixteenths in triplets, 1 eighth, *f*
44. Slurred by measures, very slow, *f*
45. 4 slurred, 4 staccato, or vice versa, *mf*
46. 2 single, 2 slurred, medium, *mf*
47. 2 double, 2 slurred, medium, *mf*
48. 3 slurred, 5 double, fast, *mf* ♫♫♫
49. 1 staccato, 2 slurred, 2 staccato, etc., fast, *mf* ♫♫♫

Scale Game: Articulation, Speed, Dynamic

50. Concerto scale, slurred, start slowly, *mf* ♫♫♫/♫♫♫
51. Concerto scale, staccato, start slowly, *mf* ♫♫♫/♫♫♫
52. Concerto scale, slurred, start fast, *mf* ♫♫♫/♫♫♫
53. Concerto scale, staccato, start fast, *mf* ♫♫♫/♫♫♫
54. Chromatic scale, low C to high C, slurred by 6, medium fast, *f*
55. Chromatic scale, low C to high C, double staccato by 6, medium fast, *f*
56. Chromatic scale, low C to high C, triple staccato by 6, medium fast, *f*
57. Chromatic scale, low C to high C, slurred by 4 or 6, medium fast, *f*
58. Chromatic scale, low C to high C, double staccato by 4 or 6, medium fast, *f*
59. Whole-tone scale, slurred, low C to high C, medium fast, *f*
60. Whole-tone scale, slurred, low C# to high C#, medium fast, *f*

SILENCE

Just as mass is subject to gravity, music is attracted by silence.

"The vase gives its shape to vacuum, and music to silence," wrote Georges Braque,[3] the great French painter who initiated Cubism and modern art with Pablo Picasso[4] in the early 1900s. Although still misunderstood and disliked by many, their art illustrates tension between volumes and lines, colors and forms, and order and chaos, sometimes to the point of deliberate ugliness.

In this sense, music is also an abstract art, meant to depict not anecdotal vignettes, but conflict between tension and release, passion and serenity, form and content, sound and silence. If our music does not express thoughts and feelings, however down-to-earth or intellectual they may be, then it is merely a bland background or an expensive noise. Composers express themselves and their inner conflicts through construction, harmony, movement and silence.

3. 1882–1963 in *Album Fondation Maeght*, Saint-Paul-de-Vence: Fondation Maeght, 1979.
4. 1881–1973.

Silence, in outer space, is total but empty,[5] whereas the silence of a rest,[6] in a musical context, is loaded. We should "play" it.

- It emphasizes a moment of tension.
- It is like a question mark (?) or an exclamation point (!).
- It is like an ellipsis (. . .).
- With a fermata, it is a fragment of suspended eternity.

In his memoir[7] Daniel Barenboim, the music director of the Chicago Symphony Orchestra,[8] and my boss for fifteen years[9] in the Orchestre de Paris, says: "The strongest element of sound, to me, is the silence before it, and the silence afterward."

- The pregnant silence before sound, when we should concentrate and meditate instead of moving frivolously. I used to find it very difficult to start *Prélude à l'Après-midi d'un Faune* or *Bolero* among coughs and chair movements.
- The moment when sound vanishes into silence, that infinite margin where everyone holds his breath, when time is suspended, when any gesture would break the charm, but where musicians turn pages loudly, suck on their reeds, or tune their violins, or when applause comes too soon and breaks the spell.

Musical sound should be set as a jewel between two intense moments of silence, before and after.

Take this passage of Beethoven's Violin Concerto (bars 28 ff.), tutti *ff*.

Silence Example 1

One can say that the rests are also *ff*. Shame on the musicians who do not respect their full value. The silence is also by Beethoven. Great composers' silence has more music than most verbose virtuosity.

There are also many examples in our flute repertoire. Let us take just two by Mozart:

5. Sound needs a medium (such as air) for its propagation.
6. In French, silence and rest are translated by the same term (*silence*). *Soupir* and *demi-soupir* (sigh and half sigh) are more evocative than "rest" and "half rest."
7. Daniel Barenboim, *A Life in Music*, edited by Michael Lewin (London: Weidenfeld & Nicolson, 1991).
8. Since 1989.
9. 1974–1989.

Silence Example 2. Andante in C Major, K. 315, measures 12–13

The asterisk (*) indicates total silence and stillness. Do not move bodily, and do not breathe perceptibly or "pump" a flute start. Time is suspended.

Silence Example 3. Mozart, Concerto in D Major,
K. 314, second movement, measure 72

Savor this suspense! Don't move! Then play the turn following the fermata, still without moving, before the beat, to signal the resolution of that rest. Here there is music even when no one plays.

In a nutshell:

Silence is a vital element of music; listen to it and live with it.

Please refer also to:

Concentration   Tension and Release

STABILITY

Stability is the foundation of flute playing. There is no possible flexibility without a sound foundation. The stronger a muscle is, the less tension it needs for its action. "Give me a fulcrum and I will lift the earth."[10]

Stability, for the flutist, implies:

- A flexible but "heavy" station on the feet, or a well-centered seat with the posterior resting on its entire surface, not on the edge of the chair.
- The center of gravity placed as low as possible and slightly forward, shoulders and elbows low. No standing at attention (except in military bands).
- Solidarity of the flute with the chin, which facilitates flexibility of the lips. If the embouchure plate is not stable, there can be no reliability in articulation. A rapid note sequence can threaten the balance of the embouchure, making slurring uncertain and staccato problematic.
- Predictable intonation. There is no totally in-tune flute; even Albert Cooper says so. But with a flute built on a reasonable scale and an ear trained by daily practice, it is possible, with flexible stability, to adapt in this respect. One should play in tune with a key more than with a tuner. A B♭ is not an A♯, nor an E♭ a D♯, nor a D♭ a C♯.

A flutist will be happy if he or she understands early the concept of chin stability. Lips should be relaxed but not loose. The chin is not jutted toward the embouchure plate. Instead it is the flute that is maintained to the chin by the fulcrums.

Fulcrums

The flute, in various forms, has been present in most civilizations, from the Stone Age[11] to the Computer Age.[12] The long shinbone became the tibia.[13] Thousands of images show the transverse flute: Greek vases, Hindu bas-reliefs, Khmer temples, Japanese etchings, Egyptian tomb walls, Renaissance ladies, African medicine men, powdered-wig gentlemen, Revolutionary fife bands, kings and court jesters, right up to the space odyssey.

Regardless of their degree of sophistication, these flutes all have something in common. They are held in the same manner:

1. By the first joint of the left forefinger.
2. By resting on the chin.
3. By the right thumb.

10. Archimedes (c. 310–250 B.C.).
11. 40,000 B.C., give or take 10,000 years.
12. 2,000 A.D. and beyond.
13. Latin name for both the bone and the instrument.

These three points I call fulcrums. They are the pivots of flute playing and the foundations of stability.

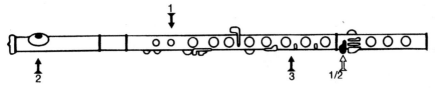

Stability Figure 1

From this diagram, one can see that the principal agent of stability is the first joint of the left index finger (fulcrum 1). It works in one direction (bringing the flute "in"). The right thumb (fulcrum 3) counterbalances it, going "out" to create an isometric point of balance at the lip plate (fulcrum 2).

The right pinky, in my view, counts for very little in stability and actually gets in the way of things except on six notes: three D♯s, 2 Es, and high A.

Two things must also be noted:

- The three fulcrums do not finger notes.
- Their action is generated on a horizontal or transversal plane, not in a vertical direction.

If you don't create stability with the points that do not make notes, you will have to compensate by holding more with the fingers that do make notes, thereby slowing down your technique.

Stability is very important. But stable does not mean tight. There is sometimes a misconception about my emphasis on stability. Some people fear that they might become cramped or tight. Quite to the contrary, I believe that loose fulcrums create instability and angst. Eventually tightness appears in the wrong places. The moving fingers grip the flute. The embouchure cramps up on staccato and wide intervals.

It is possible to vary the stability of fulcrum no. 1. This point is vital for production of low notes *f–ff staccato*, for slurred intervals *p–pp* in the third octave, and generally for tricky attacks. In the medium range, no tension is necessary.

Stability actually helps to relax the face, the lips and the fingers, and provides a sense of security under stress. Adepts of stability sometimes experience a sort of numbness at fulcrum no. 1 after considerable playing time. This is a serious problem. It might come from a nerve being compressed at the point of contact. It might result from a sudden change in the time allotted for practice, such as anxiously cramming in ten hours in two days, instead of playing five days for two hours a day. If the skin does not have time to secrete slowly its own protection,[14]

---

14. A callus.

then a finger rest made of foam or rubber, in the style of the Bopep, can be tested. I am in general not in favor of contraptions and gimmicks, but if they work, use them, especially if they prevent to play with pain. Effort, yes; pain, never.

If numbness or pain affects you, definitely go back to a looser hold on the flute, even if it means less stability. But a passing inconvenience in your left index is a small price to pay for the efficiency, reliability, and freedom afforded by the principle of stability.

In a nutshell:

Flexibility cannot be mistaken for instability, or stability for tightness. A lever needs a fulcrum that is by definition firmly fixed. Hold your flute with the points that do not finger notes.

Please refer also to:

Finger Phrasing   Little Devils
Hands   Pain and Pleasure
Instrumental Playing

STEPPING-STONES

Creators of Japanese gardens put a great amount of beauty into a small space. Their use of space and understatement is a model for musical interpretation. I love their stepping-stones: flat rocks symbolizing various stages of our existence or an imaginary river made of fine white gravel. Whatever they stand for, they are poetic images of suspended time.

There are helpful stepping-stones in interpretation also: pacing a dynamic progression and tracking a change in tempo. (See Stepping Stones ex. 1, page 225.)

The initial bar is *p* throughout. In the second bar, the primary notes are highlighted while the secondary patterns remain *p*. In the last bar, all the elements come forward. The figured-bass harmonic progression follows the same ascending dynamic progression.

In the following example, since no harmonic progression exists in the accompaniment, the performer has two possibilities:

1. Reiteration:[15] Measure 45 is louder than 44. In this case, the low notes should be enhanced first, and then the already very apparent high notes complete the progression. (See Stepping Stones ex. 2, page 225.)

15. Reiterate: repeat with insistence.

Stepping-stones Example 1. J. S. Bach, Sonata in E Minor,
BWV 1034, second movement, measures 51–54

Stepping-stones Example 2. Mozart Concerto in D Major,
K. 314, first movement, measures 43–47

2. Echo: Measure 45 is softer than 44. Here the naturally louder high notes are
dimmed to create the echo effect.

Stepping-stones Example 3. Mozart Concerto in D Major,
K. 314, first movement, measures 43–47

In a crescendo, when the agogic incites you to start the progression too soon, let the flute build it by itself. Hold back your conscious increase until the stepping-stone you have chosen to start the culmination of the swell, as in the solo in the finale of Brahms's Fourth Symphony.

In a diminuendo, on the other hand, you must resist the natural tendency of long notes to decay so that the patterns following them do not sound louder.

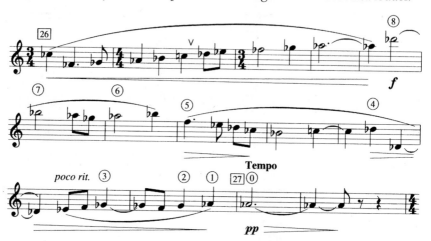

Stepping-stones Example 4. Ibert, Concerto, second movement, between 26 and 27. Reproduced with the kind permission of Alphonse Leduc publisher and owner of the world wide rights—Paris, France

(8) . (7) . . . (6) . . (5) . . . . (4) . . . . . . (3) . . . (2) . (1) . (0): The different stages are unevenly distributed: this must be taken into consideration for our pacing. Although numbers for stepping-stones may seem too materialistic for interpretation, they help keep the impulse of the phrase alive and avoid the premature collapse of the dynamics between (5) and (4). A diminuendo is well perceived when color and dynamics change on notes of the same name (here (3) G♭ – (2) G♭ (less) – (1)A♭ (still barely alive) – (0) (*morendo*). To do this, the longer notes must be kept alive to prevent the stepping-stones from appearing reinforced.

Notes of the same name or reiterated formulas are stepping-stones (see Stepping Stones ex. 5, page 227).

Color and dynamic changes are most effective on identical notes. Only stepping-stone ("skeletal") notes are shown here. In fact, this beautiful solo is made up of seven or eight notes seen under different lights. (See Stepping Stones ex. 6, page 228.)

Once the stepping-stones have been identified, any change of color on them will be well perceived. You can even decide at the last second in what way one note or pattern will differ from the others.

In the Dance of the Blessed Spirits from Gluck's *Orfeo ed Euridice*, the stepping-stones are of two sorts (see Phrasing ex. 12, page 183):

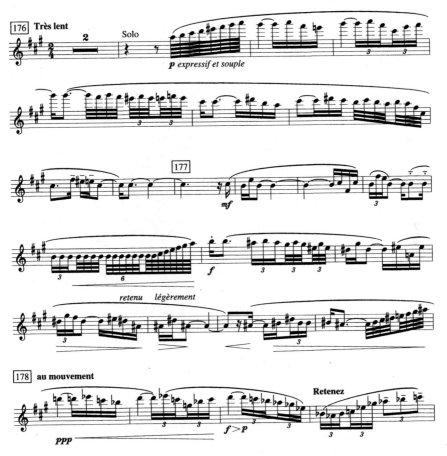

Stepping-stones Example 5. Ravel, *Daphnis et Chloé*, solo. Courtesy of
Editions Durand publisher and holder of copyrights—Paris

- Appoggiaturas indicating harmonic tension and release.
- Anacruses[16] without harmonic tension but whose very repetitiveness and direction emphasize the pleadingly insistent nature of this emotional piece.

In structuring a tempo's increase and decrease, one must recognize their onset and their outcome. To sound natural, they must be held back at first. They actually mean:

- Accelerando = slow or slower in the process of going faster.
- Rallentando = fast or faster in the process of becoming slower.[17]

---

16. A note or group of notes leading to a downbeat.
17. In Italian the suffix *-ndo* indicates the gerundive, so that the word acquires the meaning "in the process of."

Stepping-stones Example 6

Technical Stepping-Stones

I also use stepping-stones to navigate treacherous licks.[18] In fast and tricky passages, the best stepping-stones are the notes with the greatest number of fingers down on the flute: E♭s/D♯s, Ds, and eventually Es.

Stepping-stones Example 7. Beethoven Third Symphony Eroica—
Finale 17 measure after letter B

18. Pianists are very aware of this phenomenon: a black key used as a pivot among white keys will make an ideal stepping-stone.

Empty-handed C♯/D♭s provide the worst stepping-stones, even if they are placed on a rhythmic pattern. When only the left hand is concerned, the best stepping stones are Gs and A♭/G♯.

Rhythm has a lot to do with reliable finger virtuosity. Combined with stepping-stones, it provides rock-solid note security. Often stepping-stones do not coincide with a coherent rhythm. Especially in cadenza mode, there is nothing wrong with adjusting the pattern to your comfort, allowing your instrumental playing to be more efficient without altering the musical text.

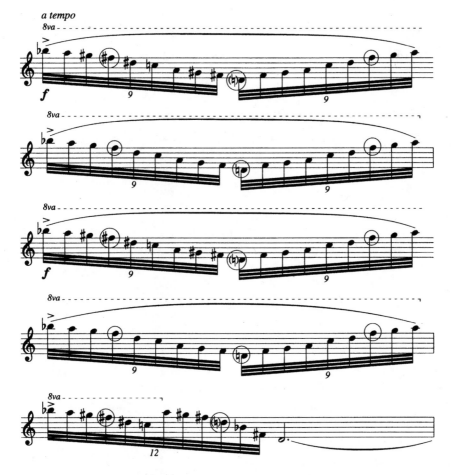

Stepping-stones Example 8. Villa-Lobos, *Bachianas Brasileiras* no. 6, second movement. Music Sales Corporation—New York

Stepping-stones are technical landfalls. They help us to orient our playing and to confirm once more that lowering fingers is more comfortable than lifting them. (Of course, we are not speaking here about slamming the stepping-stone fingers. This would result in a tighter grasp, a greater effort to lift them, and eventually a heavier virtuosity.) Even in a full cadenza or improvisation, discreet stepping-stones must be used. Under stress, things that had never gone wrong suddenly fall apart.

When little devils no. 2 or no. 3 are involved, as in E♭–D or A♭–G, either note of the two is a legitimate stepping-stone. Since these little devils tend to slam-and-squeeze, it is better to use as a stepping-stone the notes that do not implicate the little devil: D and G. This is one more reason, regardless of what most methods say, to use little devil no. 2 as little as possible, and, when doing so, to avoid tightening it. Get rid of little devil no. 2 as soon as possible (except for E and D♯/E♭) and use the other right-hand fingers for balance.

In a nutshell:

Find handfuls of fingers to frame licks. Structuring instrumental difficulties and interpretation are a technical and musical path finding. Use the whole score to track and place your stepping stones. Imagination and logic work miracles.

Please refer also to:

Bridge	Rhythm
Comfort	Score
Little Devils	Slam-and-Squeeze

STRESS

"Be patient with everyone, but above all with yourself."[19]

We must resign ourselves: stress is inherent to performing. The essence of music is conflict between tension and release, between emotion and peace, between time and space, and between joy and sorrow.

The few following thoughts are not intended as a cure for stress; that is a lure. Stress is unavoidable for an artist. It is even necessary, a source of moral achievement and beauty.

---

19. Saint François de Sales.

Let us look at stress as we flutists feel it. What person are we in its presence? How can we live with it?

Take two hypothetical flute friends, Julie and Bob. We know them. We have a pretty good notion of their playing and music making. Julie is a sensitive young lady, never quite satisfied with her qualities, but a poet at heart. Bob, on the other hand, likes to think of himself as a strong player: strong tone, strong fingers. Speeding through music, he conveys confidence and reliability. We have heard them in orchestra, in band or during master classes. One day, they each have to play their senior recital or some important competition. We hear the same Julie and the same Bob. There are a few mistakes, a certain feeling of excitement, but we recognize them. They have not changed. What has changed is their perception of themselves. When they tell us, "I played at 50 percent of my capabilities," it would be cruel for us to tell them that they were the same, or perhaps better.

When it's our turn, we will be the same musician. If one is a born performer, stress improves the performance.

When we tune in on the radio during a flute solo, we recognize the performer, if we have heard him or her before. If not, our verdict is quick. Within seconds, "I like it or I hate it." The younger the listener, the stiffer the sentence. Adoration or rejection. Yet we do not know if the performance was live or edited note by note, or if stress was in the player's soul. But we do know that we are not attracted only by literal perfection.

Making a recording or a CD is not the same as performing, since you know you can do it again. It is an agony of a different sort to decide which take to choose. It is wiser to leave that decision to someone you trust. For example, at the studio you selected takes X, Y, and Z. Three days later the tape sounds completely different to you. Now you like takes B, C, and D. Again, it is your perception that is different.

It is hard not to be judgmental about one's performance. That wrong note at letter F makes us cringe in retrospect. But the audience at large is still listening to the big picture.

One way to deal with stress is to be modest: "I am doing the best I can." When people congratulate you, don't give them a catalog of your shortcomings. Don't think you can ever be perfect; there will always be problems. Think about them after the performance. The only place where there is no excuse for mistakes is the practice room. In performance, the musical message is the issue. It's too late to correct anything.

My own constant worry is not the notes only. It is to be boring.

Come prepared and practiced—that is still the best remedy for stage fright. Hone your basics. The purpose of reliable instrumental playing, among other things, is to reassure us that we can operate well at less than full potential.

Once on stage, do not acknowledge your mistakes with faces and impatient behavior. When you do that, it shows your mind is still at the point of trouble, instead of thinking ahead to avoid the next one.

Tell yourself: "Here I am, about as prepared as I can be at this time. To be sure, unexpected things will be happening. Here is what I can do; I am willing to submit myself to my listeners with humility and simplicity."

When you think back about your faults while playing, you are trying to relive the past. You can learn from the past, but it is gone. The sky above your head is full of billions of wrong notes no one will ever catch up with.

Think ahead. If your mind stays a line back, you are headed for a worse disaster shortly. Lack of concentration is the plague of stress. Humbly and simply, again, play your piece one chunk at a time. If it has been thought out and practiced, you will not lose the sense of the whole, but you will better secure most of the isolated problems.

I applied for the first time to the Paris Conservatoire with the Hüe Fantaisie. I wanted so much to impress that the first two notes, played *ff*, came out like a big explosion (you see, to this day, I am ashamed). The jury could not help but laugh. I did not succeed. Afterward they told me that I ruined my chances not by my cracked opening, but because I thought about it during the whole piece, losing all concentration because of it.

It seems that playing wrong notes is the primary source of stress. Most people do not question their interpretation or their tone. They are very conscious of their literal inaccuracies. "Everyone complains about his luck, and no one complains about his head."[20]

One of the reasons why technical passages that went well without stress suddenly fall apart is a reflex well known to pediatricians and parents of infants: grasping. When we started to walk, Mommy and Daddy were close by, hands outstretched. When balance proved problematic, we grasped the first available finger. The drowning person does the same, grabbing at anything within reach. That ancient reflex affects us when performing under stress: the fingers grasp the instrument.

The natural position of fingers is not raised, but resting on a surface. Put your open hand on a table: you will be comfortable with the fingertips just relaxing on the tabletop. Lifting them requires a small effort.

Imagine the muscular tension necessary to do this while we are actually pressing down or grasping, doing what I call "slam-and-squeeze." I am convinced that this forceful and antagonistic muscle action plays an important part in tendinitis, carpal tunnel syndrome, tennis elbow (epicondylitis), writer's cramp—all these plagues of performing artists. The slam-and-squeeze tension has its source at the fingertips. It moves all the way up the arms to the neck and shoulders. This is where tension ends up, but it is not where it originates for a flutist. Having neck therapy[21] is excellent, but it treats the effect and not the cause.

The solution is to avoid slam-and-squeeze when you work at instrumental playing, without stress.

We need stability to avoid grasping the flute. If the baby is stable and secure,

20. La Rochefoucauld, *Maximes*.
21. Alexander technique, Feldenkrais, and others.

it does not need to hang on. For us, stability can be achieved by securing the flute with the fulcrums, elements that do not create notes:

- The first phalanx of the left forefinger, pushing toward the chest in a horizontal direction, counterbalanced by
- The tip of the right thumb, pushing out and not up.
- The chin, which should be firm.

These three points are the fulcrums of flute playing. We should think of them when stress does not affect us. If stress makes us tense up a little more on the fulcrums, it will not affect us as much as our grasping the note-creating fingers.

The right pinky (little devil no. 2) is a source of great tension if it is pressed tightly. It is weak, and its action is contrary to the movement of the other fingers of the right hand. It should not contribute to stability, in spite of what most fingering charts indicate. It is mandatory for six notes only. It cramps up easily, especially under stress, when it is sometimes impossible to lift.

The necessary stability is provided by the transversal force of both arms (strong muscles) instead of the vertical "slam-and-squeeze" of the fingers (weaker muscles).

Another effect of stress is the imprecision of an embouchure that is constantly in motion, or jawboning. Movements attempted under stress tend to be erratic. If you need a particular position of the lips and the chin for every note you play, stress will make you do too much or too little and your playing will lose some of its reliability at the wrong moment. If your embouchure is stable in general, and you don't constantly move it except for tuning and color, you will not exaggerate or minimize chin and lip movements because of stage fright.

Dry Mouth

What to do when our mouth is dry? Biting our tongue during a rest can help. It is a very personal thing. Citrus juices might induce too much salivation. Drinking ice-cold water just before we play or during a performance might not be such a good idea. Washing the mouth out feels good on the spot, but wiping out natural mucus might actually increase the dryness later on.

My ritual used to be to take a small mouthful of warm milk sweetened with honey. The organic quality of both worked well for my mucus and me, or maybe it was just my head. We all have our rituals about preparing to play. By all means, keep yours. Don't change your normal routine. Avoid irritating foods and drinks but eat normally. An empty stomach is just as bad as stuffing yourself. Nerves affect saliva secretion. A moderate food intake triggers the digestive processes, one of which is salivation.

Brushing your teeth might contribute to stopping saliva flow, depending on the brand of toothpaste. Do what works for you, but oral hygiene, in this case, takes a back seat to performance efficiency and comfort. After all, the matter at hand is not an intimate date.

The foul taste of tap water and of the ghastly chemicals added to it are an offense to the mouth. Sip a little uncarbonated spring water, but use it at room temperature. Ice has a constricting effect. Acidity might help, but soft drinks are also chemical and bubbly.

Preparation

In the days preceding a performance, do not take any special medication (tranquilizers, beta-blockers, and such). But if you are on some kind of treatment, don't interrupt it either.

When we are worried or upset our spoken voice changes: it becomes coarse or forced. At the slightest nervous tension, the throat tightens and squeezes the air column, producing a choked sound. The same phenomenon occurs when we lift our shoulders, in an instinctive defensive gesture or because of poor posture.

Don't try to sleep longer than usual the night before. Insomnia might make you even more anguished. Live normally.

I am not a fanatic of warm-ups. Today's practice will not pay off tonight but six months hence. When somebody is panicked for a concert or cancels a lesson, warm-ups are usually not the reason, but lack of timely preparation is.

We should be striving to use very little actual force in the weak muscles.[22] Strong muscles[23] do need a few movements to loosen up, but that can be done even without flute in hand.

My concern about playing close to performance is twofold. First, it gives you a false sense of security and of duty accomplished. Second, the material, hopefully, should have been thoroughly prepared way ahead of time. Played and played again at the last minute, it could lose some of its freshness and spontaneity. Rediscovering the music on the stage after a few hours' break might not be such a bad idea. Besides, performance events are unpredictable. Prepare yourself mentally for the unexpected instead of rehashing once more. Accidents happen where you least expect them. What crashes in concert is difficult to predict, and in fact the dreaded passages often work better because they have been practiced more.

In spite of all the admonitions above, the prime rule is to do what makes you comfortable. It does not mean that your routine cannot evolve with your experience.

On the day of the concert, go out and see the world. A walk in the woods, the smell of rain, a movie, or a museum—these are all good soul pacifiers. The music is constantly with you anyway, so watching interesting or beautiful things might add input to your interpretation. I try to avoid television; it numbs the mind. But all of this is personal preference. Discover your own.

Be yourself, use what you have learned about the flute, about music, and about

22. Lip, finger and intercostal muscles.
23. Abdominal, thigh, and left arm muscles.

yourself (which all comes to the same thing), don't worry about a wrong note (it's too late), have fun, be emotional and . . . go for it.

If you have a tendency to slam-and-squeeze, stress will only aggravate the problem. Like the drowning person or the teetering infant, you will grab at anything within reach. Unfortunately, it's the flute. But if your normal practice has taught you to balance the instrument with the non-note-producing fulcrums, you probably will increase that stability instead of fighting to lift the slammed note-producing fingers off the keys.

Shaking

Stress can actually make us shake:

- The sound can develop a nasty goat quiver. Knowing one's own vibrato helps control that. If you can, definitely use a conscious vibrato instead of trying to stop the sound from shaking by playing without any tone animation.
- Fingers experience shaking, often in so-called easy passages, long notes, and slow movements. It is usually possible to use a silent key as a rest so that at least one finger of each hand is on the flute.

Short Breath

In my case, shortness of breath is a definite aspect of performance stress. If it is also your problem and if you have the choice, start your recital with something that has some motion instead of supposedly easy long phrases. In your practice, plan for an extra breath instead of going for the world-record apnea. In spite of our temptation to breathe like a whale, a huge breath is hard to control. If the music permits, it is better to take small gasps more often—the fishbowl breath.

When drawing up your program for a recital or an audition, avoid starting with a slow movement, even if you feel it is easier. First play something that has some movement to it and allows for short phrases so that your breaths are easily placed.

Wet Hands

What about wet hands? Quantz[24] advises us to stick our fingers into our powdered wig. The closest we can get to that is using some talcum powder, the same that dries a baby's bum. But experiment with it before the actual need arises.

24. Johann Joachim Quantz, *Essay of a Method for Playing the Transverse Flute, Accompanied by Several Remarks of Service for the Improvement of Good Taste in Practical Music*, trans. and with introduction and notes by Edward R. Reilly (London: Faber and Faber, 1966).

Concentration and Relaxation

One of the goals of practice is to achieve the greatest concentration with total relaxation. Ask an unsuspecting person to relax: the shoulders fall, the hands hang by the side, the body goes into a slouch, the eyes lose their spark, sleep is close at hand. The personality is all but snuffed out. Now tell the same person to concentrate: every muscle tightens, the forehead wrinkles, the neck stiffens, the eyes glow, the body stands at attention. The person is awake and ready for action, but nervous tension threatens to hinder performance.

We cannot relax everything at once. If we did, our instrumental playing would fall apart; the flute would float out of control.

Relaxation, to be productive, must come with concentration. You can relax only after you know what muscles, what actions and thoughts actually hinder your playing. You can fix only what you know does not work. It is a sort of journey toward the inside, a survey of one's physical and nervous capabilities, a selective use of our muscles.

To understand relaxation, first work on something that does not require force or induce stress: slow arpeggios or intervals. At the points of passage, hold down the fingers that do not move, but relieve the pressure on the one(s) that will give you the interval, usually the key closest to the embouchure. Never slam the fingers on the way down: this will make you tenser and will make the lifting of the fingers harder. Lifting is harder than slamming, so concentrate on applying less pressure on the way down and more speed on the way up, while the inactive fingers hold the flute.

Mental concentration helps us to know which areas need stability, so that other obstacles can relax. Feeling your center of gravity brings tension away from the obvious places. We breathe better, blow better, and tire less, because the center of gravity is an inexhaustible source of power and pleasure.

When difficulty arises, nervous tension builds up, causing constriction of the throat, and you try to produce the tone with too much or too little air and to control tone with excessive jaw or lip action. Observe your own process of yawning and its effect upon breathing as well as upon blowing. Concentrate on inducing your own yawning: the ensuing feeling of comfort is the essence of relaxation.

> ### *In a nutshell:*
>
> Practice is the best remedy for stress. The thought process of stress control and relaxation starts with awareness of every aspect of playing. A conscious loosening of the obstacles in the air column (tight throat, unsteady chin, pinched lips) leads to a freer flow of air. Stability of the fulcrums takes the pressure off grasping fingers. Don't warm up too long. Do what makes you comfortable. Before playing, look at beauty: a face, a painting, a film.

> ### *Please refer also to:*
>
> Air column   Posture
> Blowing   Practice
> Breathing   Silent keys
> Center of Gravity   Slam-and-Squeeze
> Fulcrums   Yawning
> Muscles, Strong and Weak

STYLE

Once instrumental playing has received some answers to its problems, once the grammar of phrasing and interpretation has matured, there remains an elusive question: What is style?

Some people's idea of lifestyle is to go for the richest and most ostentatious. The same thing happens in music, in fashion, and in cooking. The more stuff you add, the more the neighbors and the colleagues will be impressed.

Beware of musical editions and improved foodstuffs. It is hard these days to find anything that has not been improved. Improved milk, improved bread, improved soap, improved sugar; and, of course, improved music. Mahler reorchestrated Schumann, and even Beethoven, did he not? Why then cannot editors do likewise with our most cherished repertoire?

How would anyone think of improving a classical painting? Yet some nudes were painted over by order of the church, supposedly to preserve a sick kind of morality.

Everybody claims that simple and fresh food is the best. Yet a fast-food chain advertises its sandwich as having "five meats and three cheeses, everything on it." You get more for your money. But in the process, you lose contact with the essential: the taste of individual content.

On a recent flight, I was served a salad with a small container of dressing. I had always thought that salad dressing was simple, made from basic ingredients according to one's preference, a bit more of this, a bit less of that. This one must have been "improved." The label indicated: "Ingredients: soybean oil, sour cream (cream, milk, locust bean gum, carageenan, enzymes), water, vinegar, eggs, lemon juice from concentrate, egg yolks, cucumbers, corn syrup solids, salt, sugar, herbs and spices, onion, mustard flour, natural flavor,[25] xanthan gum (food fiber), and garlic."

Phew! All that for one ounce (twenty-eight grams) of "Naturally Fresh."

Flute style is sometimes like that: the ingredients are added to the basic mix to

---

25. No mention of what kind.

"improve" it: stuff the low notes here, put in a good buzz there, you must cut through at any cost. As a listener, I do not like the flute to reach my ears with the sound of a trombone. I have nothing against the trombone, may I add, but I prefer the flute to sound like itself, poetic and fragile, instead of this bazooka that some recent mouthpieces are trying to turn it into. Let your flute play its own color. Dark and soft in the low notes, brilliant and lyrical in the third octave, warm and human in the middle range.

The works of the seventeenth and eighteenth centuries, under the very general phrase "baroque music," are an example of how styles can vary. With the best of intentions, J. S. Bach was edited with metronome tempos and dynamics of the romantic era, then performed by full Wagnerian orchestras and huge organs.

Before 1800, performance styles varied from one province to the next. The Hanover A was not the Coethen A. Harpsichord tuning[26] was a personal preference until J. S. Bach laid the groundwork for equal temperament.[27] Some historical organs of the same period are tuned to a very high pitch, some to a very low one.

The Rothenburg flute did not prevail in France or Italy. Hotteterre called his instrument a *flûte allemande*,[28] but it came from La Couture-Bousset, in Normandy. How can anyone claim absolute authenticity? And is it so absolutely desirable?

For my taste, in matters of style, less is more. Don't try to say too much. "Style is a very simple way of saying very complicated things."[29] In musical interpretation, good style is doing as little as possible.

Simplicity is not easy: "For vain and cold souls, complication and difficulty are beauty."[30]

We cannot express what we have not felt. Once we have learned and studied the basic elements of style (rhythm, tempo, and form), analyzed the historic elements (instrument characteristics and pitch) and understood compositional parameters (structure and harmony), we must go back to simplicity. Most of the musicians I admire, conductors, soloists, singers, have a quality of inimitable simplicity. In their care, music becomes evident.

The concert as we know it is a relatively recent historical event. There was a time when the church considered musical instruments pagan and their presence near the altar sacrilegious. Only the voice was holy. Plainchant[31] was not accompanied; in fact, to this day, "a cappella"[32] means without instrumental support. In medieval Europe, the church was the center of popular life: it towered over the

---

26. Sometimes called tablature.

27. Roughly speaking, a tuning system where the octave is divided into twelve semitones.

28. German flute, i.e., transverse flute.

29. Jean Cocteau (1889–1963), poet and playwright.

30. Henri Beyle, alias Stendhal (1783–1842), French writer, in *Le rouge et le noir* (The Red and the Black).

31. An unmeasured unison line of musical support for liturgical text.

32. Literally, "in chapel style."

market place, surrounded by shops, trades, taverns and places of pleasure. Even today, the market is the heart of the European city. Instruments were the realm of the street, never crossing the threshold of the place of worship. On the steps leading to the church, drums, tambourines, and cymbals marked the beat, and instruments, especially winds, carried the tunes. These were essentially dances, slow or fast, whose names described their geographical origin or rhythmic character (siciliano, gavotte, sarabande, polonaise, bourrée, passacaille, rigaudon, etc.). Religious pageants and *chansons de geste*[33] told the stories of saints and heroes. Court music was, meanwhile, the art of the troubadour,[34] who told legends, tales of love, and poems, accompanied by a lute or a harp, among the inner circle of the nobility.

The great artistic upheaval of the Renaissance was bound to break down these barriers. Migrations brought foreign influence, and merchants became rich burghers competing with the lords of the land for the musicians' services. Slowly, the church's austerity gave way to worldly and lavish services, where instrumental music found its place.

This description is, of course, schematic. What it attempts to show is how medieval music evolved into baroque and classical forms and eventually into romanticism and modern concepts of composition. Music cannot be arbitrarily compartmentalized. The rhythms and characters of the last two centuries' music relate to baroque music, which has its roots in medieval sacred singing and dance forms. Even if they have lost their dance names or religious implications along the way to metronome indications, it is vital to know, as a general rule, that phrasing relates to the voice and rhythm to instrumental dance.

The great merit of the baroque revival is more than the pro forma "authenticity" of period instruments. It is the quest for these stylistic roots. For our appreciation of style, we must rely not only on the sacrosanct metronome. In many cases, it is only an indication. More important are the inner character of the pulse and the hierarchy of beats.

Grace Notes

After 1800, roughly speaking, grace notes are consistently indicated and played short. Appoggiaturas are written out.

Things are not quite as clear before 1800. The general rule was that grace notes were to be played on the beat and leaned upon[35] for at least half of the written duration of the note following. Thus, the grace note or appoggiatura should have more emphasis than the resolution.

---

33. Epic and heroic poems of the European Middle Ages that narrated in the form of plays the achievements of historical or legendary characters.
34. Lyrical poet.
35. Appoggiatura, from the Italian *Appoggiare*, "to lean."

However, there were notable exceptions to this as to every rule. These are often ignored today, giving rise to confusion disguised as correctness.

Ornamentation

Many things have been written about baroque ornamentation, so much so that it becomes synonymous with baroque style. As early as 1750, Quantz warned against drowning out the music's structure with excessive ornamentation. He cites as example a movement by Tartini. It is so florid as to be a meaningless succession of scales, frills, and trills obscuring the substance, if there was any.

The fact that Tartini[36] was an "authentic" baroque artist and that he gave de facto "historical performances" does not mean that they should be imitated. In any case, the tree should not hide the forest.

For a detailed description of embellishments (or *agréments*, as ornaments are also called), there are manuals by Geoffroy-Dechaume,[37] Jean-Claude Veilhan,[38] Saint-Aroman, and others, and modern versions of Quantz,[39] Hottetterre, C. P. E. Bach, Couperin, Leopold Mozart, and still others. More complete and "authentic" than I could ever be in this small book, they still differ on many issues.

One of the few bits of common advice they give is the elusive "good taste," *le bon goût*. It is, in fact, what we call style, that combination of refinement devoid of ostentatiousness, of simplicity deprived of arrogance, of sincerity divested of pomposity.

In a nutshell:

Treat music with respect and simplicity. Good style is never emphatic or redundant. Every period has its excesses. Indulgence in pomposity and decoration is a harbinger of decadence.

Please refer also to:

Accents	Hierarchy of Beats
Appoggiatura	Upbeat
Grace Notes	

---

36. Giuseppe Tartini (1692–1770).

37. Antoine Geoffroy-Dechaume, Les "secrets" de la musique ancienne: Recherches sur l'interprétation, XVIe, XVIIe, XVIIIe siècles (Paris: Fasquelle, 1964).

38. Jean-Claude Veilhan, The Rules of Musical Interpretation in the Baroque Era (17th–18th Centuries) Common to All Instruments (Paris: Alphonse Leduc, 1979).

39. Johann Joachim Quantz, Essay of a Method for Playing the Transverse Flute, Accompanied by Several Remarks of Service for the Improvement of Good Taste in Practical Music, trans. with introduction and notes by Edward R. Reilly (London: Faber and Faber, 1966).

TECHNIQUE

"Everyone complains about technique, and no one about musicality."

Technique is like money: it creates problems mostly when you don't have any.

Usually technique implies mere finger speed. When you hear someone say, "Miss X has fantastic technique," you immediately infer that her fingers move very fast but that her music making is altogether a bore. This confusion between technique and superficial velocity is very common. When the comment is, "Mr. Z is very musical," the implication is that he cannot move fast.

My teaching ideas stress instrumental playing as much as if not more than repertoire. I tell my students that before they can revolutionize interpretation, they owe music good instrumental playing. Thinking and studying both simultaneously is even better.

In fact, finger velocity is only one aspect of instrumental playing, a phrase that I use more readily than technique. There are as many techniques as there are facets of flute playing: blowing and breathing techniques, technique of articulation and attacks, tone technique, phrasing technique, even technique of expression. The border is thin: Where does music start? Where does instrumental playing end?

There is no relevant instrumental playing without a musical project.

There is no credible interpretation without reliable instrumental playing.

Instrumental playing's various elements cannot be disconnected: finger practice this morning, staccato next, tone tonight (without vibrato until tomorrow.) Unfortunately, technique is seen as playing all the notes, at any price, as fast as possible, without any other concern.

How can instrumental playing be improved? The basis of the French flute school has always been the simultaneous practice of scales, articulation, and tone equality. From the gospels of flute playing[1] is derived my own Scale Game. Sound, along with intonation, vibrato, and finger smoothness can be worked out together on my intervals, derived in part from *De la sonorité*.[2] Each arpeggio, interval, and scale is only a few seconds long. This timing is deliberate—fifteen seconds of concentration are more profitable than fifteen minutes of senseless repetition. The exercises should be studied easily and comfortably, without stress or nervousness.

Pleasure, Patience, and Perfection should replace Speed, Stress, and Sloppiness.

1. Henry Altès, *Célèbre méthode de flûte*, facsimile ed. by Jean-Pierre Rampal and Alain Marion (Paris: Allo Music, 1977); and Paul Taffanel and Philippe Gaubert, *Dix-sept exercices journaliers de mécanisme de flûte* (Paris: Alphonse Leduc, 1923).

2. Marcel Moyse, *De la sonorité: Art et Technique* (Paris: Alphonse Leduc, 1931).

Scale Game

Speed will eventually come, but first I demand clean attacks, a beautiful tone at all tempos, no breaks in the slurring or cracks in the staccato, stability of the embouchure on the chin, a wide range of dynamics, and more.

The modulating bridge between keys, like everything else, should be musical—always very slow, legato, and phrased so that timbre is controlled and modulating notes are in tune.

Reichert

Play arpeggios in all keys.[3] Again, speed in not the first consideration. Rather, play legato (slurred) slowly, take time on the harmonic tensions, and always refer intonation to tonality.

I don't like to assign "finger-twisters" in long repetitious series. They are the opposite of comfort, and they contribute to stress and frustration in practice. One must be a saint or a masochist to persist day after day on painful and tedious exercises. I am neither.

Often one hears the matter-of-fact statement, "So-and-so is a natural," or "So-and-so sings or plays naturally." It might be natural to sing in the shower or blow into a noisy toy, but there is nothing more unnatural than singing opera or playing an instrument. It is the fruit of mature thought and experience. The greatest compliment, for a musician, is about the apparent ease and simplicity of his performance. Artists know they are the result of polished and sophisticated instrumental playing.

In a nutshell:

Technique is more than finger speed. It is the domination of every aspect of instrumental playing. Slow pieces need fingers as much as difficult passages require tone control. Play simple patterns, but play them perfectly.

Please refer also to:

Articulation	Intonation, Intonations
Instrumental Playing	Practicing
Intervals	Scale Game

---

3. Mathieu-André Reichert (1830–c.1875), *Sept exercices journaliers* (Mainz: Schott,), no. 2 and no. 4.

TEMPO

Are you sometimes uncomfortable listening or playing, without being able to define why? Often it is because the pulse of the music, the tempo, does not feel right. Tempo, like politics, has its ideologues and its terrorists. Verdicts and victims fall upon the altars of Truth and Beauty as decreed by a few.

In ensemble playing, some (conductors as well as musicians) are inflexible. The wisest are those who know how to convince, or how to bend, or both. "If you can't lick 'em, join 'em!" An imposed tempo may work, but what pleasure, what swing when it is lived with together!

A good conductor or group leader feels the general response, the instrumental mass, and the acoustics. He should deal with the tempo accordingly, without putting a number on it once and for all. When one is a participant in a group, one must strive to accommodate the general pulse even if it does not feel right. In the last resort, "the boss is always right."

I do not think there is only one valid tempo marking. The tempo corresponds to a number of parameters, of which adrenalin and a fast heartbeat are not the least.

Don't hide behind the umbrella of a metronome marking. Take it for what it is: an indication, an idea. I have worked enough with great composers (Poulenc, Rivier, Ibert, Messiaen, Jolivet, and Boulez, among others) to know that they never conduct or play their works at the fixed tempi they wrote themselves. And these are alive or were until recently. So don't let yourselves be imposed upon for the tempi of the past masters! Don't take editions for granted. They are respectable as a good player's opinion, but not as the gospel. Use your own judgment. Use your head. Use your heart and your heartbeat.

Before setting up your beloved metronome, look at the music, and consider the character of the piece (allegro, andante, andantino, etc.) more than the metronome indication: is it rigorous, light, austere, proud, martial, tender, stark, ornate, sensuous, serene, passionate, religious, farcical, idyllic, ironic, or what?

"Speed is an objective element, tempo a subjective notion; tempo is not equivalent to speed."[4] Most of the following explanations will use examples taken from Mozart, because Mozart is forever relevant and actual.

In a letter to his father, Mozart speaks of playing in time ("auf dem Takt") as the first order of priority. From there can be achieved "the most important, the hardest, and the main thing in music . . . , namely the tempo" (das notwendigste und härteste und die Hauptsache in der Musik . . . , nämlich das Tempo).[5] "It is the interpreter's first responsibility to establish an order strict enough that all the liberties he will take in its framework will be felt by the listener as manifestations of the very essence of the musical art, the transmutation into sounds of all which in life is spontaneous, unrational, unpredictable."[6]

4. Jean-Pierre Marty, *The Tempo Indications of Mozart* (New-Haven: Yale University Press, 1988).
5. Mozart, letter dated Augsburg, October 24, 1777, quoted in Marty.
6. Marty.

When a passage (or a movement) feels awkward, the right tempo might be found by changing the basic pulse.[7] Sometimes this common denominator might seem far from the apparent character of the piece. This is, however, just an experimental procedure.

A clue to the character is sometimes given by the composer's qualifications, say, of an adagio or allegro, for instance: Mozart, K. 313, *maestoso* (solemn), *ma non troppo* (but not too much), *K 314, aperto* (open); and so on.

The first approach to a work should, therefore, be to understand the meaning of these markings before jumping to the metronome. Most common locutions are in Italian. Sometimes they are in German, but they are seldom in French.[8] The next step is to figure out the spirit of the pulse. Do not always assess it on the basis of the opening solo. The metronome marking is sometimes misleading. Try to find the structure and the rhythmic pulse of a passage without worrying about the written measure. In other words, in a fast movement in 4/4, think of the music in 2/2, with a slow and flexible half note, then in 8/8, with bouncing and crisp eighth notes:

Tempo Example 1. Mozart, Concerto in D Major, K. 314, first movement

A tempo that comfortably accommodates this passage has a good chance of feeling right, for you at least, from the top. It is already very important. You will eventually have to yield to the tyranny of a metronome marking or to a beat imposed by someone else, usually a conductor. Unfortunately, you will have to follow him as a last resort. When we are playing under someone's lead, our *raison d'être* is to be able to follow that beat without afterthoughts.

Sometimes, a 2/4 felt in one beat per measure will fly better:

7. From C to 2/2, from 4/4 to 12/16, etc.
8. A helpful tool is the *Pocket Dictionary of Musical Terms* (New York: Schirmer, 1905).

Tempo Example 2. Mozart, Concerto in D Major, K. 314, third movement

The comical character and pulse come from the fact that if there is any rhythmic emphasis, it comes in the middle of the measure, as if suspended in midair, not on the downbeat. Compare it to the aria "Welche Wonne, welche Lust," from *Abduction from the Seraglio*.

Tempo Example 3. Mozart, *Abduction from the Seraglio*

Likewise for the Rondeau in Mozart's Flute Quartet, K. 298:

Mozart indicates playfully: "Allegretto grazioso, mà non troppo presto, però non troppo adagio. Così-così con molto garbo ed espressione" (Graceful allegretto but not too fast, however not too slow. Just so-so with a lot of charm and expression). Try to put a metronome marking on that!

In slow movements in 3/4, for instance, think a steady sixteenth-note pulse and then a quarter or an eighth note:

This tranquil flow of time should bring us closer to the right tempo. The sign of a good tempo is our pleasure and our comfort.

RONDEAU

Allegretto grazioso,

Mà non troppo presto, però non troppo adagio.
Così-così - con molto garbo ed espressione.

Tempo Example 4

Tempo Example 5. Mozart Concerto in D Major, K. 314, second movement *Andante*

Tempo Example 6. Mozart Quartet in D Major, K. 285, second movement

When thirty-second notes are present, they must flow without too much emphasis, so that the other values (sixteenths, eighths, and quarters) do not lose direction. Imitate the pulse of the accompaniment.

Often the "good tempo" is found upon the first reading of a piece, or upon returning to a familiar work months after setting it aside. Old friends and well-worn clothes feel like that also. It is because candor is intact. The natural measure finds its pulse spontaneously. Yet once study is undertaken again, tempo comfort is not felt as well. Once again we must try to find a flow of the tempo other than the literal measure.

"One never really learns anything until one can forget it."[9] Repertoire should be studied a long time ahead, so that we can forget it a little and then discover it again.

How can we find or build a tempo when we are the one responsible?

In a fast movement, the maximum speed is one that can integrate the fastest flurries of notes. One cannot shift down, as with a gearbox, just to make things easier.

This is the purpose of concerto scales in the Debost Scale Game.

In a largo or an adagio, where breath is one of the prevailing problems, tempo will be the difference between success and failure. Slower does not mean more expressive, any more than faster is a proof of virtuosity. Speed is not in itself a determining element of interpretation, since obviously different people have different tastes and response. That is one of the reasons why I am generally opposed to basing everything on the metronome.

In everything we play, we think about the beginning as emblematic of the whole piece. Yet it does not always give us a tempo that feels right. There is always a passage, however insignificant it might be, that feels good and fits all the other musical ideas.

Dance forms of the baroque period and before do not carry specific tempo markings, for the excellent reason that the metronome had not yet been invented. But the tempo was implicit from tradition and from the very steps of each dance. The name of the dance (menuetto, bourrée, gavotte, etc.) corresponded to precise dance steps (that were sometimes put into law by monarchy).[10] There was a small window of tempo that could accommodate them. A slow, pompous minuet or a subdivided sicilienne was just as inappropriate as a funny funeral march or a jumpy pavane.

Most of the classic and romantic instrumental music for orchestral and chamber ensembles derives from these dance forms, without actually naming them. Their study helps greatly to find our own tempo.

9. John Krell, *Kincaidiana: A Flute Player's Notebook* (Culver City, Calif.: Trio Publications, 1973).

10. The Paris Opéra, formerly Théâtre Royal, still has detailed instructions for the minuet bearing the royal seal of Louis XIV: "Dance as I say, or else!" Today it would be "Play my metronome tempo, or else!"

```
┌─────────────────────────────────────────────┐
│                                               │
│              In a nutshell:                   │
│                                               │
│  Tempo is a reflection of the character of    │
│  music. Find the tempo of a piece not only    │
│  with a metronome, but by working from a      │
│  passage whose beat flows naturally and       │
│  accommodates all the musical elements,       │
│  fast and slow.                               │
│                                               │
│            Please refer also to:              │
│                                               │
│      Character         Languages              │
│      Comfort           Metronome              │
│      Hierarchy of Beats  Rhythm               │
│                                               │
└─────────────────────────────────────────────┘
```

TONGUING

There is almost a holy war over showing the tip of the tongue. Some say never, never. Others say ever, ever.

According to learned opinions, French tonguing is faster (better?) because the language is dryer and more glib than English. There might be some truth to that. The best tonguing comes to those who practice. There is no gimmick. If your work is productive and satisfactory, who cares if you put your tongue between your lips or in your backpack?

Nevertheless, a few logical points must be addressed:

- Cracking notes. Why does it happen?
- Tone quality. Tonguing, whatever the speed, is a brief interruption of tone.
- Dynamics. Tonguing should have no effect on loudness.
- Tempo. Tonguing must not alter the tempo.
- Variety. There is no single tonguing for everything.

Tonguing covers many distinct actions: the onset of the tone (attack), and single, composite single, double, triple, and composite triple tonguing.

Confusion often exists between the onset of the sound (attack) and the action of the tongue in repeated staccato.[11] First, a simple principle: air hitting the breaking edge of the embouchure hole creates turbulence, which is the physical source of the flute sound. Second, air has a natural tendency to scatter as soon as it is not channeled. And third, focus is the best angle of attack, neither too tight nor too open.

For these reasons, the breaking edge must[12] receive a narrow air brush that will

11. "Staccato" means detached or untied, as opposed to "legato," meaning tied or slurred.
12. Except for special effects.

disperse the smallest possible volume of air at the optimal pressure. Too much volume will create an unfocused, breathy sound,[13] an excessive expenditure of air, and fuzzy tonguing. Too much air pressure will produce a thin, pinched, hissing sound[14] and explosive attacks at the octave or beyond.

At the onset of long notes or at the initial note of a slurred passage, the tongue does not act as percussion. It works as a valve that stops the air until it is pulled back. Its movement is from front to back, not as a hammer from the back to the teeth or lips. On delicate attacks, pressure is built up behind the tongue, and release of the airflow starts with the nose so there is no explosion. This is sometimes called "French tonguing." It is the source of misunderstanding. If the tip of the tongue does not show, then it is back in the mouth, and the air brush is not stopped. The air must then be held back instead of flowing slightly through the nose, just as a violin bow would be in motion just before touching the string.

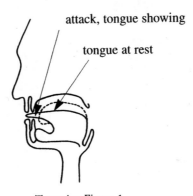

attack, tongue showing

tongue at rest

Tonguing Figure 1

For staccato (repeated tonguing), however, the action of the tongue is not the same. It would be ridiculous for the tongue to show on every backward and forward movement, traveling a great distance from the mouth cavity to the outside of the lips. This is not what "French" tonguing is about.

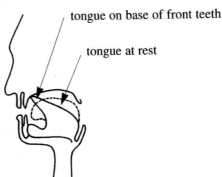

tongue on base of front teeth

tongue at rest

Tonguing Figure 2

13. "Turbo-sound."
14. "Gas-leak sound."

It must be remembered that loud staccato does not require more movement than soft. The tone is loud or soft, but the tongue movements are about the same for all dynamics. Only a psychological ambiguity equates soft tongue movement with playing *p*. Quite the contrary: when the note is short, less time is spent on it, and therefore it is perceived as softer. Strangely, tonguing works better when we are almost out of breath because we have to support more to compensate.

We must not forget also that the sound is interrupted at each note. Dynamics are brought down to the lower level: *f* becomes *mf*, *p* falls to *pp*. We must judge by what we hear, not by what we think we're doing.

Single Tonguing

In single tonguing, we must make sure that all the notes have the same quality as the attack. Try to avoid holes between notes, and even though they are staccato, think of the continuity of the sound. Practice Scale Game no. 4 in single tonguing, making sure than no note is broken. It does not have to be fast, but each note must be perfectly emitted. You can have in mind a work with single tonguing that you are working on at that time.

From the moment the tempo becomes too fast for comfort in single tonguing, you should be able to switch to double or composite tonguing without anybody (not even yourself) noticing. It's nobody's business what happens inside your mouth.

Tummy Tonguing

Support is vital. Practice it with air impulses but without the tongue, as in Scale Game no. 5. Of course, it is not really tonguing, but it helps you to feel how the abdominal muscles work in the production of single tonguing.

Double Tonguing

The previous remarks apply to double tonguing as well: the position of the tongue is the same for the *ti* part. For the *ki* or *gui*, you should use the syllable that brings the tongue closest to the front teeth. It is logical to assume that the shorter the distance traveled by the tongue, the less the dispersion of air and the greater the reliability of the result. The choice of *gui* or *ki* is each flutist's preference according to mouth cavity, tooth shape, and taste. But there is no gimmick: tonguing must be practiced patiently on the Scale Game (no. 8, no. 9, no. 12, etc.).

At first, one must not seek speed but above all clarity. Breaths, very defined, should be placed after the upper tonic, after the lower tonic (preceding the modulating link), and after the arrival note (first note of the following scale).

The weak part of double tonguing (the *ki* in *tikitiki*) can be practiced by playing a scale using only the *ki*, as in Scale Game no. 9.

Once you are ready to increase the speed of tonguing, practice the scales in short bursts separated by rests, as in Scale Game no. 26 and no. 28.

Doubling (Repeating Each Note)

This is the most effective way to place one's double tonguing. Practice on Scale Game no. 12 and no. 42. First the rhythm must be physically established.[15] It will provide the common denominator for tongue and fingers.

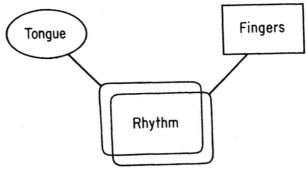

Tonguing Figure 3

Be careful to avoid emphasizing notes "in slices of two." Insert once in a while one measure in single tonguing to recall the even succession of attacks. (This recommendation actually applies to the different modes of execution of the scales.) Tempo must be felt every four notes, that is, eight times per bar. Since speed is not required, breathings are left up to the possibilities of the subject; the second of the two notes can be omitted to breathe.

Tripling (Three Times on the Same Note)

The same remarks apply as for doubling. Practice Scale Game no. 13 and no. 43.

Composite Tonguing

One form of composite tonguing consists of using different syllables in a running flow of staccato.

15. For example, by bouncing on tiptoe or relating to a march tempo. The metronome is often advised here. I think that rhythm comes from within, as a living thing, not through a machine.

Baroque composite tonguing seems out of fashion today. It was in current use in the old treatises, Quantz[16] and Hotteterre,[17] and it is among the first lessons in the Altès *Méthode*.[18]

Tonguing Example 1. Altès, *Methode, tidi tidi*

It is a very simple procedure, consisting of using two or more different syllables to articulate, even if the tempo does not require fast tonguing. The rhythmic placement comes naturally. Do you remember skipping when you were a child? Well, composite tonguing has some of that: you find your natural rhythm, one foot (syllable) doing the short rhythm, the other the long.

Tonguing Example 2. Mozart, Concerto in G Major, K. 313, first movement, *ti ti tidi*

Tonguing Example 3. Stamitz, Concerto in G Major, op. 29, first movement

Tonguing Example 4. Sonata in E Minor, BWV 1034,
second movement, *tigidi tigidi*

16. Johann Joachim Quantz, *Versuch einer Anweisung die Flöte traversiere zu spielen; mit verschiedenen, zur Beförderung des guten Geschmackes im der praktischen Musik dienlichen Anmerkungen begleitet, und mit Exempeln erläutert* (Berlin: Johann Friedrich Voss, 1752).

17. Jacques Hotteterre dit Le Romain, *L'Art de préluder sur la flûte allemande et autres instruments (The Art of Prelude on the transverse flute and other instruments)* (Paris, 1719).

18. Henry Altès, *Célèbre méthode de flûte* (Paris: Alphonse Leduc and Paris: Allo Music, 1977).

Tonguing Example 5.   J. S. Bach Suite no. 2 in B Minor, last movement

Tonguing Example 6.   Prokofiev, Sonata in D Major, op. 94, first movement, after double bar, *titigidi titigidi*

Flutter Tonguing

What is flutter tonguing? A very rapid repetition of the same note, creating a tremolo effect. It is perceived by the listener as a shivering sound, regardless of the way it is produced, whether from the actual tongue or from another area, such as the throat. There are people who do this effect without thinking about it, whereas most do not produce it easily.

There are as many names for flutter tonguing as there are musical languages: *Flatterzung* (German), *frullato* (Italian; literally, whipped), and *tremolo dental* or *tremolo guttural* (French). The French terms imply that there are two kinds of tremolo: one with the tongue fluttering just behind the teeth, the other produced somewhere further back in the throat area (soft palate) and uvula, that little hanging piece of flesh that always seems to be flapping in the wind.

To be honest, I don't use flutter tonguing per se. I am one of those people who have had to find an alternate way to flutter tongue: if I do it by rolling my tongue, I get a very weak sound. I also lose it totally when I try to go below low G. I am not sure that flutter tongue can be taught. Personal experiments will probably be just as good as my suggestions.

Coming back to national tongues, many languages have a natural guttural consonant: The German *ch* (*Bach*, *leicht*), the Spanish *jota* (*jóven*, *navaja*), the Russian *kh* (*Tchekhov*, *Khatchaturian*), the Hebrew *kh* (*khalil*[19]), the Arabic *kh* (*khalifa*), and so on. The ability to pronounce and produce these sounds helped me for flutter tongue. That is where I started.

19. Meaning "flute"!

French is a mostly dental language, but it uses a semi-guttural r (*Paris*, *rue*) that is quite useful, although not so much so as the previous examples. Unfortunately, English does not use the throat sound. As far as I know, English speakers need to have a working knowledge of the guttural consonant to find an alternative for flutter tongue. Worst of all, the Japanese have trouble distinguishing between Rs and Ls. Where else would you hear, "Jean-Piel Lampar was a glate fruit prayer?"

Whereas the "real" flutter tongue is an added action of the tongue to a normal flute sound, the throat version requires more air, as if one were trying to clear one's throat to get rid of something stuck in it. The same applies to harmonics and double (sometimes triple) notes commonly required in music of the twentieth century. The issue here is to produce not a fine sound, but a deliberately different or even ugly one. The notes are basically failed ones that are kept going by a lot of air speed and little focus. Because of this increased quantity of spent air, throat flutter cannot be sustained for very long and it must be supported and accelerated by the abdominal belt.

The simplest exercise I know is to try to master this technique is to emulate gargling. When I had a sore throat, as a child, I was given medicine (usually foul tasting) that I had to gargle, tilting my head back slightly. To avoid swallowing it, I had to produce a kind of grumble in my vocal cords. It had to be supported by air, like speaking with the voice.

After gargling with a liquid, try to do it with a dry throat but still uttering and sustaining a vocal noise like "aarrr" or "aach." When you are comfortable with that, try producing the same effect without the vocal cords. The flute sound should be relatively efficient because the inside of the mouth is not affected as when the tongue flaps about in there.

Throat flutter has definite qualities. In my case, at least, it will work equally throughout the range of the flute, even in the low notes. I can use more dynamics, even playing softly. I can even slow it down. It works also with the alto flute in G, a problem with real flutter tonguing.

Since every flutist and every language have their own peculiarities, there might be other ways. But don't get bogged down with the words flutter tongue. If you can produce the effect by different means, by all means try it!

In a nutshell:

The tongue does not produce sound. It shapes articulation just as a valve closes or vents a fluid. Practice your tonguing on scales with many syllables. Adapt it to the music you are playing.

> ### Please refer also to:
>
> | | |
> |---|---|
> | Articulation | Scale Game |
> | Attacks | Dynamics |
> | Low Register | |

TRILLS

Even when a trill is performed with one finger, there are still three problems: how to make it smooth, how to start it, and how to terminate it.

One clue for smoothing the trill itself is to focus one's energy not on the shaking finger, but on the stability of the flute. If force is used in the trilling finger, that is, if it comes down hard on the instrument, it is all the more difficult to lift it. This slows the trill and makes it bumpy.

How can this be helped? Since the trill is performed by one hand, it is the non-trilling hand that should provide stability:

- If you are playing a trill with a finger of the right hand, the left can anchor the stability without risk through some energy applied by the first joint of the left index against the embouchure plate and all of the left fingers resting on the flute.
- When the left hand is the triller, it might seem more difficult to stabilize with the right, which is mostly off the flute. One solution is to use one right finger in a "silent" position, that is, on a non–tone producing key. The B♭ lever helps to stabilize for G–A, G♯–A, or D–E♭ trills. Using the right ring finger as a "silent" balance for A–B or B–C trills helps release the tension in the trilling finger.
- Lever trills such as G–A♭, D–E♭, and C♯–D are activated by the left or right pinky, both notoriously weak little devils. My suggestion is to stabilize the flute with the stationary fingers while working the pinky as far away from the rod as possible, because, the lever being longer, its action is softer and smoother. The last thing you want to do is cramp up on the moving finger.

The start of a trill is a matter of style. Roughly speaking, music composed before 1800 almost always requires that the upper note start the trills. When this is indicated by a grace note, it is often an appoggiatura, meaning that it is leaned upon with more or less insistence to create harmonic tension and expression. Personal taste plays an important part here. There are exceptions to this rule, since, obviously, styles are not unified by decree. Trills belong to the family of ornaments, or *agréments* in French, which implies that they must not interfere with the line or phrase and become an entity unto themselves. Granted, this is a bit vague, but François Couperin-le-Grand,[20] the king's composer in the first half of the eighteenth century, indicates that ornaments should follow *le bon goût*—good taste, whatever that is. Johann Joachim Quantz[21] gives an example by Tartini of how not to ornament: a deluge of runs and trills drowning out a simple melody. However, to each his own bad taste. Herr Professor Quantz was a serious Prussian, rigorous even in ornamentation. At the conclusion of most baroque episodes, a cadential trill (started from the upper note) is implied, even if it is not indicated.

I do not require trills to be metered in practice. Rather, they should be free flying, in the manner described above, while the non-trilling fingers provide static balance. Metered or free, be careful to stay close to the keys and to avoid slam-and-squeeze.

Even if the trill is free, it is a good idea to count its duration, so that its termination is neither early nor hesitant. Actually, this counting is necessary. Because of nerves during performance, we have a tendency to shorten their duration. Besides, it is almost as difficult to stop a trill as to keep from cramping on it. Therefore, it is best to let a trill run almost on its own without stopping it, but counting it. The first note of the termination very naturally interrupts the movement of the trilling finger. Sometimes the terminations are written out. In classical concertos such as those by Mozart, the terminations of cadential trills, indicated by grace notes, can be played at the latest possible moment, almost on the following beat.

In a nutshell:

Trills are ornaments. They must not be more important than the main musical discourse. Loosen the trilling finger and balance with the fulcrums and the silent keys.

Please refer also to:

Appoggiatura	Silent Keys
Fulcrums	Stability
Hands	

TUNING

This vital activity is often a pretense even in major orchestras. First, a few sobering principles: There is no such thing as an in-tune flute. The last fashionable instrument, the X schema, the Z scale, are at best a workable approximation of

---

20. 1668–1733; in the foreword to *Concerts Royaux* (Paris: Editions Musicales Transatlantiques, 1963).

21. Quantz.

perfect tuning that actually does not exist. Nobody holds the final truth. There are also fanatics in this respect.

Beware of the usual excuses: "I have not played yet (or I have played too much)"; or: "It's too cold (or too hot)." You might get the obvious answer: "It's your ears that are cold." It is not always "the others' fault," nor always your own.

So what can be done? Generally, knowing yourself, be ready to adapt, and never think that you are right compared to everyone else.

Find an instrument whose sound you love, then take other points into consideration:

- It must be built to the prevailing pitch of your musical environment.[22]
- The relationship between the notes should be reasonably balanced. Some flutes whose low notes have been raised play C#2 and D2 uncontrollably sharp.
- The tone hole placement on the tube always results from a compromise, so tuning must take into consideration the characteristic of each instrument.
- Know your playing tendencies—which notes you tend to play sharp or flat under varying dynamics.
- Some instruments tune sharp and play flat, and vice versa. The simple act of matching one pitch is no guarantee.

"Know thyself," says the moralist . . . and know thy flute.

Cold air is also heavier than our lung air. That is why we warm our flutes in a cold environment. Hot air, of which we are full, is lighter and helps to raise the pitch. This has more influence on intonation than the length of the tube.

The length of the tube is important, of course, and pulling out or pushing in the head joint helps. However, the ambient temperature inside the tube affects the height of the pitch, because cold air is denser than hot, resulting in a flatter pitch.

Fatigue or stress make some play sharper because of nerves, and some flatter because of less support.

Often, when the "tuning A" is in tune, the A above the staff is flat.

Here are some practical suggestions:

- For the actual tuning with the oboe or piano, in general, listen to the note before matching it by playing with the pitch giver. As soon as you play, you do hear some beats, but your tone hides the reference tone. Listen first.
- Tune *mf* and *p* on A1 and its octave, then on D2 and D1.
- Also check C# (above the staff) *f* and *pp*. This note's pitch can go sharp and flat in short order.
- Since you are going to use vibrato in actual playing, use a moderate vibrato for tuning. I know that some people advise against this. My rationale is that vibrato, which is a modulation in the pitch, affects our sound in different ways. A straight tone will feel flat and lifeless, resulting in a sharper tuning. Some players' vibrato may dip more than rise above the reference pitch, and vice versa. Our individual tone has its own center. A well-focused tone always sounds more in tune. Sometimes we perceive ourselves as playing

22. In the United States and Canada, A = 440–442 cycles per second; in France, Italy, and Switzerland, A = 442–444; in Germany, A = 444–448; and in the United Kingdom, A = 438–440.

sharp or flat because our tone's center has a brighter or darker timbre, which affects our compatibility with other instruments in actual playing.

- In the course of music making, verify your tuning as often as possible by comparison.
- The influence of dynamics cannot be ignored. Everyone knows that *f* will raise the pitch and *p* will pull it lower, which does not always work the same way with oboes, clarinets, and bassoons, your immediate neighbors. Learn how to keep up your air speed in *p* and to lower your center of gravity in *f*. It takes more energy to play soft than loud. So if you must jut your chin, it should not be to play louder, but to keep the pitch from dropping on soft notes and releases. When you play loud, lower your shoulders and your jaw while opening the throat, and let the flute play out.

In a nutshell:

Tuning is a constant quest. Taking an A on a tuner is not enough. Never feel you are always right, or always wrong. Parameters of tuning: temperature, range, the musical environment, and you.

Please refer also to:

Air speed	Dynamics
Acoustics	
Angle of Attack	Intonation, Intonations

UNUSUAL TRILL FINGERINGS

All trills are assumed to be slurred. Only fingered keys are shown. The first note is the basic fingering. Arrows show the trilling finger(s).

  darker, softer

Unusual trills Figure 1

  starting on E♭

Unusual trills Figure 2

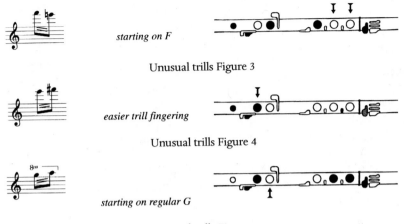

starting on F

Unusual trills Figure 3

easier trill fingering

Unusual trills Figure 4

starting on regular G

Unusual trills Figure 5

Note: This trill fingering does not work without the D♯/E♭ key.

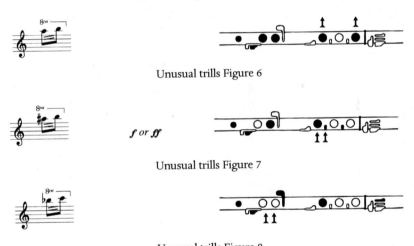

Unusual trills Figure 6

f or ff

Unusual trills Figure 7

Unusual trills Figure 8

VIBRATO

What Is Vibrato?

There are many theories. Extensive measurements[1] show that the diaphragm has no role in vibrato. Since you cannot produce vibrato with your lips or your chin, its mechanism must initiate somewhere in the throat area. This not mean that it needs to be of the nanny goat variety, very fast and very narrow. In fact, it is safe to say that vibrato is a modulation in the pitch of the flute tone, making it rise and fall in a more or less controlled fashion.

String players do the same thing more visibly. But it confirms the fact that vibrato is not spontaneous. String players show us it is a oscillation of the finger tips on the fingerboard.

What Is Good Vibrato?

I think that vibrato is wrong when it is the first thing I notice in someone's playing or singing. I often say that vibrato must be "inside the tone." Figuratively, let us symbolize the tone as parallel lines:

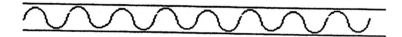

Vibrato Figure 1. Tone without vibrato

Vibrato should be "inside the tone." It gives more density, economy, and intensity to the tone, whatever the dynamics.

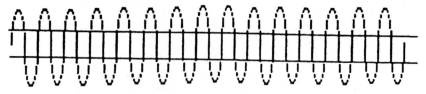

Vibrato Figure 2. Tone with "inside" vibrato

Vibrato should not go "out of the tone," whatever its speed:

Vibrato Figure 3. Tone with excessive vibrato

1. Jochen Gärtner, *The Vibrato, with Particular Consideration as Given to the Situation of the Flutist: Historical Development, New Physiological Discoveries, and Presentation of an Integrated Method of Instruction* (Regensburg: Gustav Verlag, 1981).

All the curves "out of the tone" are heard as parasitic air noises, and indeed they are wasted air and energy.

However, when the vibrato is "inside the tone" but too slow, its undulation has a "wa-wa" effect.

Vibrato Figure 4. Tone with "wa-wa" vibrato

How Can Vibrato Be Practiced?

Most of the time, vibrato is a natural expression of someone's personality, like one's tone of voice, and should not be tampered with, just controlled.

But when it is absent or out of control, then it must be started artificially by practicing a sort of humming *mf* on easy notes, middle D or middle G (hmm . . . hmm . . . hmm . . . etc.) in an eighth-note rhythm, *a tempo giusto.*

In practice, vibrato should be used and experimented with in tone exercises such as Intervals. I know of few things as boring and unpleasant as long tones without vibrato. And a turn-off is never a good pedagogic tool. If you are going to play with vibrato, then practice with vibrato.

In an interval, vibrate the slur more than the head of the notes. If a slurred interval is wider than a fourth or a fifth, especially, the first note needs to be nourished just before fingering the second note. This way, the interval needs little or no lipping, but it does need air speed and vibrato to pass smoothly.

Tuning with or without Vibrato?

I know that many people recommend tuning without vibrato. I think that since most music will be played with vibrato, one should tune with it. A excessively fast vibrato will make the tone seem sharp, while one with no vibrato seems flat. Tune with a tone you will use. And give your electronic tuner a rest.

When to Use Vibrato?

One of the purposes of vibrato is to animate the tone, to help carry it through a phrase or toward silence. It helps sensitive legato playing.[2] In soft dynamics (*pp* or *ppp*) the tone has less natural energy. Vibrato will keep the sound alive and carry energy through the intervals within a phrase. It also helps to taper into silence, the hidden face of music. Our natural reflex when playing *pp* or *ppp* is often to stop animating the tone with vibrato, destroying the link between notes and the approaches of harmonic and melodic tension. In *f* or *ff* playing, vibrato

---

2. Legato, let us not forget, is not some kind of mushy semi-tonguing; it means "tied" in Italian, i.e., slurred.

comes naturally, often almost too much. Control it then. It is always more difficult and tiring to play soft than loud.

Vibrato should almost always be used and have the direction of the phrase. For
instance, long notes should not systematically drop off or start without vibrato,
like the D in this excerpt.

Vibrato Example 1. Ibert, Concerto, second movement Adagio

Don't use vibrato only on long notes. In slow movements, it will help shape
passing notes and connect them. On the other hand, in a fast *f* passage, vibrato
will help you avoid rushing by filling out the runs.

Vibrato Example 2. J. S. Bach, Sonata in E Minor,
BWV 1034, last movement, measures 30–31

When to Use Less or No Vibrato

When you are playing loud, the natural tendency for the vibrato is to be bigger
too. But an uncontrolled vibrato can actually waste the energy of a large sound.
It can become obnoxious and increase the tendency to go sharp or to sound
forced. So we must moderate our vibrato in strong dynamics to keep maximum
projection without sounding shrill.

Vibrato Example 3. Brahms, Symphony no. 1, Finale

Use less or no vibrato when harmonic and melodic tension are building toward
a phrasing accent, indicated, for instance, by a leading tone (circles on measures

10 and 12) or a wide dissonant interval from a diminished seventh chord built on a leading tone (circle on measure 14). These tension points (circled) would be weakened by excessive vibrato up to the accent. Thereafter, vibrato is welcome like sunshine after a passing cloud. Vibrato should be present on the release of harmonic tension, but not always on its build-up. It acts like the compression of a coil spring. Energy is stored during build-up and is let go upon release, where it oscillates, giving an image of vibrato. In other instances, the sign > is an indication that one note should be highlighted, if for only a fleeting moment. Vibrato will convey that flash of color, giving it a slightly longer duration and the fugitive impression of life.

Vibrato Example 4. Mozart, Quartet in D Major, K. 285, second movement

The release of a long high note poses at least three problems: intonation, breath management, and the risk of falling to a lower level for lack of support. Such is the case for the last note at the end of Enesco's Cantabile, a long high G held *pp* for two measures. Vibrato is going to help us in this endeavor. It will keep the sound alive while we use *Tenuto, Sostenuto, Ritenuto*. Air speed combined with vibrato will sustain the intonation. At the very end of the taper, where sound meets silence and when we are about to run out of breath, the sound will still be animated by a mental crescendo and vibrato. Otherwise, the perfect diminuendo would be *morendo* (dying), before the note has collapsed to the lower octave.

In a nutshell:

Resonance goes to the head, vibrato comes from the heart. Don't vibrate with the diaphragm. Keep vibrato inside the tone and keep it alive even more in soft than in loud dynamics. Carry notes and intervals through phrases by using vibrato.

> *Please refer also to:*
>
> Appoggiatura   Resonance
> Intervals   Tension
> Phrasing   *Tenuto, Sostenuto, Ritenuto*

WARM-UPS

I take issue, with all due respect, with the term "warm-up." I do agree that if this activity makes one feel good, then, by all means, do it. Yet warm-ups are more an affair of nerves than of muscles. If flute playing were a muscular activity like running or weight lifting, I would be the first to recommend stretching and aerobics. But it is my opinion that long-term practice and short-term mental concentration are a better tool to dominate our nerves. You should be able to play at short notice without warm-ups. Practice is a long-term investment.

The hours preceding the performance are for thinking about the meaning of the music, its character, and its content. It is too late to correct instrumental flaws. It works just as well to read the score without playing it, or go over the memorizing mentally, and to save one's energy and concentration. Better still, read a book, look at pictures for an hour in a museum, or even go to a movie. In a word, reflect.

Another practical reason for not being dependent on warm-ups: at school, the time slot for band or orchestra rehearsal might be between classes. Your private lesson may be right after you get home. When you enter professional life, you have to drive from one gig to the next and play. The day you have to play is often the one you have the least time to warm-up. When I hear that you should do warm-ups for thirty or forty-five minutes before playing, I find that totally unrealistic. We have to develop our playing in order to function at the drop of a cleaning rod regardless of the size of our shoes or what we have eaten. The public (and the conductor) are not interested in the fact that you barely made it on time and did not go through your rituals.

Another flaw of the sacrosanct warm-ups: they consist mostly of slow long tones played in such a way that they do not require any concentration, because they are "easy," one thinks. Psychologically, we feel that we have done something worthwhile, when all we have done is deal with our guilt machine, which is already something. Nonetheless, when we have "stored" bad habits or self-defeating actions such as wrong posture, sloppy scale patterns, cramped embouchure, slamming fingers, loud breaths (the list goes on), it's too late to do anything about them the day of the performance.

Have you noticed that every player has his own flourish or gestures before starting? Warm-ups are a ritual, a fetish, an amulet that we hope will conjure up a good omen and reward the good boys and girls we wish we were. So be it. If it helps our morale and nerves, at least it's useful. My motto is, "If it works, do it." Let us not forget, however, that our long-term construction of instrumental playing is the most important: the education of precise reflexes in the movement of tongue and fingers as much as in the production and development of sound.

If you must do warm-ups, play the Taffanel-Gaubert daily exercise no. 4 (the Debost Scale Game) with your best tone, in an unchallenging tempo, listening and thinking. Or play intervals with a concentration on finger perfection. Do not isolate instrumental playing from music. Do not separate fingers from sound, slurring from articulation, and the voice of the heart from the calculations of the mind.

What you have stored away by careful and patient work stays with you, even after many years, ready to be called back. No amount of short-term, on-the-spot warm-ups can make that possible. This week's practice is next year's warm-ups. Today's warm-ups won't pay off tonight.

In a nutshell:

The purpose of practicing is the long-term benefit: to be in reasonable shape all the time, not just tonight. Playing basics consistently pays off in the long run. Thoughtless and last-minute warm-ups are useless. Today's practice is next year's warm-ups.

Please refer also to:

Finger Antagonisms	Scale Game
Intervals	Tonguing
Posture	Tuning
Practicing	

YAWNING

We have all experienced the feeling. Under nervous tension, the throat tightens, producing a choked sound. Poor posture, such as high shoulders, has the same effect.

How can we remedy this situation? Let's observe the process of yawning. Through an involuntary motion, the shoulders drop, the throat opens, the ears pop. A sense of well-being sets in, and the abdomen's movement allows the lungs to fill up completely upon inhaling.

Yawning is the language of the body telling us to relax, to forget about our problems, to feel good and to go to sleep. We can hardly do that just before going on stage. I experience this yawning just before performing. It's the only good thing about stage fright.

Everything is connected back in the throat area. Our ears pop when we change altitudes in order to balance the pressure on either side of the eardrums. We can also do this by blowing our nose, swallowing, or yawning.

Once we have observed the involuntary pleasures of inhaling as we yawn, we can try to emulate it consciously when we blow. If we are able to open the throat as we play, our sound is likely to broaden also. When you are working on tone, try to open your nostrils and have the impression that you are pulling your ears outward.

In a nutshell:

Enjoy yawning. It helps you understand the mechanics of breathing. Apply your pleasure to playing also. Open your throat, your nose, and your ears.

Please refer also to:

Air Column	Posture
Nose	Shoulders

ZEAL IN FORM OF CONCLUSION

"Earnestness or fervor in advancing a cause or rendering service. Hearty or persistent endeavor."[1]

For one who dedicates his love to music, as an amateur in the best sense of the word,[2] or his life as a professional, the challenge is in self-improvement for the sake of art.

My advice to aspiring professionals would be for them to put themselves to the test as often as possible. Do not wait until you are completely ready to undertake the goals of ambition. There is no such thing as being completely ready. No artist can stop growing—not until he dies. Competitions are a case in point. The important part of a contest, outside of the eventual prize, is self-improvement. It is the reward of the also-ran. Trial and failure demand as much as trial and success. Competitions help you learn more about yourself than anything else. The day

1. *The Concise Oxford Dictionary* (New York: Oxford University Press, 1990).
2. From the Italian *amare*, to love.

after you have won, or failed, you are the same person. This is true of prizes, diplomas, distinctions, and decorations.

It is just as difficult to aspire to a lesser position as to a lofty one. Go for the top, which you will never reach: "Be realistic, demand the impossible."[3]

Always try to perform and compete with musicians who you think are better than you are. As in tennis or chess, you play better and learn more with the best.

If you lose the contest, instead of complaining about politics or preferential treatment, congratulate the winner and move on. If you felt you were very good, then, somehow, he or she must have been even better.

Have a sense of humor: "The only perfectly honest competitions I know are those I won." Never mourn the past. Prepare for the future.

Don't have contempt for any form of music. You might think that only the greatest masterpieces deserve your care, but they will cut you down to size more than repertoire you look down upon. Beethoven thought he was a dwarf next to Bach.

Technically difficult works take hours, but masterpieces take years.

Enjoy playing the flute for itself as much as serving music. There is reward in not limiting oneself to Bach and Mozart. "Instrumental pieces are designed to show your qualities. Bach and Mozart show your defects."[4]

Some of the advice in this book may seem foreign to musical art in its purest form. The advancement of instrumental playing is only a means to an end: music. Many of my students have thought, at one time or another, that my emphasis on the flute-playing craft was limiting their artistic development. As should be obvious by now, I think one cannot separate skill from imagination, nor skillful playing from interpretation.

I will go even further. The reason most of us started the flute was the simple pleasure of playing it and playing with it. As we became adults, music grew into our *raison d'être*, and we saw instrumental problems as just an obstacle to be overcome on the path of our "tender Art."[5] But what if, in the process, we had lost the ancient delight that brought us to the flute in the first place and the zeal to play an instrument for its own sake?

I hope that the thoughts and advice in this book will help some to rekindle the pleasure of flute playing and renew the old candor.

Paris 1996
Munich 2000
Oberlin 2001

3. Graffitti on Paris wall, May 1968.
4. Crunelle.
5. "Du, holde Kunst, Ich danke dir" (Thou, tender Art, I thank thee): a poem by Schober, set to music by Franz Schubert.

BIBLIOGRAPHY

Anthology, A Pedagogy, The flutist's handbook assembled by Martha Rearick with articles by Frances Blaisdell, Michel Debost, Angeleita Floyd, Katherine Borst Jones and Christopher Weait, Jeffrey Khaner, Alexander Murray, Carol Kniebush Noe, Donald Peck, Fenwick Smith, Albert Tipton, Ransom Wilson, Bradley Garner, Roger Mather, Toshio Takahashi, Carol Wincenz, Jeanne Baxtresser, Leone Buyse, Robert Dick, Walfrid Kujala, Anita Miller Rieder, Mark Thomas, Jim Walker, John Wion, Trevor Wye, Sarah Baird Fouse, and Mary Stolper. Santa Barbara, CA: National Flute Association, 1998.

Artaud, Pierre-Yves, and Gérard Geay. *Present Day Flutes: Treatise on Contemporary Techniques of Transverse Flutes for the Use of Composers and Performers.* Introduced by Olivier Messiaen (in French and English). Paris: Editions Jobert/Editions Musicales Transatlantiques, 1980.

Auer, Leopold. *Violin Playing as I Teach It.* New York: Dover, 1921.

Averitt, Frances Lapp. *An Intonation Method for Flutists Based on the Use of Difference Tones.* Winchester, WV: Shenandoah College (available from the author), 1983.

Bach, Carl Philip Emmanuel. *Essay on the True Art of Playing Keyboard Instruments.* Translated by William Mitchell. New York: 1949.

Bartolozzi, Bruno. *New Sounds for Woodwinds.* Translated and edited by Reginald S. Brindle. Oxford University Press, 1967.

Beethoven, Ludwig van. *Edition encyclopédique des neuf symphonies.* Edited by Igor Markevitch. Paris: Editions van de Velde, 1982–85.

Boehm, Theobald. *The Flute and Flute-Playing in Acoustical, Technical, and Artistic Aspects.* Translated and annotated by Dayton C. Miller. Cleveland: Savage Press, 1908.

Castellani, Marcello, and Elio Durante. *Del portar della lingua negli instrumenti di fiato, per una corretta interpretazione delle sollabe articolarie nella trattatistica dei sec. XVI–XVIII.* Firenze: Studio per Edizioni Scelte, 1979.

The Concise Oxford Dictionary. 8th ed. New York: Oxford University Press, 1990.

Coltman, John W. "Mouth Resonance Effects in the Flute." *Journal of the Acoustical Society of America* 54, no. 2 (1973): 417–20.

Cooper, Albert. *The Flute.* 2d enlarged ed. London: 1984.

Dorgeuille, Claude. *L'ecole Française de flûte.* Paris: Collection Euterpe, 1994.

Gärtner, Jochen. *The Vibrato: With Particular Consideration Given to the Situation of the Flutist: Historical Development, New Physiological Discoveries, and Presentation of an Integrated Method of Instruction.* Regensburg: Gustav Verlag, 1981.

Geoffroy-Dechaume, Antoine. *Les "secrets" de la musique ancienne: Recherches sur l'interprétation (XVIe, XVIIe, XVIIIe siècles).* Paris: Fasquelle, 1964.

Girard, Adrien. *Histoire et richesses de la flûte.* Paris: Librairie Gründ, 1953.

Hoppenot, Dominique. *Le Violon Intérieur.* Paris: Editions van de Velde, 1981.

Krell, John. *Kincaidiana: A Flute Player's Notebook.* Culver City, Calif.: Trio Associates, 1973.

Kujala, Walfrid. *The Flutist's Progress.* Vols. 1 and 2. Winnetka, Ill.: Progress pp Press, 1970.

———. *The Flutist's Vade Mecum: Of Scales, Arpeggios, Trills, and Fingering Technique.* Winnetka, Ill.: Progress pp Press, 1994.

Lorenzo, Leonardo de. *My Complete Story of the Flute: The Instrument, the Performer, the Music.* Rev. and expanded ed. Lubbock: Texas Tech University Press, 1992.

Le Roy, René, with Claude Dorgeuille. *Traité de la Flûte: Historique, technique et pédagogique.* Paris: Éditions Musicales Transatlantiques, 1966.

McCutchan, Ann. *Marcel Moyse: Voice of the Flute.* Portland, Ore.: Amadeus Press, 1994.

Margolis, Simeon. *Johns Hopkins Symptoms and Remedies.* New York: Rebus, 1995.

Marty, Jean-Pierre. *The Tempo Indications of Mozart.* New Haven: Yale University Press, 1986.

Michel, François et al. *Encyclopédie de la Musique.* Paris: Éditions Fasquelle, 1958.

Miller, Richard. *The Structure of Singing: System and Art in Vocal Technique.* New York: Schirmer Books, 1986.

Moyse, Marcel. *De la sonorité: Art et Technique.* Paris: Alphonse Leduc, 1934.

Nyfenger, Thomas. *Music and the Flute.* Published by the Author, 1986.

Ory, Isabelle. *La flûte traversière* (in French and English). Paris: Éditions van de Velde, 1992.

Quantz, Johann Joachim. *Essay of a Method for Playing the Transverse Flute, Accompanied by Several Remarks of Service for the Improvement of Good Taste in Practical Music.* Translated with introduction and notes by Edward R. Reilly. London: Faber and Faber, 1966.

Reichert, Matheus André. *Sept Exercices Journaliers, op. 5.* Mainz: Schott, 1873; Paris: Alphonse Leduc, 1950.

Riemann, Hugo. *Musikalische Dynamik und Agogik* (1884). Hamburg: D. Rahter, 1884.

Ricquier, Michel. *Traité méthodique de pédagogie instrumentale.* Preface by Maurice André. Paris: Gérard Billaudot, 1982.

Rockstro, Richard S. *A Treatise on the Construction, the History, and the Practice of the Flute.* London: Rudall, Carte, 1890.

Stravinsky, Igor. *Poetics of Music in the Form of Six Lessons.* Trans. Arthur Knodel and Ingolf Dahl. Cambridge, Mass.: Harvard University Press, 1970.

Toff, Nancy. *The Book of the Flute.* New York: Oxford University Press, 1996.

———. *The Development of the Modern Flute.* Bloomington: University of Illinois Press, 1986.

Travell, Janet G., and David G. Simons. *Myofascial Pain and Dysfunction.* Philadelphia: Williams and Wilkins, 1982.

Veilhan, Jean-Claude. *The Rules of Musical Interpretation in the Baroque Era (17th–18th Centuries) Common to All Instruments.* Paris: Alphonse Leduc, 1979.

Welch, Christopher. *History of the Boehm Flute.* With von Schafhäutl, *Life of Boehm,* and an appendix containing the attack originally made on Boehm and other papers relating to the Boehm-Gordon controversy. London: Rudall, Carte, 1882.

Wood, Alexander. *The Physics of Music.* Revised by J. M. Bowsher. London: Methuen, 1961.

Wye, Trevor. *Marcel Moyse, An Extraordinary Man: A Musical Biography.* Cedar Falls, Iowa: Winzer Press, 1993.

Wysham, Henry Clay. *The Evolution of the Boehm Flute: An Essay on the Development of the "Reed Primeval" to the Perfect System of Theobald Boehm.* S.I.: S.n., [189–].

INDEX

Ab key, as stepping stone, 229–230
abdominal muscles
  during breathing, 15–18, 46–47, 61–62
  for correct posture, 54–55, 185, 187
  isometrics of, 141, 165–166
  playing applications of, 23–25, 40, 42, 59
  in tone production, 33, 59, 167
accelerando, as stepping stone, 227
accents
  as agogic component, 12, 14
  appoggiatura expression of, 21–23
  breathing strategies for, 51–52
  hierarchy of, 109–110
  interpretation of, 120, 123–128
  release of, 125, 263
  sf and sfp vs., 124–125, 127
  in syncopation, 126–127
  vibrato with, 262–263
accompaniment
  breathing strategies for, 41, 51–52
  freedom in, 5–11, 91–94, 212
  interpretation in, 8, 11, 114–119, 120, 171
acoustics, 10, 83, 205–206
adagio, 120, 178, 180
agogic, 12–13, 171
  accents and, 125–126
air bag, for circular blowing, 57
air brush, 4, 54, 66
  air speed and, 17–18
  embouchure relation to, 69–70
  focus and, 89–90
air column, 4, 14–18, 32–33
air management, 4. See also breathing
  focus during, 88–90
  isometrics of, 16–17, 141, 166
  for long phrases, 38–43, 47
  tonguing and, 248–250
air speed, 4
  control factors of, 17–18, 54, 64–66
  focus for, 89–90
  for intervals, 130–131, 146
  jawboning and, 17, 143, 146–147
air temperature
  air speed and, 17–18
  for flute maintenance, 87
  influence of, 66, 204, 257
alignment
  with embouchure, 18–19

  of foot joint, 19–20
  hand position and, 19–20, 37, 101
  of head joint, 20, 69, 86
  of wrists (See specific hand)
allegretto, interpretation of, 121, 179, 245–246
allegro
  hierarchy of beats for, 109–110
  interpretation of, 115, 118–119, 245
alphabetical system, for notes, 168–169
altitude, as agogic variable, 13
American music, composers of, 193
anacruses, 178, 227
anapestic rhythm, in Scale Game, 217
anarchy, freedom vs., 90
andante
  hierarchy of beats for, 109–110
  phrasing of, 116, 178, 180, 182
andantino, interpretation of, 116–117, 181
annotations, articulation of, 29
anxiety. See stress
apnea, 4, 47
  causes of, 41, 166, 235
appoggiatura
  energy expression in, 21–22
  graces notes in, 97–98, 100
  interpretation of, 21, 81, 120, 227
appoggio, 4, 23, 141
  diaphragm role in, 62–63
  in dynamic control, 64–65
arm muscles. See also left arm
  maximizing use of, 163–165
  playing applications of, 40, 59, 145
arpeggios, 211, 242
  air column and, 16–17
  as practice strategy, 188, 190, 211
art, mission of, 111–112, 267
Art Nouveau music, composers of, 192
articulation, 28–29, 198, 200
  breathing strategies for, 42, 50–51
  left forefinger role in, 24, 40
  linguistical perspectives of, 26–27
  practice strategies for, 27–29, 218–219
  tonguing of, 27–29, 167, 252, 254
ascending intervals, air speed and, 17–18
ascending notes, 25–26, 31
atmospheric pressure, in breathing, 46
AT&T (articulation, tonguing, technique), 198, 200

271

medication, stress and, 234
medieval music, style variations of, 238–239
melodic memory, durability of, 162
memorizing, 161
memory
    skill development and, 160–161
    types of, 162–163
metal flutes, wood *vs.*, 82–83, 86
metronome
    in discipline of rubato, 211–212
    limitations of, 179, 188, 215, 247
    for tempo marking, 243–245, 247–248
    traditions regarding, 199, 203, 208–209, 239
middle breath
    strategies for, 5, 44–45, 52
modern music, composers of, 192
mood, as agogic effect, 12–13
mouth
    in air column, 15–16
    during breathing, 46–47
    in circular blowing, 57–58
muscle groups. *See specific group*
muscle strength
    air management and, 15–18
    in appoggio, 23–24
    importance of, 145, 147
    for intonation, 166–168
    isometrics of, 140–142
    maximizing use of, 166–168
    stress and, 233–234
music theory, teaching of, 35, 173–176,
    209–210
musical art
    compartmentalization of, 3–4
    zeal for, 266–267
musical notation. *See* notes and notation
musical periods
    composers of, 192–193
    in concert programs, 193–194
musical sound
    resonance of (*see* resonance)
    as vibration, 14, 153, 204
musical terms
    for dynamics, 64–66
    interpretation of, 91, 114–119, 122
musicality
    finger phrasing as, 81–82, 87
    traditions regarding, 88, 200, 241

natural energy, in *piano*, 64
neck tension, 164, 170
nervous tension. *See* stress
noisy finger technique. *See* slam-and-squeeze

nose
    in air column, 15, 58
    resonance and, 204, 206
notes and notation
    for beginners, 35
    naming systems for, 27, 30–31, 97, 168–169
    as stepping stones, 228–230
    tempo interpretation for, 243–248
numbness, with stability of flute, 223–224

oboe
    breathing strategies and, 41, 57
    orchestral relationship with, 138
    tuning to, 257–258
octaves
    intervals and, 128–132, 136
    intonation and, 136, 138–139
offset G alignment, advantages of, 19
onset, 30–31. *See also* attacks
oral hygiene, dry mouth and, 233
orchestra
    concert programs for, 192–194
    freedom in, 91–94, 172
    instrumental tuning in, 136–138
    interpretation in, 31, 114–122
ornamentation
    grace notes for, 98, 100
    as style, 240, 255
overuse syndrome, causes of, 145, 170

pacing
    of concerts, 193–194
    of phrases, 179–183, 226
    stepping stones for, 224, 226
pads, care of, 87
pain
    causes during playing, 145, 164, 169–171
    with stability of flute, 223–224
panting, as breathing strategy, 46–47
Paris Conservatoire, 173–176
pectoral muscles, in air management, 166
percussion
    with keys, 153
    with tonguing, 30, 249
performance anxiety. *See* stress
performance preparation, 234–235
pharynx, resonance and, 204
photographic memory, durability of, 162–163
phrases and phrasing, 176–184, 200
    in accompaniment, 6–8, 212
    in articulation, 27
    in artistic interpretation, 111–114, 122–123
    breathing strategies for, 38–42, 47–51

phrases and phrasing (*continued*)
    components of, 176–177, 182
    finger role in (*see* finger phrasing)
    freedom for, 91–92, 95–96, 182
    grammatical analysis of, 177, 182, 184
    harmonics in, 176–177, 179–180
    key technique for, 148–153
    linguistics of, 177, 182, 184
    pacing of, 179–183, 226
    posture and muscle control for, 36, 40–43
    release in, 176–177
    rubato and, 213–214
    smoothing: with bridge, 52–53, 75; in intervals, 81–82, 132–133, 146; with trills, 255
    upbeats as beginning of, 177–178
    vibrato during, 261–262
pianissimo, 33–34, 64
piano. *See* keyboard
piano, 33–34, 64
piccolo, fingerings for, 172
pinky position. *See specific pinky*
pitch. *See also* intonation
    adjusting to subtle differences of, 55, 139–140
    concerns about perfect, 134–135
    modulation of (*see* vibrato)
    tuning and, 257–258
placebo effect, 87
pleasure, playing strategies for, 169–172, 266–267
positioning. *See* posture; *specific body part*
posture, 195–196
    for breathing, 44, 46, 186
    correct guidelines for, 36, 184–187, 222
    isometrics of, 54–56, 140–142
    for phrasing, 36, 40–43
powder, for wet hands, 235
practice and practice strategies
    for articulation, 27–29
    for attacks, 31–32
    for beginners, 35–36, 38, 74
    for blowing, 42–43
    for breathing, 48–49, 51, 189
    common-sense principles for, 91, 187–189
    for concentration, 60
    études as, 71–72, 188, 190
    for intervals, 128–133
    memory disciplines for, 160–163
    pleasurable *vs.* painful, 169–172
    purpose of, 236, 264–265
    for relative intonation, 135–138
    repertoire as, 201–203

    scales as (*see* scales)
    schedule for, 190, 202–203, 215–216
    sight-reading as, 189–190
    as stress reduction, 234, 236, 264–265
    for tonguing, 250–251
    traditions regarding, 91, 197–198
professors, of Paris Conservatoire, 173–176
programs
    for concerts, 192–194
    proving too much in, 192
    for recitals, 191–192, 235
progression, as agogic variable, 12–13, 65
projection, techniques for, 64
Pythagorean scale, for intonation, 135–136, 138

rallentando, as stepping stone, 227
range, impact on articulation, 28
reading, as practice strategy, 60, 71–72, 133
recitals, programs for, 191–192, 235
recording(s)
    of CDs, 231
    use of, 6, 13, 198–199, 208
redundancy, as teaching component, 3
reed instruments
    breathing for, 41, 43, 57
    tuning to, 257–258
reflexes
    in attacks, 31, 34
    breathing, 57–59, 61–62
    control of, 108
reiteration, as stepping stone, 224–226
relaxation
    antagonism of, 59–60, 164, 232, 235
    of lips, 154–155
    of muscle groups, 164–165
    for stress reduction, 59–60, 236
    with yawning, 236, 265–266
release
    as dynamic element, 66–68
    interpretation of, 119–120, 122, 200
    in phrasing, 176–177, 226–227
    playing applications of, 21–22, 125, 128, 212–214, 222
    rest during, 211
repair, of flutes, 86–87
repertoire, as practice strategy, 201–202, 216, 247
repetitive strain injury (RSI), 145, 170, 232
resolution
    of appoggiatura, 21–22
    breathing strategies for, 39, 48, 50–52